BY THE TIME ANNE CAPUTE WENT ON TRIAL
FOR FIRST-DEGREE MURDER
SHE HAD LOST HER JOB, HER SAVINGS,
AND THREE CLOSE FRIENDS.
HER MARRIAGE WAS DOOMED, SHE WAS
FORTY THOUSAND DOLLARS IN DEBT,
AND HER DAUGHTERS WERE CLOSE TO
EMOTIONAL COLLAPSE.

Since childhood, Anne Capute had wanted to be a
nurse. When her dream came true, nursing was as
wonderful as she had imagined. She hadn't cared
about the low pay, the long hours, the drudgery of a
job few would ever thank her for doing. All she had
ever cared about was the opportunity to help and to
heal. Then came the shocking day when she was
indicted for murder.

Not even Anne's defense attorney knew about the
loaded gun that his client had concealed in her
pocketbook during the closing days of the trial. For
Anne was convinced that the verdict would go against
her. And, rather than spend the rest of her days in
prison, she had plans to take her own life. . . .

FATAL DOSAGE

Fatal Dosage

Gary Provost

BANTAM BOOKS
TORONTO • NEW YORK • LONDON • SYDNEY • AUCKLAND

FATAL DOSAGE is a true story based on interviews, research and court testimony. In the interest of protecting the privacy of certain persons, some of the information is conveyed through the fictitious composite character, Bonnie Dumalek.

FATAL DOSAGE

A Bantam Book / December 1985

Grateful acknowledgment is extended to the Enterprise Publishing Co. Brockton, MA, and Taunton Daily Gazette, Taunton, MA, for permission to reproduce photos of the Anne Capute trial.

For Gail,
My Honey,
My Sunshine,
My Life.

Acknowledgments

I would like to thank the following people for their help in the creation of this book:

Barbara Bartol, Mary Bauer, Anne Capute, Charles Capute, Meredith Capute, Heather Grant Florence, Ted Gay, Don Harwood, Jon Matson, James Morton, Donna Piscatelli, Meredith Piscitelli, Pat Piscitelli, Gail Provost, Lawrence Ross, Donna Ruvituso, Paul Stevens, Lori Wantman, Susan Wantman.

And a special thank you to Linda Price, my editor at Bantam, who got me on the right track and helped me stay there.

Author's Note

The people, places and events in this book are all true.

Courtroom interrogations are lengthy, tedious, and repetitive. In order to wring what I hope is compelling dialogue from 25 volumes of court transcript I have, of course, had to cut and compress. However, every word of courtroom dialogue in this book was spoken in the courtroom and all of the courtroom scenes are true representations of what was said and what it meant.

To spare a few minor characters from embarrassment I have created Bonnie Dumalek, a fictitious name for a composite character. All other names are real.

Chapter One

Somebody had been stealing drugs from the medication closet at Morton Hospital. It had been going on for months, mysterious shortages of Tylenol Codeine. The tablets were pain-killers, and they were addictive.

Anne Capute, a licensed practical nurse, had stolen one tablet. She stole it when a nurse's aide had arrived for work almost in tears from the pain of an abscessed tooth. Anne, feeling sorry for the girl and anxious to stop her pain, got the key to the medication closet. She took one Tylenol Codeine tablet from a patient's drawer and gave it to the girl.

And so when they came to get Anne at ten-thirty on the night of May 22, 1980, her first thought was, Oh, God, they're going to accuse me of stealing drugs.

"They" came first in the form of Nurse Lorraine Hickey, a stout, gray-haired woman who was the clinical manager of surgical ward 2, known as S-2. Anne, with a half hour left on her shift, was standing at the nurses' station looking at a chart. Nurse Hickey, as precise in speech as in motion, approached Anne and said, "Anne. Costello wants to see you."

"God wants to see me? What for?" Anne said. She sounded flippant, but she was scared, and before the words had even stumbled from her mouth, she could feel fear rattling inside her. Being invited to Costello's office was like suddenly being thrown back to Catholic elementary school and sent to the mother superior's office.

"Just come with me to her office," Hickey said. Before Anne could ask another question, Hickey swung around and marched back down the corridor of S-2.

The pills, Anne thought, the goddamn pills. Her heart thundered in her chest as she struggled to keep up with Hickey. Anne was sure that they were going to accuse her of stealing pills, that they were going to take her license away. The frightening thought became more and more real. She thought she would be sick. Anne had spent the first forty years of her life wanting nothing as much as she wanted to be a nurse, and she had spent only the past three years actually being a nurse, and now she was afraid it would be taken away from her. Anne was a mother even more than she was a nurse, and her worry now was for her three teenaged daughters at home and the things they would have to do without if she got fired.

Hickey didn't take the elevator. Anne followed her down two flights of stairs and out the back door of Morton's main building, one of three buildings sprawled across two city blocks in downtown Taunton, Massachusetts. The night was balmy, and Anne could hear the rumble of traffic behind her as she followed Hickey across the parking lot toward the small brick administration building. Anne's heart fluttered. It wasn't just the fear of being accused of stealing pills that was getting to her. It was Costello. The idea of being brought before Costello for anything at all was terrifying.

To the nursing staff Maureen Costello was known, respectfully, as the "Iron Maiden," and was a person to be reckoned with. Her title was assistant administrator for nursing services. But the title was not nearly as intimidating as the person. A licensed practical nurse, Anne Capute was on the bottom step of the nursing hierarchy at Morton. Maureen Costello was at the top.

Anne had met Maureen Costello only once, a few days after Anne had been hired. She and ten other new employees were led into a conference room, where they sat at a long wooden table, with Maureen Costello presiding. She greeted the new employees, she told them in detail who she was, and she rattled off a list of her professional credits that almost bowled Anne over.

The list included service with some of the best hospitals in the nation. By comparison, Anne felt like two cents. Costello had spent her entire adult life succeeding gloriously in a world that Anne had only dreamed of entering. When Costello finished reciting her list of credits, she had asked each person at the table who he or she was and what that person hoped to get from his or her job at Morton. After that first day Anne watched in admiration as the Iron Maiden patrolled the wards like some visiting general. Anne soon realized that the assistant administrator for nursing services remembered every word that had been spoken at that first meeting. Anne was in total awe of the woman.

By the time Nurse Hickey led Anne into the administration building on the night of May 22, and they entered Maureen Costello's office on the first floor, Anne was breathless. She was forty-three and recklessly overweight.

Maureen Costello's office was small and well-ordered. Costello sat calmly behind her assistant administrator for nursing services placard. When Anne entered the room, Costello stood and greeted her. Costello is a small woman, trim, attractive, a woman not easily ruffled. Though she had worn nursing whites for many years, she now wore the suit and blouse of a professional manager.

"Take a seat, please," Maureen Costello said, exuding graciousness without warmth. Anne came in and sat in a metal office chair in front of Costello's desk. Automatically she glanced down to see if her white shoes were properly polished.

Sitting to Anne's right in front of Costello was Noel "Tom" Bosanquet, director of personnel for Morton Hospital.

"You know Mr. Bosanquet," Costello said. Anne nodded. "Tom is here as an employee advocate. He'll give you support whenever needed."

"Employee advocate?" "Support?" The words activated an alarm button in Anne's mind. Here it comes, she thought, the goddamn pills. Anne noticed that Nurse Hickey was staying in the office, hovering just beyond Anne's shoulder. A phrase rushed back to Anne from girlhood afternoons spent watching cowboys-and-Indians movies at the Rivoli Theater: They've got us surrounded.

They sat—Anne Capute, Lorraine Hickey, Maureen Costello, Tom Bosanquet—for a single silent moment that ticked with tension. Everyone fidgeted. It seemed as if they all wished they were someplace else.

"Anne," Maureen Costello finally said, "we're here on a pretty serious matter, and we need your help in sorting out the information."

"Sure," Anne said, "shoot." This was typical of a frightened Anne, shielding herself with some flippant remark at the most inappropriate time.

"Anne, can you tell us about Norma Leanues?" Costello said.

The name Norma Leanues was music to Anne's

ears. She was thrilled to hear the name of a patient, any patient, because to her that meant she was facing Costello over a patient-related matter, not those damned missing pills. Anne felt ridiculous for having been so afraid. This whole thing was probably about some minor infraction in filling out forms or something equally insignificant. The knot in Anne's stomach began to unravel. She rolled her eyes toward the ceiling as if to say, Thank you, God, for getting me out of this mess.

It was a small thing, but it was one of many small things that would take on importance later. Maureen Costello saw this rolling of Anne's eyes and took it as proof that the name Norma Leanues had special significance to Anne. Eventually Costello would so testify in court.

Anne told Costello that Norma Leanues had been a very frightened patient, and with good reason. Afflicted by cancer, Norma lived in constant pain. Anne said that most of the medication given to Norma Leanues had not stopped the pain.

"How was she on May sixteenth?" Costello asked. "Friday?"

"In exquisite pain," Anne said. "Exquisite" was a word Anne used often to describe pain. It sounded right to her. She had even looked it up in the dictionary once to be sure she was using it correctly. When she found that "exquisite" could mean "intense," she continued to use it in reference to pain.

Costello asked, "How do you know she was in pain?"

"She cried out a lot so we'd hear her," Anne said.

Costello looked down at her desk, where Norma Leanues's medical records were spread out. Among them were the narcotics proof-of-use sheet, the medication chart for Norma Leanues. And the nurse's notes. Costello read out loud the nurse's notes that Anne had written for the three-to-eleven-thirty shift on Friday, May 16.

After one medication note Anne had written, "with poor results."

"What does 'with poor results' mean?" Costello asked.

"She wasn't able to swallow all of her oral medication," Anne said. "She was suffering, she was in agony."

As she spoke, Anne began to get edgy again. Her fingers began to tremble. Why, she wondered, would it take four people to discuss a minor infraction? Anne didn't know what was going on, but once more she began to feel that her lifelong dream of being a nurse was threatened.

"It says here 'crying all the time.' What does that mean?" Costello asked.

"Tears were streaming down her face," Anne said, "and she was clutching her chest." Anne searched Costello's face for some hint of what this was all about but found nothing.

Bosanquet and Hickey were silent.

"Did Dr. Hillier make the rounds that night?" Costello asked.

"Yes," Anne said. "Around seven o'clock."

"Were you with him?"

"I wasn't on rounds with him. I was with Nancy Robbins. She was talking to Dr. Hillier. He seemed to be in a rush. In fact, I had to hold his sleeve so that Nancy could ask him some questions."

"Can you tell us about that conversation?" Costello asked.

"There's not much to tell," Anne thought, never imagining that the conversation with Hillier would affect her whole life and career. "Nancy told Dr.

Hillier that the morphine solution was not helping Mrs. Leanues, and she asked if we could try some other medication. Hillier said "Sure, give her anything she wants, just make her comfortable—"

Costello broke in abruptly. "Is that *exactly* how Dr. Hillier said it?" she asked. Costello looked at her intensely.

"Well . . . yes," she said. "'Give her anything she wants anytime, just make her comfortable. She'll be dead in twenty-four to forty-eight hours.'"

"Then what happened?" Costello asked.

Hickey and Bosanquet leaned forward.

"Well, Nancy said, 'How about morphine, fifteen milligrams, subcutaneous, no time limit?' Then Nancy went to the desk to write the order, and I went to the medication closet to get the fifteen milligrams of morphine and also the ten milligrams of Valium, intramuscular, which Dr. Hillier had ordered for Mrs. Leanues."

"Did the Valium and morphine help Mrs. Leanues?" Costello asked.

"Not much," Anne said. "She was still crying out in pain."

Costello studied her notes again. To Anne it looked as if she were trying to figure out a word for a crossword puzzle. "Anne, tell me about the rest of the evening."

Anne shifted in her chair. "I finished up with the other patients about ten P.M.," she said. "When I got back to Leanues she was in a lot of pain."

"Vital signs?" Costello asked.

"Blood pressure about a hundred eight over seventy, I think, pulse about a hundred to a hundred twenty, respiration around eighteen."

"Was she having trouble breathing?"

"No."

"Then what?"

"She was crying out in pain," Anne said. For an instant Anne's memory was haunted by the sounds of Norma Leanues's tragic wailing. "So I gave her thirty milligrams of morphine."

"Did you realize the order was for fifteen milligrams?" Costello asked.

"Yes."

"Then why did you give her thirty?"

Anne shifted again in her chair. Her hands, clammy with sweat, clutched the arms of the chair.

"Anne, why did you give her thirty?" Costello asked again.

"I wanted to make her comfortable."

For a minute nobody spoke. Costello stared down at her charts. Bosanquet and Hickey glanced around the room, looked at their hands, looked at the floor, looked at the ceiling, looked everywhere except into Anne's eyes. Anne squirmed. In her mind she reran the images she had of Norma Leanues, like a coach studying game films to find mistakes. Anne found none. It seemed as if everybody else in the room knew something she didn't.

"Anne, what about Saturday night?" Costello finally asked. "Were you assigned to Mrs. Leanues?"

"Yes."

"Did you specifically request that assignment?"

"Yes."

"You did?"

"I mean no," Anne said. "I mean I didn't request Leanues. But I did ask for the same assignment. It's easier if you have the same assignment on consecutive nights."

"How was Mrs. Leanues that night?"

"She was going down."

"What do you mean?"

"She'd gotten worse," Anne said. "Her color was

lousy, blood pressure about a hundred over sixty, rapid pulse, respirations twelve to sixteen."

"Was she still crying out?"

"She was moaning," Anne said. "She was obviously in pain."

"How could you tell that?"

"She had tears streaming down her face and she was clutching at her chest the way she had before."

"Clutching her chest?" Costello said. "That could mean she was having difficulty breathing. You gave her thirty milligrams of morphine s.c. at five P.M.?"

"Yes."

"Why?"

"I thought she needed it."

"Did Nancy Robbins know about the dose of morphine you were giving?"

"Yes," Anne said.

"I see," Costello said. She looked at her nurse's notes and medication records again.

"'Morphine sulfate, 30 milligrams, s.c., right arm, with poor results at 7 P.M.,'" Costello read. "'Morphine sulfate, 30 milligrams, s.c., left leg muscles, with fair results at 8 P.M. 9:15, morphine sulfate, 30 milligrams, s.c. in the right thigh. 10:15, morphine sulfate, 30 milligrams, s.c., in the left arm with apnea 10 seconds in duration.'"

Costello stared at Anne. "Anne," she said. "What does 'apnea ten seconds in duration' mean to you?"

"Huh? Well it means she wasn't breathing for ten seconds at a time. What else could it mean?"

"Nothing," Costello said. "I just wanted to be sure we are clear about this."

Costello read the last entry on Anne's nurse's notes for Saturday. Written just hours before Norma Leanues died, it stated: "'11:15, morphine sulfate, 45 milligrams, s.c. in right arm, nail beds are bluish, extremities warm, apnea 10 to 15 seconds in duration. Not responding. Condition very poor. Valium 10 milligrams, IM times two at 6 P.M. and 9:45.'"

When she finished reading, Costello leaned back in her chair. She stared grimly across the desk at Anne as if to ask, Well, is it true? Are these numbers correct? And Anne, frightened, shaken, stared help-lessly back. All the numbers were correct.

"Anne," Costello said, "do you know the effects of that dosage on a patient?"

Anne pushed herself up in her chair. Once more dredging up a wisecrack, she grinned and said, "My God, it would be enough to kill an elephant!"

Costello was not amused.

"Why did you give her all this medication, Anne?"

"I wanted to keep her comfortable."

"In the notes it says she was unresponsive. So how did you know she was in pain?"

"She had tears streaming down her face and she was clutching her chest." Anne's hands fell limp in her lap, and her body slumped once more into the hard office chair. She could feel the weight of the narrow room on her.

For another hour they covered the same ground, line by painful line. "How much morphine did you give her?" Costello asked. "What did Leanues look like? Why did you give her this medication?" And Anne once again tried to make them all understand the pain of a dying woman. "There were tears in her eyes, tears streaming down her face, and she was always clutching her chest."

"Do you know the effects of morphine?" Costello asked.

"Yes," she said, gripping the arms of the chair. Her voice cracked. "It's a CNS depressant, it's a narcotic, respirations have to be watched carefully."

"And Valium?" Costello said. "Do you know the effects of Valium?"

"Yes," Anne said, "yes." She was so scared. "Same thing, respirations have to be watched."

There were more questions covering the same ground, and Anne kept trying to explain about the tears streaming down Norma Leanues's face and the trembling little hands futilely clutching at her chest as if to strangle the pain. Anne could not imagine what further explanation was needed. And after an hour of being badgered and forced to recall Norma's pain, Anne started crying.

"I didn't want her to feel any more pain," Anne said.

Tom Bosanquet spoke. His voice floated softly on the tension in the room. "What do you mean by that?" he said.

"I wanted her to be comfortable, not to suffer. . . ." Anne sobbed. "I . . ." and then the immense implication of Bosanquet's question struck with all the shocking force of a rock crashing through the window. The truth hit Anne. These people were not looking for "help in sorting out the information."

"WELL, I KILLED HER!" Anne cried. "I must have killed her, I guess that's plain to everybody in this room."

"Now, Anne," Costello said, her icy surface melting slightly, "we're not trying to make you think that."

"Well, I do feel that way," Anne snapped.

"We just want to find out what happened. We'll support you in any way we can. Do you understand our concern?"

Anne did not answer. She was drowning in her own tears. Her first desperate thoughts were of money. Losing her job would mean losing her paycheck, and the bills were already piling up at home. Even with Charlie working full time as a carpenter and Anne working a full week at the hospital, they were lucky if they could keep up with all the expenses.

"Do you understand our concern?" Costello repeated.

"Yes, yes," Anne muttered through her sobs, but she didn't really understand much of anything. As far as she could see, she hadn't done anything wrong. She had merely followed doctor's orders and her own conscience, just as any other nurse would. She was allowing herself to be bullied, but she didn't know how to fight back.

"Do you have any questions?" she heard Costello ask.

"What's going to happen to me?" Anne asked.

Costello answered, "I don't know. But I have to put you on administrative suspension for three days. I'll get back to you by next Wednesday."

"Do you think you're being treated fairly?" Bosanquet asked.

"Yes, I'm being treated fairly," Anne said, delivering her words in an icy monotone.

"Do you want a ride home?"

"No," Anne cried, feeling as if someone close to her had just died. She searched her mind for some cutting remark with which to slash out at these people, something that would make them ashamed of themselves. But at that moment Anne was just too weak, too thoroughly beaten to fight back.

For a long time Anne just sat, slumped in the office chair, her head down, her eyes closed and wet. No one spoke. She was worried, she was embarrassed, and she was angry. She wanted no more than to take care of her patients and work on that bottom step of the hierarchy at Morton Hospital. And now they were trying to kick her off of it.

Finally she wiped her tears and she walked out of the office. It was almost midnight.

Chapter Two

What will become of me? Anne wondered as she walked across the Morton parking lot. She was still in a state of shock. As she drove out of the parking lot she could almost imagine the face of the Iron Maiden hovering over the windshield.

Meredith! Anne thought suddenly, and for a moment her worries about herself were pushed away by worries about her youngest daughter. Meredith had come running in after school that day, terribly upset and crying over some incident with her friends. Poor Meredith, Anne thought. Twelve years old. What a miserable age. Anne had spent the hours before work holding Meredith's hand and comforting her, but the girl had still been depressed when Anne left for Morton. Being a mother had always been Anne's number one job. It occurred to her that motherhood was the one dream they couldn't take away from her, as she thought now about the dream they *could* take away, the dream she had held most of her life. *To be a nurse,* that was the dream, and it was a dream that had never been out of sight but always out of reach.

Anne Capute was born in Boston on January 25,

1937. The name on her birth certificate was Mary
Patricia Larue. It wasn't until she was forty that she
started calling herself Anne. Her family was poor,
and Anne's father, an alcoholic, ran away from the
family before Anne had even entered school. One
brother died in infancy. Another was adopted by
Anne's grandmother because Anne's mother's job as a
hairdresser couldn't support them all.

When Anne was five years old she moved from
the Back Bay to Jamaica Plain, a blue-collar section of
Boston. There Anne shared an apartment with her
mother, stepfather, and a half sister, Marilyn. And
there Anne dreamed of becoming a nurse.

As a kid Anne played nurse, bandaging up her
friends who had skinned their knees or were willing
to make believe they had. Anne always seemed to
know about things such as elevating a swollen ankle,
applying pressure in the right place, and the importance of cleaning wounds. Anne was a fat kid, which
occasionally made her the victim of thoughtless children's taunts, so perhaps she craved love just a little
more, and perhaps she got that love when she tended
to her make-believe patients. More than anything
else, she liked the feeling of being needed.

Anne outgrew her nurse games but never her
nurse dream. As a teenager she was devoted to
paperback novels about dedicated nurses and doctors
who saved lives together and fell in love. When
someone in the family was sick it was always Anne
who would run to the store for medicine and then
come home and put the soup on the stove.

It would not have taken much money to put
Anne through nursing school after high school. If she
had been born into a family that could have tucked
away a few dollars every week or could have qualified
for a bank loan, and if she could have afforded to stay
unemployed for an extra year or two, Anne might

have become a nurse at age twenty. And by May 1980 maybe Anne Capute would have been assistant administrator for nursing services. But it didn't work out that way.

On her sixteenth birthday Anne dropped out of Jamaica Plain High School so she could get a job and bring home some badly needed money. She worked first at a bakery, where she spent two years stringing up brown boxes of doughnuts and eclairs and asking customers whether they wanted their bread sliced. This was the first in a long line of low-paying jobs that occupied Anne's life for the next twenty-four years but never nourished her soul. Anne made friends at the bakery, as she did at all her jobs, but she never quite got what she yearned for most: the chance to help people who really needed help.

When Anne was nineteen years old and working at a wholesale drug firm in Boston she got married, and before she was old enough to vote, she was the mother of a baby girl, Barbara. The baby gave Anne what she needed most, someone to love her and need her. But now the dream that had dangled for so long just beyond Anne's fingertips was abandoned for a long, long time.

Anne blossomed in motherhood. It was the thing she was best at, and in it she found the greatest joys of her life. She loved to take care of her baby. With Barbara and with the babies that came later—Susan, then Lori, then Meredith—Anne found pleasure in the daily routine of changing diapers, boiling bottles, and picking bits of cereal out of her little girls' hair. But despite her affinity for mothering, Anne could not stay home with the kids. There was never enough money, and Anne had to work full time at a variety of jobs all the time that her kids were growing up.

Anne worked as a typist, then as a keypunch operator, then as a commercial scheduler, then as a

keypunch operator again, then as a lunch counter
manager, and then this and then that, grinding out
the years at jobs that were just that, jobs.

Anne's personality inspired a variety of feelings
among her coworkers. Some say she was a loud and
aggressive woman who had an annoyingly thunder-
ous laugh and could be counted on to say the wrong
thing at the wrong time. Others describe her as a witty
and spontaneous woman, and the kindest person
imaginable. "She was the kind of gal who would cut
off her right arm and give it to you if you told her you
really needed it," says one man who worked with her
for two years. Many of the people Anne worked with
described her as a shy and insecure woman who
constantly sought approval, someone who needed to
be loved and who loved to be needed.

In 1975 Anne Capute was thirty-eight years old.
She had four daughters and was into the eighth year
of her third marriage, a marriage that had brought
her three stepsons. She had also given up the Catholic
faith of her childhood and converted to Judaism.
Like many women her age, Anne had postponed her
dream for so long that it often seemed more like a
memory than a plan. But she was actually closer than
ever before to doing the kind of work she'd long
dreamed about.

She was living in Plympton, in southeastern
Massachusetts, and while the kids were at school,
Anne drove a school bus. In her free time she did
volunteer work as a nurse's aide at Jordan Hospital in
nearby Kingston. During this period two significant
things happened that finally brought Anne to the
point where she could say out loud, "Damn it, I want
to be a nurse, and I'm going to be a nurse."

The first significant event happened on Anne's
first night as a volunteer at Jordan. Here is how she
later described it to a friend:

"I happened to be at the right place at the right time. My very first night I got a patient with a gunshot wound, and I was fascinated. I always wanted to do nursing, but I had always wondered if I could handle certain aspects of it. I knew that blood and guts was no problem. But somebody vomiting? I wasn't so sure about that, and I worried about how I'd handle it. Urination and bowel movements was never a problem, not after you've had children. But anyway, this guy had eaten just before he got shot, and he must have really pigged out, because he just started vomiting, and he vomited all over the place. I mean, copious amounts. And I handled it. I really handled it well. And I came out of the hospital that night feeling so good I knew vomiting wouldn't be a problem. It was like I had cleared the last hurdle, at least in my mind."

The other formative event happened on November 6, 1975, when a reckless young driver named Daniel Walker used the last few seconds of his life to speed around a curve on Route 27 in Kingston, on the wrong side of the highway. He slammed head-on into a loaded school bus. Anne was not the driver; her bus was a minute or two behind. Walker's car was instantly crushed into a tangle of jagged steel. Though none of the twenty-eight passengers was killed, several were injured, as was the driver. A few kids had their teeth knocked out, some were bleeding, many were crying. When Walker's car erupted in flames someone started screaming hysterically, "The bus is going to explode!"

Anne arrived at the accident first. She jumped out of her own bus and rushed into the bus that had been hit. She calmed the kids and quickly sorted out the injured ones. One kid with a bloody nose was lying flat, but Anne, realizing he could strangle on his own blood, turned him on his side. When the police, firemen, and medical technicians arrived, Anne helped get the kids into ambulances and taken to Jordan Hospital. She was a heroine.

Anne was cited for her heroic effort by the school district and the junior high school.

"Without her presence of mind, quick thinking, and alert action, the situation could have been much worse than it was," wrote Edward Uburtis, chairman of the regional school committee.

Anne was delighted with her own response to the crisis. The praise she received gave her the self-confidence she so badly needed as she hovered at the brink of forty. The school bus incident convinced her that she had what it takes to be a nurse. Two weeks later she told her family that she wanted to enter nursing school at the Lemuel Shattuck Hospital in Jamaica Plain.

"We all thought it was great," her daughter Lori says. "We knew that Ma had this nurse dream. She had always had it, and so we all tried to support her. We knew money would be tight. Not the tuition expenses; that wasn't much because it was a state school, but Ma had to give up her bus driving job. So we just cut back on things. Instead of the electric heat, we got a wood stove, and so forth. We all just took the point of view that it was for one year and we could somehow make it."

Despite Anne's self-confidence and her family's support, there was still a major obstacle. Anne was not a high-school graduate. Mary Patricia Capute was not qualified to start nursing school at Lemuel Shattuck. She could have qualified by taking a high-school-equivalency examination, but she didn't know that. So she took a more expedient route. She lied.

Mary Patricia Capute sent for the high-school transcript of a girl she had known years before, a girl named Anne Wall, who had graduated from Mission

Hill High School in Boston. Claiming the transcript as her own, she submitted it along with her application for nursing school, and for that reason she was obliged to go by the name "Anne." The false transcript was the only deception. Anne took all her own entrance exams.

Anne was accepted for the 1976–77 term at Lemuel Shattuck, where she entered an accelerated one-year program. At first she commuted between home in Plympton and Shattuck in Boston. But it was forty-eight miles each way. In addition to the hours of driving, studying, and cooking, Anne still had three girls to raise. Barbara was living with Anne's mother, and Charlie's boys had all joined the service, but Susan, Lori, and Meredith were still at home. Anne knew she wasn't going to make it. And so she made a major decision: She told the family she wanted to move out of the house for a year and into a dormitory at Shattuck.

"We were really bummed out over that," Anne's daughter Susan says, "but this was Ma's nurse dream, and we knew we had to give her whatever she needed. Mostly it meant a lot more baby-sitting for Lori and me. We were fifteen or sixteen then and we were into hanging out with the gang, and now it meant we'd have to come home and baby-sit Meredith, because she was only eight. Lori and I used to get home from school around ten past two. Meredith was cool until nighttime, so Lori and I would go out and hang around with our friends in the afternoon but then we'd have to get home and make supper . . . Charlie has to have supper on the table when he gets home. Lori and I would fight about whose turn it was to make supper, but I think things stayed pretty much normal. This was our experimenting stage, with the cigarettes and the joints. And it was Charlie's mania stage. He didn't have any experience raising girls. He had raised three boys, and they had all gone into the service. He was pretty much into the double standard about what girls could do, I mean as far as staying out late and that sort of thing. He was very strict and overprotective. But basically, we all just took care of each other while Ma was in school."

Anne came home on weekends. The family survived. And on August 27, 1977, Anne Capute, finishing up in the top third of her class, was graduated from Lemuel Shattuck in a candelight ceremony with her mother, her stepfather, her four daughters, and her husband all there to congratulate her. In December she received her L.P.N. license. The dream had come true. She was a nurse.

After graduation Anne worked for a year at Lemuel Shattuck on the 3:00 P.M. to 11:00 P.M. shift, commuting between home and the hospital.

Anne's years at Lemuel Shattuck were immensely rewarding. She was forging a lifelong dream. And she was needed. When she went to work for Lemuel Shattuck she applied to work with terminal patients. She had become inspired by a course on death and dying, was excited about the work of Elisabeth Kübler-Ross, and talked often about death.

"So many of us stare away from death and don't want to talk about it," Anne told a friend. "We all want it to go away." She blamed society's attitude, which aggravated the isolation experienced by people who are dying. "Everybody," she said, "wants to avoid the subject and act as if death doesn't exist."

During her career at Lemuel Shattuck, Anne was reprimanded only once. She had a cancer patient who had become needle-addictive, a situation that occurs when a patient has been given so many injections that the patient feels shots are necessary for his or her well-being. Anne, following another nurse's advice, gave the patient a subcutaneous injection of sterile water.

However, Anne's overall record at Lemuel Shattuck was excellent and when, tired of commuting a hundred miles a day, she left the hospital, she had no difficulty obtaining work, first for several temporary medical services and then for Morton, where she started work as an L.P.N. in December 1978.

I still have what it takes to be a nurse, Anne thought somewhat bitterly at twelve-thirty in the morning of May 23 as she turned onto Maple Street in Plympton.

As she pulled into the dirt driveway, Anne noticed a small, insignificant thing that bothered her. Her right headlight was out of line. Its beam landed on the work shed in the yard about a foot and a half above the light from the left headlight. Damn cars, she thought, they suck the life out of you. She'd have to get it fixed, at least before the next inspection period. They'd probably charge her three bucks, and then four bucks for the sticker, and then who knows what mysterious life-threatening mechanical disease they'd find festering under her 1978 Fairmount.

Anne stared out at the lopsided headlights and thought grimly about the money it would cost to line up her lights. No matter how hard you worked or how many bills you paid, there was always one more. If it wasn't braces for the girls it was a broken faucet or the long-distance phone bill or the car insurance or something. She tried to remember whether Costello had said she would be paid for the three-day suspension. Probably not. With these worries pressing like the point of a pistol at the back of her neck, Anne crawled out of her car and plodded into the house.

The house was a three-bedroom raised ranch house that Charlie had built in 1974. Plympton is a

sparsely populated town, mostly farms, where most of
the people have firewood piled up on their porch and
a small stand of trees to separate them from the
nearest neighbors.

When Anne entered the house, her maternal
instinct impelled her directly to Meredith's bedroom.
Sometimes when Meredith was distressed she'd stay
awake late into the night. Anne wanted to be sure her
little girl was all right. Anne snapped on the hall light
and peeked into Meredith's room. Meredith, caught
in the glow of light from the hall, was sleeping
peacefully. Anne stared at her for a moment. Sleeping children always looked so beautiful. Then Anne
turned off the light. She kicked off her shoes and
padded into the small living room. There was no
noise except for the occasional distant noises of some
animal in the woods behind the house. Moonlight
poured through the front windows, filling the room
with shadows that only deepened her sadness.

Charlie and the girls were asleep, Anne knew.
She could *feel* them sleeping, the way she could feel
an entire ward of sleeping patients. Anne turned on
the television set, but its glow only enhanced her
loneliness, so she shut it off quickly. There was
nobody to talk to. There was nobody to tell how
unfairly she was being treated.

There was God, of course, but in recent years the
idea of a God you could talk to was becoming harder
for Anne to believe in. Each day's work at the hospital
with sick and dying patients, sometimes children,
made the idea of a personal and merciful God more
difficult to embrace.

Anne sat in the dark and smoked for a while, and
when she crushed out her third cigarette she decided
she had to talk to Charlie. Now. Just wake him up and
tell him. She would rather have talked to Susan or
Lori. But Charlie's the one she should talk to, she

thought. He was her husband. And though the years had drained most of the love from their marriage, Anne knew that at a time like this you were supposed to talk to your husband, not your kids. And she wanted to do the right thing. Besides, she thought, as she walked quietly to the bedroom, the girls have to get up and go to school in the morning.

"Charlie," she called from the doorway. Charlie's beefy body was stretched almost diagonally across the bed. He was snoring softly.

"Wake up," Anne said. Still trembling, she walked into the room and pressed the button on the bedside lamp. She sat on the bed and poked Charlie.

She knew that money would be the first thing Charlie would ask about. Then she comforted herself with the knowledge that at least it was the start of "the feast season." Charlie was a carpenter, a builder of houses, and he earned 70 percent of his income between May and October. "Charlie, wake up!"

Charlie bolted up in the bed. He was startled. "What? What is it?" he said. He glanced around as if he expected to see the house on fire. "What? What? What the hell are you waking me up for?"

Anne knew she had dragged her husband out of a deep sleep. Because his work was outdoors and physically hard, Charlie usually slept as if he'd been drugged. It had always annoyed Anne that Charlie rarely woke up when she got home at night. She could turn on lamps, undress, crawl into bed, and he would never miss a snore.

"I've been suspended," she said.

"Suspended? What do you mean, suspended?"

"Suspended," Anne snapped, annoyed that Charlie hadn't grasped the whole situation immediately. "From Morton. For three days."

"Anne, what the hell did you do?"

"Nothing."

"Oh, sure! Will you get paid?"

"I don't know."

"Didn't you ask?"

"I didn't think of it."

"Oh, great! That's three days' pay. We need that."

"I might get paid," Anne said. "I don't know."

"So, what did you do?"

"I didn't do anything," Anne said.

"You must have done something."

"It's some kind of misunderstanding," Anne said. "It's about medication, that's all. A woman died, and—"

"Died?" Charlie said. His eyes widened.

"Yeah, she died, Charlie," Anne said. "That's what people do at hospitals sometimes, they die. Norma Leanues. She died of cancer. But we gave her a lot of morphine, you know, to keep her comfortable."

"Who?" Charlie asked.

"Me and Nancy Robbins. The woman was terminal, so Hillier said to make her comfortable."

"Did Nancy Robbins get suspended, too?" Charlie asked. He seemed somewhat suspicious.

"I don't know," Anne said. "Probably."

"Well, if you didn't do anything wrong, then why are you being suspended?" Charlie asked.

"What do you mean?" Anne asked coldly. She could feel her anger building. She didn't need another cross-examination.

"Well, they don't just go around suspending people for the hell of it, do they? You must have done something."

That was the thing with Charlie, Anne thought, he was always so cowed by authority, always so certain that the big wheels were right and the little guy was wrong. Oh, sure, he'd rave and rant at the President on the TV news, but let a small-town cop pull Charlie over for a ticket and it was "Yes, sir" this and "Yes, sir" that. Anne hated that meekness in Charlie almost as much as she hated it in herself.

"I did do *something*," Anne said. "I gave the woman enough morphine to kill an elephant. But it was on Dr. Hillier's orders."

"Then why are they suspending you?" Charlie asked.

By now he was sitting up and rubbing his beard. Anne could see his eyes shifting from side to side. She knew he was still thinking about the money.

"I don't know," she said. "It's just a lot of morphine, that's all. Hillier's in Europe. I guess they haven't talked to him. Maybe he's coming back in three days; maybe that's why it's three days. I don't know."

"But you did what they say you did? You gave the woman the drugs?"

"Charlie, of course I gave her the drugs. The woman was in excruciating pain, so I gave her a lot of morphine, that's all. She was terminal."

Anne waited for Charlie to put his arms around her and say, "Gee, hon, you must feel pretty lousy." She waited for a warm spot on his shoulder where she could burrow in and weep. But Charlie just stared at her as if she were a stupid little girl who would have to be punished. Anne stared back, and Charlie looked so old to her, so pale and tired of life.

"Anne, why did you do a stupid thing like that?" he said.

His words sliced into her. It wasn't a question, it was a comment. Charlie turned his back on her and went to sleep.

Chapter Three

In the morning Anne did not mention the suspension until all the girls were up. Only Susan, eighteen, Lori, seventeen, and twelve-year-old Meredith, her only child by Charlie, lived with Anne. Barbara, the oldest, lived nearby, in Kingston, with Anne's mother.

Charlie had already gone off to work. It was bright and peaceful in the kitchen. The radio played softly, and sunlight poured in through the wide glass doors that faced onto the back porch. The girls, still sleepy, gathered at the breakfast table and burrowed into bowls of cereal. Anne stood by the kitchen counter fussing around with the coffee pot. During the night the problem had shrunk to manageable size in Anne's mind, and now the idea of losing her license over this Leanues thing seemed pretty far-fetched, but she was still nervous about telling the girls.

"I guess Morton must be pretty happy with my work," she finally announced. "They gave me a vacation. Starting today."

"A vacation?" Susan said.

"Well, it's not exactly a vacation. It's more like a three-day suspension."

"Suspension?" Lori said. "What for?"

"I raped a patient," Anne said. She poured her coffee and joined the girls at the table. "Believe me, it was worth it. This guy could have won the Neil Diamond look-alike contest. And he was already in bed."

"Good for you, Ma," Susan said.

"Yeah, Ma, great, congratulations," Lori said. "Now tell us the truth. Why were you suspended?"

"A woman died."

"Who?"

"Her name was Norma Leanues," Anne said.

"What did she die of?"

"Cancer," Anne said. Then she told them about Norma, the pain, the morphine, and the late-night interrogation in Costello's office.

When Anne finished telling her story, the girls responded the way she knew they would, with love and concern. Anne could feel it rolling like a wave across the breakfast table.

"You must feel pretty awful," Lori said.

"I'll be okay," Anne said.

"What a bunch of assholes!" Susan said, and the other girls joined in, quickly defending their mother by saying nasty things about Maureen Costello and Lorraine Hickey and "them," meaning the hospital in general. Soon everybody was laughing.

"Hey, this is no big deal," Susan said. "Remember the time Ma totaled the truck and walked calmly in here and tossed the pieces on the kitchen table? Now, that was a big deal!"

The girls laughed again. Except for Lori. Anne felt as if the ordeal was over. She relaxed and lit her first cigarette of the day.

Susan and Meredith continued to talk and ask questions, but Lori, silent and grim-faced, stared into a bowl of shredded wheat. Lori didn't say anything at the time, it seemed silly to get all worked up over a three-day suspension, but that morning Lori was convinced that something dreadful loomed over the family.

After the girls left for school, Anne put on a Neil Diamond album and started singing along with it.

The emotional support of her daughters and their good humor had washed away the bitterness she felt over Charlie's "Why did you do a stupid thing like that?" remark. She decided she'd make the most of the three-day suspension. She'd bake a cake, call friends, read a book, go for a walk in the woods, and catch up with the housework. No longer was she scared. It was, she thought, simply a breakdown in communications. A doctor had given verbal medication orders for a dying woman. The woman had died while the doctor was away, so of course the hospital wanted to take precautions. Soon Dr. Hillier would return from Europe and explain that Anne was following doctor's orders, and that would be the end of it.

On Monday Nancy Robbins called. Nancy had been suspended, too. And so had Judy Foley, an R.N., and Pat Courcey, an L.P.N. Nancy sounded annoyed but not overly concerned.

"Don't worry," she told Anne. "We wouldn't have gotten suspended at all except that they've got a JC team coming in next month and they want to make sure we're all going to be good little girls. They're just trying to show us they can be tough."

"JC" was shorthand for the Joint Committee on Accreditation, which inspects hospitals periodically to make sure standards are being maintained.

"They just don't understand what it means to be a nurse," Nancy said. "You have to serve administration, you have to serve the doctor, and you have to serve the patient. You do what's right for one, and you get in trouble with the other."

"Yes," Anne said, "you try to take care of your patients, and they suspend you."

The talked for a few minutes about reprimands. Nancy had been bawled out before—not about drugs, but she had drifted into some gray area in the hospital's regulations. Anne confessed about the sterile-water incident at Lemuel Shattuck, and Nancy told Anne that Judy Foley had been reprimanded once.

"What for?"

"Poor Judy," Nancy said, "would you believe it? She caught hell once for *under*medicating a patient. Now she gets suspended for overmedicating a patient. She must think they're all crazy."

"They are," Anne said. "They are."

On Tuesday Maureen Costello called. The three days were up, but Costello asked Anne to stay away from the hospital for a while longer.

"We're all very concerned about you, Anne," she said, "but you can't come back to work yet." She said that Pat Courcey had been reinstated, but that Nancy Robbins and Judy Foley were still on suspension.

Maureen Costello called the next day.

And the day after that.

And the day after that.

Each conversation was like the one before it. "Don't come back to work yet," Costello would tell Anne. "But what is going on?" Anne would ask, and Costello, choosing her words with all the precision of a dentist choosing which bit to place in a drill, would answer, "Well the matter is quite sensitive and I really cannot discuss it."

So Anne drank a lot of coffee and smoked. She stretched out on the living room couch and read *Salem's Lot* by Stephen King. Six days passed and she still was not back at work. She baked two cakes, and seven days had gone by. She finished *Salem's Lot* and started reading *Carrie* after nine days. She brushed a new coat of stain on the gun cabinet in Meredith's room on the tenth day. Anne pored over the bills, choosing which to pay and which to ignore, after twelve days had passed. Then thirteen days and fourteen and fifteen passed. May faded into June and still Anne was in the dark.

Then one day, when the three-day suspension had swollen to three weeks, the phone rang and Anne heard Maureen Costello say in the grimmest possible tones, "Anne, you had better check on your malpractice insurance."

"Malpractice insurance? I don't have any," Anne said.

"Then you'd better get a lawyer," Costello said.

"I don't even know any lawyers."

"Ask around," Maureen Costello said. "Find someone who's right for you."·

"I can't afford a lawyer." Anne's heart was pounding. "What do I need a lawyer for? I didn't do anything."

"You probably won't need one," Costello said, "but it's best to have someone handy to protect your interests."

"What interests?" Anne said. "What are you talking about? I just want to come back to work. Have you talked to Dr. Hillier? Has he explained everything? I just want to come back to work."

"Perhaps it will work out that way."

"What the hell is going on?" Anne said. She had wound the telephone cord so tightly around her hands that she had red welts running across her fingers. "Is it malpractice? Is that it? Is someone suing?"

"I can't discuss it, Anne."

"Is the Leanues family suing for malpractice? Is that it?"

"Really, Anne, I have to maintain confidentiality about all of this."

"Is Hillier in trouble? Has anyone else been suspended?"

"Try not to worry," Costello said.

"Not worry?" Anne started to cry.

"Anne, we've had to turn this matter over to the district attorney."

"The district attorney?"

"It's only a formality. We're required by law to notify the district attorney if there might have been a case of overmedication."

"Oh, God!"

"Anne, it's best not to get emotional."

"Not get emotional? Mrs. Costello, I'm out of work, I've got bills to pay, I don't know what on earth you people are doing with my life. You're telling me to get a lawyer. And you tell me not to get emotional."

"I know this is difficult for you, Anne."

"Difficult? It's not difficult. It's horrible. I'm worried, Mrs. Costello, I'm worried. Just tell me one thing."

"What?"

"What is going on? I mean, what exactly is going on? Just tell me that. I don't understand what's happening. I can handle it, if I know. What is this all about?"

There was a long silence on the phone. For a moment Anne thought it had gone dead. Then the voice of the Iron Maiden replied. Coolly, carefully examining each syllable of each word before she delivered it, Maureen Costello said, "Anne, your interest and the hospital's interest have diverged. Get a lawyer."

The following week Anne received a letter from Maureen Costello.

"Dear Anne," it said, "In accordance with our discussions I have concluded that your employment is terminated effective May 22, 1980, as a result of your nursing performance relative to Norma Leanues."

For the first time in her life, Anne had been fired.

Chapter Four

The events that led to Anne Capute's firing began in December 1979, when Norma Leanues fell down in a parking lot at work.

Norma was fifty-one years old. She and her husband, Edward, were both conscientious blue-collar workers. She was a spot welder at the Triad Company in Chartley, and he worked as a custodian at Taunton High School. They had raised four children. Linda and Cheryl had married and moved out; Edward and Jeffrey still lived at 20 Shores Avenue in Taunton, which had been home to Norma and her husband for more than two decades.

It was two weeks before Christmas 1979 that Norma fell and fractured her thighbone. Her personal doctor, Robert Hillier, was an orthopedic surgeon on staff at Morton Hospital, and when he examined Norma at Morton, Hillier suspected that something had weakened her thighbone. It had broken too easily.

Hillier found cancer in Norma's thighbone. He removed a tumor and inserted a nail plate to support the bone. But Norma's ordeal was only beginning. The tumor was metastatic; it had spread to the thigh from someplace else. During the weeks that followed, Norma was put through dozens of tests. The doctors probed, prodded, and poked at every inch of her body, but they couldn't find the primary site of the cancer. They knew Norma had cancer; they just didn't know where it had originated.

In March 1980 Norma started to lose feeling in her legs. Her husband urged her to see Dr. Hillier, but she refused. Finally Edward Leanues called Dr. Hillier, against his wife's wishes. On April 30 Dr. Hillier admitted Norma to Morton Hospital.

Norma got worse. She lost control of her bladder. Her legs became more numb. Hillier concluded that a cancerous tumor was swelling in Norma's spinal cord and gradually paralyzing her. Norma was presented with a choice of paralysis or surgery. She chose surgery. On May 6 Hillier operated on her, removing most of the tumor from her spine. This tumor was also metastatic. The spine was not the primary site of the cancer.

Later Dr. Hillier would tell a jury that he had never given up on Norma Leanues, that he had plans for more tests and further treatment, that he fully intended to save her life. But after the spine operation Norma's nurses began to perceive Norma as a dying woman. Whether Hillier projected the image of Leanues as a doomed woman is arguable. But what is important is that Norma was believed to be terminal and was treated as such.

During the two weeks following the spine operation Norma Leanues experienced a good deal of what is referred to in nurses' notes as "discomfort." In fact she was in severe, often excruciating pain. Relief came from drugs, most notably morphine sulfate.

On Mother's Day Norma's whole family went to the hospital to visit her. She was happy to see them all together, and she was in good spirits. But after that, things got worse.

On the night of Friday, May 16, there was a conversation concerning the medication for Norma

Leanues. It's the conversation that Anne later recounted in Costello's office. Anne, Nancy Robbins,
and Robert Hillier were present, but their reports of
the conversation vary.

Here is how Dr. Robert Hillier describes it:

"As I was leaving the hospital I spoke to Nurse
Capute and Nurse Robbins. I was in front of the
nursing station on the second floor. Anne said that
the morphine solution that Mrs. Leanues was taking
did not appear to be effective. The morphine solution
was taken PO, orally. It was a combination of morphine and alcohol, which Mrs. Leanues drank from a
cup several times a day. Drugs taken orally are usually
the least effective, and the solution can gradually lose
its power. Anne said Mrs. Leanues was still having
considerable pain, and we discussed the best thing to
do. We decided we were going to proceed with a shot
that would be given in addition to the solution if the
solution did not work. I decided to go with fifteen
milligrams of morphine by shot every three hours, as
needed, for pain, in addition to the oral solution, if
the patient was in extreme pain.

"The shot was to be used only if the oral
medication was not working and only at a frequency
of every three hours, no shorter than that. But it
could be used, let's say, every eight or every ten hours.
Anne said, 'Don't worry, Dr. Hillier, we will take good
care of Mrs. Leanues,' and I went out of the hospital
to my office, called the answering service, and transferred Mrs. Leanues to Dr. Pottier because I was
leaving the hospital for a week."

Nancy Robbins describes the conversation this
way:

"I saw Dr. Hillier outside of Mrs. Leanues's room.
Anne Capute was also present. The nurses on the day
shift had asked me to speak to Dr. Hillier about

changing the morphine solution to the s.c. type, so I told Dr. Hillier and I told him that Mrs. Leanues was having trouble swallowing. Dr. Hillier said, 'Fine, give it to her s.c. So I asked him how much morphine he wanted Mrs. Leanues to have. He said, 'Give her whatever she needs to make her comfortable. She's only got twenty-four to forty-eight hours to live.' I asked him again what dose he wanted. He said, 'Well, let's see, 40 cc's equals about ten to fifteen milligrams of morphine s.c., so give her that,' and I said, 'Well, how about if I write morphine, fifteen milligrams, s.c., no time limit, like other doctors do, keep her comfortable. Is that all right with you, Dr. Hillier?' He said that was fine. Then I asked him about changing the Valium order from PO to an IM, intramuscular, order, and he said again that was fine. Then I proceeded to write the order, and while I was writing it, Anne went off to get the medication. I wrote the order just the way I had repeated it to Dr. Hillier. 'Morphine, fifteen milligrams, IM, prn, no time limit, keep patient comfortable.'"

Nancy Robbins wrote the medication order she describes, but Dr. Hillier never signed it.

During the next thirty-six hours Norma Leanues was given morphine by several nurses, and each nurse who medicated Leanues correctly entered the amount of morphine into the medication records and nurse's notes.

When Edward Leanues visited his wife on that weekend, she was sinking fast. On Friday night she didn't wake up for him. He went back to the hospital on Saturday morning. His wife was still unconscious. He shook her but she didn't wake up. He came again during Saturday afternoon visiting hours. Still Norma slept. At midnight Saturday, when Edward finished his shift as a custodian at Taunton High School, he came again to be near his wife.

"I just sat there and listened to Norma's breathing," he says. "It was like her breaths were getting further and further apart. And she finally stopped breathing. I shook her and I noticed her eyes were half open. I waited for her to take another breath and it just never came."

And so early on May 18, with her husband at her side, Norma Leanues died. Dr. David H. Pottier signed the death certificate, listing the causes of death as cancer, primary source unknown.

Dr. Robert Hillier was vacationing in Paris.

The information about Norma Leanues's medication was of no great concern to anyone until L.P.N. Vicki McKenna discovered it two days after Norma died. On that day, Tuesday, May 20, Anne Capute and Vicki McKenna had a short conversation at the nurses' station on S-2. Here is how Vicki McKenna recalls the conversation:

"Anne told me she had taken care of Norma Leanues over the weekend, and she asked me if I knew that Norma had died. I said yes. Anne said, 'I promised her husband she wouldn't suffer. If you had a hundred twenty milligrams of morphine you would die, too.' Then I said, 'I suppose I would.'"

Later that evening Vicki went to the medication closet to get some morphine for a patient.

"And when I opened up the narcotic book I noticed that Norma Leanues's name had been written time after time on the narcotic sheet," Vicki says. "I checked the dates, and the dates were all the same, and the time was within an hour apart. That is when I realized that Norma Leanues had been given medication that was far above the normal dosage. I have never seen a patient given medication like that. The effect of that much morphine would be respiratory failure.."

Vicki McKenna, shocked by the large doses of morphine, decided to report it. She tried to call her supervisor, Fran Silva, but could not reach her at home. Vicki called Ms. Silva all day Wednesday but still couldn't get her. On Thursday morning Vicki McKenna called Lorraine Hickey. That afternoon Vicki went to the hospital and told Hickey about the medication charts and the conversation with Anne. Lorraine Hickey passed the information on to Maureen Costello. The information was moving its way up the Morton Hospital hierarchy. Early that evening Maureen Costello brought it to the top, Larry Ross.

Larry Ross is the administrator of Morton Hospital. He's the boss. Ross is a huge man who dominates every room he enters. He's good-natured, candid, and intensely dedicated to the Morton staff, which is, he says, "like family."

"Maureen Costello called me at home around dinnertime," he says. "She told me what Lorraine Hickey had told her that Vicki McKenna had told Lorraine. By this time Maureen and Lorraine had gone over the Leanues medical chart, and Maureen wanted to know whether or not we should contact our legal counsel. I told her there was nothing we could do that evening but that she and I would sit down first thing in the morning and talk about what had happened.

"Then Maureen said she would like to talk to a couple of the nurses who were involved in the case, because they were on duty that night and it would be helpful to interview them before she met with me in the morning."

That was May 22, the night Maureen Costello interviewed Anne at ten-thirty.

On Friday morning Costello reported to Larry Ross. Ross telephoned Nelson Ross, an attorney for the hospital, and told him what was going on. The attorney said the medical examiner and the district attorney would have to be notified.

By Sunday morning Dr. Hillier had returned from Paris. Ross called him at home.

"When I talked with Hillier that Sunday morning I asked him if he recalled giving an order with regards to changing Mrs. Leanues's medication. I said, 'There's no written or signed order by you in the chart, just a verbal order taken down by Nancy Robbins,' and I read him what was written and asked him if that was what he ordered in the chart. Hillier's response was, 'I don't remember exactly, but I don't think that's what I said.' I told him that as attending physician he was the one who should notify the medical examiner. He said that he would."

The information was spread in many directions. Dr. Hillier notified the medical examiner. The hospital's attorneys notified District Attorney Ronald Pina. And somebody notified the press.

Chapter Five

Anne came into the house one afternoon lugging two bags of groceries.

"Well, I got one," she said. She came into the living room where her friend Warren Magee was helping Susan with homework. Warren was like a member of the family. He was a tall, charming, and extremely intelligent black man who was engaged to Anne's friend Beth Whitehead. Warren dropped in often.

"Got what?" he asked.

"A damn lawyer," Anne said. She put her groceries on the coffee table.

"What's his name?" Warren asked.

"David Elliott."

"Who the hell is David Elliott?"

"He's a lawyer, that's all," Anne said. "He seemed all right. To tell you the truth, I've got no use for any of them, but Costello says get a lawyer, so I got a lawyer."

"You didn't get Piscitelli?" Warren said. He frowned.

"Pisci . . . whoeee?"

"Pat Piscitelli," Warren said. "The guy I've been telling you about."

"Oh, come on, Warren, I'm not going to schlep all the way to Boston just for a lawyer when I probably don't even need one."

"Brockton," Warren said, "not Boston. He's in Brockton. They call him the Bailey of Brockton. You know, like F. Lee Bailey."

"Well that's still a half-hour drive. This guy's ten minutes away, in Hanover."

"How did you choose him?"

"I picked his name out of a phone book," Anne said.

"Very scientific," Warren said.

Anne smiled and turned to Susan. "Your turn to cook supper," she said, "Come on, I'll help you," and she led Susan into the kitchen.

After a few minutes Warren drifted in. He lit up his pipe, then stood by the kitchen counter with his arms folded and took on that wise expression he always got when he was about to tell Anne something for her own good.

"I still think you should get Piscitelli," he said. "He's good. He once got five acquittals in a row in murder cases."

"Yes, well this isn't a murder case," Anne said, poking him gently in the ribs.

"You never know," Warren said.

"It's a case of me getting fired," Anne said. "Oh, excuse me, not 'fired,' 'Terminated'! I'm getting terminated, not fired." She laughed. "It sounds like they're going to give me rat poison or something."

"Piscitelli handled Albert Desalvo," Warren said. "The Boston Strangler. He was going to defend him, except that Desalvo got a shiv in the chest in Walpole State Prison."

"Warren, I love you dearly, but buzz off," Anne said. "I don't need some big-deal lawyer. I'm going to go in and get officially terminated, that's all. Then Leanues's lawyers will probably sue everybody in sight for a hundred million dollars or something and it will drag on for years."

"Don't forget that the district attorney has all those medical records," Warren said.

Anne let out a hearty laugh. "What are they going to do, accuse three nurses of murder?"

"Maybe," Warren said. "Pina's ambitious. Something like this would get him a lot of publicity."

"Wouldn't that be a riot?" Anne said. "Imagine me helping someone get into Congress."

Soon Warren plodded back into the living room and sat alone. This disturbed Anne. Warren was a troubled soul who had been hospitalized for depression, and he was inclined from time to time to sink silently into inexplicable sadness.

"You and Charlie going fishing this weekend?" she called, but Warren did not answer.

"We could use some fish, a lot of it," she said. "I'm running out of money for groceries." Still Warren did not respond. Anne, thinking that Warren was hurt because she hadn't taken his advice, walked into the living room and sat beside him. "Tell you what, pal," she said, putting an arm around him. "I'll make you a promise. If I ever need a lawyer again I'll go to this Piscitelli guy."

Warren still seemed kind of down. But after a minute the shine returned to his eyes and he smiled. "Good," he said, and he relit his pipe. "Just don't let anybody with a shiv get behind you."

Anne was dismissed from Morton Hospital in Maureen Costello's office on a sunny morning in the middle of June. David Elliott's first official job as Anne's lawyer was to escort her to the formal firing.

It was a painful moment for Anne. Still in awe of the assistant administrator for nursing services, Anne had dressed up in a skirt and blouse and heels. She wanted to go out with dignity. Elliott was having back problems, and he kept trying to draw Costello into his joking.

"Hey, you got a good chiropractor here? My back's killing me," he said, while Costello, as stiff and formal as ever, slid forms across the desk to Anne and carefully explained what each one was. Anne signed the forms, and kept her head up. Despite everything, Anne still sought Costello's respect.

When the papers were signed, Costello led Anne and Elliott into the hallway. She put her arm around Anne and said, "Anne, I want you to know that all of us here at Morton are praying for you."

"Imagine that!" Anne said when the Iron Maiden

was gone. "She just fired me and now she's praying for me."

When they got outside, Anne stood in the parking lot between the administration building and the hospital's main building, clutching the papers that said she was no longer a nurse at Morton Hospital. She stared up at the second floor and thought about the lucky women up there who were taking care of their patients, and her eyes filled with tears.

"Come on, let's get out of this place," she said to Elliott. "Hospitals give me the creeps."

Chapter Six

During the first week of June Ted Gay, managing editor of the *Taunton Daily Gazette*, received a package of information about the Leanues medication and Morton's investigation. Early on the morning of Monday, June 9, Gay, who has never revealed his source, put in a call to Morton administrator Larry Ross. He told Ross that the *Gazette* intended to run a story on the morphine dosage. He asked Ross for comments. Ross told Gay the hospital would have nothing to say on the matter until the investigation was over.

When Larry Ross hung up he knew he had to tell the Leanues family what was going on. He certainly didn't want them reading it in the newspaper. Ross drove to 20 Shores Avenue in Taunton, the small house that Norma and Edward Leanues had shared for more than twenty years. He rang the bell and was met at the door by Edward Leanues, a small, gray-haired man who was still in shock over the loss of his wife.

"Is it about my wife's bill?" Leanues asked.

"No," Ross said. "Something else."

The two men went in and sat in the Leanues living room. Ross told Leanues about the medication and the suspension of the nurses. He explained that there would be a story in the afternoon paper.

"I felt so bad for him," Larry Ross says. "Mr. Leanues didn't say it, but the impression I got from him was a feeling of 'My wife is dead. Why are you doing this to me? She's gone and there's nothing we can do, so let her rest in peace.' I was there for about half an hour. He really didn't say much of anything. He wept most of the time. In fourteen years at the hospital that was the hardest thing I ever had to do."

That afternoon the *Taunton Daily Gazette* broke the story:

DA PROBES POSSIBLE "MERCY" DEATH
OF PATIENT AT MORTON

At five o'clock that day Anne was in the living room reading when Susan came rushing into the house.

"Ma, Ma, it's on the radio," she said. "It's on the radio, I heard it on the car radio."

"What?"

"About you," Susan said. "It's on the radio that you were suspended. They're calling it a mercy killing."

"Oh, no," Anne said. This was the most frightening development yet.

"I mean they didn't say your name, but they said three nurses had been suspended."

While Anne and Susan were talking, the phone rang. It was Beth Whitehead, Anne's nursing friend from her days at Jordan Hospital.

"Anne, do you know they're talking about you on the radio?" Beth said.

"I just heard," Anne said. "It's scary. It's . . . it's crazy."

The next day Neil Downing, a staff reporter with the *Gazette,* wrote a story, LEANUES SHOCKED BY MATE ORDEAL and the *Brockton Enterprise* ran a headline, MORTON SUSPENDS NURSES IN WOMAN'S DEATH. The story was then picked up by newspapers in Boston, New Bedford, and Providence. By the end of the week the wire services had spread it across the country.

Anne was not in the dark anymore. During the summer of 1980, if she wanted to find out what was going on, all she had to do was pick up the daily newspaper. On June 12 she read a story in the *Brockton Enterprise* by Paul Stevens, one of the reporters who would follow the case to the end:

HOSPITAL TO PROVIDE RECORDS
IN POSSIBLE MERCY KILLING

Records dealing with the suspected mercy killing on May 18 of a 51-year-old woman cancer patient were due to be released by the administration of Morton Hospital early this afternoon to the Bristol County district attorney's office. . . .

A few days later, Anne read:

MORTON HOSPITAL VICTIM
BODY TO BE EXHUMED

Then:

EXHUMED BODY RE-INTERRED AFTER AUTOPSY

The body of a terminal cancer patient exhumed for an autopsy was re-interred at St. Joseph's Cemetery Friday as authorities subpoenaed seven people in an alleged "mercy killing" investigation. . . . Medical examiner Dr. William Bennet Jr. told United Press International "We have a better knowledge of what the situation is than we had before. It looks as though we've arrived at something."

Anne read:

HOSPITAL DEATH PROBERS
MULL THEIR NEXT MOVE

State detectives investigating the circumstances surrounding the May 18 death of 51-year-old Norma C. Leanues, suspected mercy killing victim, met with District Attorney Ronald A. Pina today to go over evidence to date and decide their next move in the puzzling case.

And:

GRAND JURY READY TO REVIEW
SUSPECTED "MERCY KILLING"

The Bristol County grand jury is being convened Tuesday at the New Bedford courthouse to review evidence in the suspected mercy killing of Norma C. Leanues, 51-year-old victim of terminal cancer.

Beth Whitehead brought Anne the paper that said:

"MERCY KILLING" PROBE BEGINS

. . . Pina said last week there was evidence Mrs. Leanues's death was due to a deliberate overdose of morphine and that hospital officials may have tried to cover up the fact.

Throughout the summer the headlines continued, but still Anne's name did not appear in the paper. It was always "three nurses were suspended from Morton Hospital," and for that she was grateful. It was getting so that she was afraid to look at the newspaper. But she always knew what was happening. She was still a nurse, and she took temporary jobs through a medical personnel service, and inevitably she heard other nurses talking about the case. Sometimes Anne told them that she was one of the three nurses, and sometimes she didn't. She felt terribly embarrassed, as if she were being scolded in public.

On June 21 a headline said:

EXPERT SAYS CANCER
DID NOT KILL WOMAN

A Harvard-trained expert on cancer said Friday that in his opinion—based on his study of medical records and the autopsy report—Norma C. Leanues died from causes other than cancer. Dr. Robert J. Greene, asked if he thought the death of the Taunton woman was of suspicious origin said: "I think you can say that, yes."

At the beginning of August Anne read:

MORTON HOSPITAL PERSONNEL
TESTIFY BEFORE GRAND JURY

The story noted that of the four nurses suspended, one had been reinstated and the other three had been fired. But still no names were mentioned.

Late on the afternoon of August 8 Beth Whitehead came into Anne's house, somewhat wild-eyed and angry, waving a folded newspaper in Anne's face. Warren Magee was with her.

"Anne, have you seen this? Have you?" Beth asked. She walked right past Anne and stood in the middle of the kitchen.

"Don't show it to me," Anne said. "I don't want to see any more newspapers." Anne had just gotten home from one of her temporary nursing assignments, and both women were in nurse's whites.

"It's outrageous," Beth said, "that's what it is." She opened the paper. It was the *Taunton Daily Gazette* brandishing a headline that said, MERCY KILLING OR MISTAKE? "Listen to this," Beth said, "just listen to what they're saying." She started reading from the newspaper, all the time pacing across Anne's kitchen. Anne slumped into a kitchen chair.

"Quote," Beth said, "'I just wanted to stop her suffering. She had enough morphine sulfate to kill an elephant. I knew I had killed her the next morning.' Unquote."

"I don't believe it," Anne said. It was the first time she had ever heard herself quoted in the newspaper.

Beth continued, making angry faces at the paper as she read:

Those words were those of a licensed practical nurse at Morton Hospital, Taunton.
The time: the evening of May 22. The
occasion: the beginning of Morton Hospital's
internal probe into the circumstances surrounding the death of 51-year-old cancer
patient Norma C. Leanues, suspected victim
of fatal doses of morphine.

The information given by the L.P.N. in
her own words was sent anonymously
through the mails to the district attorney in a
packet postmarked July 17 from Mansfield.

Her remarks were contained in a photo-
copy of a hand-written account of an interrogation of nurses by hospital officials that
began four days after Mrs. Leanues died.
Three other photocopies of reports of the
hospital's internal investigation of Mrs.
Leanues's death also were contained in the
packet.

Beth went on. Anne looked at Warren. He was
standing with his arms folded, and his eyes were
moving. Anne loved to watch Warren's eyes when he
was trying to figure something out; she loved the way
his mind worked. Beth read the entire story. It
contained quotes from Nancy Robbins's interview
also, identifying the nurses only as "the L.P.N." and
"the R.N." Warren said nothing. When he finished
figuring out whatever he was working on, his eyes
grew still and he took on an expression that said to
Anne, "See, I told you this would get worse."

"Well," Beth said when she finished reading, "did
you say those things, Anne?" She threw the paper
down on the kitchen table.

"Some of them," Anne said. "I said the elephant
thing. But I was, you know, kidding. You know how I
am."

"What about this?" Beth said. She snatched the paper off the table and found the paragraph she wanted. "Did you say this? 'I just wanted to put an end to her agony. She suffered such pain. I didn't think of it as killing her. I mean, I was not trying out for "euthanasia nurse." ' "

"I don't remember," Anne said. "I don't remember. I might have. It sounds like me, doesn't it."

Anne lit a cigarette. She was starting to feel relaxed even though she knew the situation was becoming increasingly serious. Beth seemed really upset, and Anne didn't want to make matters worse by getting emotional. Anne had felt for some time that she had no control over the situation, and she was tired of worrying about it.

"Costello should be fired for this," Beth said. She paced again. "She should be thrown out of that hospital. What right has she got to do this, leaking stories to the newspapers? It's outrageous."

"It wasn't Costello," Anne said.

"Of course it was," Beth said. "Who else?"

"It wasn't Costello," Anne said. "If I'm certain of anything, I'm certain of that. She's not that kind of person. She's a lady."

"Then who? Who would do a thing like that?"

"I don't know," Anne said. "It could have been a lot of people. Tom Bosanquet and Lorraine Hickey were there. It could have been one of them. It could have been the medical examiner, or one of the detectives."

"Or none of them," Warren said.

"Huh?"

"Aren't you overlooking the obvious?" Warren said.

"Who?"

"Who has the most to gain from this story?"

"I don't know." Anne laughed. "It sure as hell wasn't me."

"It could have been our friend the D.A., or someone in his office," Warren said.

"The district's attorney's office? Why would they do a thing like that? It doesn't make sense."

"It's been said that he's ambitious. Maybe he wants to move on to higher office," Warren said. "In order to do that a district attorney needs publicity. In order to get publicity he needs a juicy murder trial. In order to get a murder trial he needs an indictment from the grand jury. This story could help. Grand juries are not locked up. They read the papers. Maybe one of his staff people did it without telling him."

"But it doesn't make any sense," Anne said. "He got an anonymous package too."

"Did he?"

"That's what it says."

"Well, maybe," Warren said. "But I find it a little strange that on July seventeenth someone would send him a package containing information which he had already received in early June when the hospital turned over all the records of their investigation. And incidentally, all the people you mentioned would have known the D.A. already had the information. In any case, how would the newspaper know that their package contained the same thing as his package unless he or someone in his office told them what was in his package? And most of all I would find it strange if the newspaper ran a story like this based on nothing but a bunch of papers submitted anonymously. They could have come from anybody. So the newspaper had to verify that they came from the hospital records. The hospital sure as hell wouldn't help them print a story like this. It had to be the D.A.'s office."

The three friends were quiet for a while, letting Warren's conclusions settle on them. Then Warren spoke again.

"I would say it's time to call Piscitelli," Warren said.

"Anybody want a cup of coffee?" Anne said.

"Coffee?" Beth said. "Anne, they are smearing your name across the front page like you're some kind of murderer, and you're just sitting there taking coffee orders."

"They haven't mentioned my name yet," Anne said.

"They will," Beth said.

"How about you, Warren? You want some coffee?"

"Piscitelli," Warren sternly replied.

"Sorry, honey, we're all out of Piscitelli. I've got coffee and I've got tea."

"Anne, you have got to call Piscitelli."

"What for, for God's sake? It's almost over," Anne said.

"Is it?"

"Of course it is, Warren. The grand jury is supposed to finish up in a few days."

"What if they indict you?"

"Indict me? Warren, don't be ridiculous. They're not going to indict three nurses for murder."

On Tuesday, August 12, Anne didn't work. She was at home washing dishes when the phone rang. She was annoyed, thinking it was another bill collector. They had been hounding her. With her wet, soapy hands she grabbed the phone receiver on the kitchen wall and hollered into it a rather gruff "Hello."

The man on the other end was a reporter, and he asked her if she wanted to make any comments.

"Comments about what?" she said.

"About the fact that you've been indicted for first-degree murder," he said.

Chapter Seven

Anne woke up screaming.

"Don't lock me in!" she hollered into the dark. She felt a hand grab her. "No!" she cried, recoiling. Her heart pounded in her chest. Then Anne realized it was Charlie's hand reaching to comfort her, and she was in her own bed. She fell into Charlie's arms and wept.

"What happened, hon?" Charlie whispered.

"A nightmare," Anne replied, sobbing. Her body was still cold from the terror. "I was in a small room, it was gray, and there was no door and no windows. Just walls. I had this incredible feeling of claustrophobia. I felt so doomed."

Charlie pulled her close to him in the bed. He patted her shoulder. "It's okay, it's okay," he said. "Just a nightmare."

"I don't want to go to prison," Anne said. "I didn't do anything." It was the first time Anne talked about prison. The idea of being locked up had always seemed absurd. Now it was dangerously real.

"You won't go to prison, hon. You won't."

After a few minutes Anne's trembling stopped, and when the sound of her own heartbeat faded she heard only the sound of Charlie's stiff hand flapping in neat, steady beats against her shoulder. She felt like a child, and she snuggled deeper into Charlie's arms and inhaled the warmth of his body.

"I couldn't bear to go to prison," she whispered. "I just couldn't bear it."

Charlie's response was to wrap his arms more tightly around her, as if to say, I won't let them take you away. This saddened Anne. She knew that things were not good between her and Charlie, and what was worse, she knew that she was past the point of even wanting them to be good.

The dream lingered. To be in prison must be the worst thing in the world, Anne thought. Worse than death, certainly. She had always been an outdoorswoman, a lover of fresh air and wide skies and long walks in the woods.

"Charlie," she whispered.

"Yeah?"

"Remember the time we went hunting in Maine, and Phil drove a hundred miles past the cottage?"

"Sure do," Charlie said. "I thought Phil would shit a brick, he was so mad at himself."

In the dark they chuckled, and Anne tried to recall other funny incidents from their past, trying to push back the gray walls of her dream. But the memories just wouldn't come, and soon she heard Charlie's breathing change and she knew he was asleep. For a long time she stayed in the warm cocoon of his arms. But she was unable to sleep that way, and finally she pulled away and rolled back to her side of the bed. She thought about running away—to northern California or Montana, someplace big and open. With such dreams replacing the memory of the nightmare, Anne tried to get some sleep. She was being arraigned for murder in the morning.

It was August 13. Anne met her lawyer, David Elliott, at the courthouse in New Bedford.

While Anne and Elliott waited in the lobby at the back of the court, Anne stayed close to the coffee and Coke machines as if they were a pair of friends. There was something reassuring about vending machines: They were familiar; they were part of her real world, not the world of courts, judges, and prisons. She was nervous, but David Elliott told her not to worry.

As she and Elliott were talking, a court officer came to Anne and tapped her on the shoulder. "Would you come with me," the officer said.

"What? What for?" Anne said. She felt a jolt of panic move through her. What was happening? Were they going to drag her off to prison without a trial?

"Fingerprinting," the officer said.

"Fingerprinting? You mean, like a criminal?" She couldn't believe it. She turned to Elliott as the officer led her away. "Nobody told me about this," she said.

The officer took her into a small side room and he rolled her fingers across an ink pad and firmly pressed each one onto a fingerprint chart. Anne felt humiliated. Then the officer told her he had to take her picture. He smiled weakly, as if to say, Sorry, lady, it's just my job.

The camera wasn't working right, so Anne had to adjust the flash attachment for her own mug shot. She was feeling self-conscious about her weight, and she stuck out her jaw hoping it would stretch the skin under her chin and make her look less fleshy, but it merely made her look tough and defiant.

Nancy Robbins and Judy Foley arrived with their lawyers. After the two nurses were fingerprinted and photographed, everybody went upstairs. They were led into the second-floor courtroom. The three nurses stood in the prisoners' dock, and the charges were read:

At the Superior Court holden at New Bedford within and for the County of Bristol, for the transaction of criminal business, on the second Tuesday of August in the year of Our Lord one thousand nine hundred and eighty. The jurors for the Commonwealth on their oath present that Anne Capute, on or about the seventeenth day of May in the year of Our Lord one thousand nine hundred and eighty, at Taunton, in the County of Bristol aforesaid did assault and beat one Norma C. Leanues with intent to murder her, and by such assault and beating did kill and murder the said Norma C. Leanues.

Anne was shocked at the formal, archaic language of the indictment.

Murder, assault, and beat, Anne thought. I barely laid a finger on her.

In addition to the murder charges, each nurse was charged with a drug violation. Specifically, the indictments read in part, "did knowingly or intentionally dispense a Class B controlled substance, to wit: Morphine-sulfate in violation of Section 32, Chapter 94C of the General Laws of the Commonwealth."

Anne had been to the courthouse once before—in June, when she had testified before the grand jury. Anne's grand jury testimony, like that of Nancy Robbins and Judy Foley, consisted of two sentences repeated after every question from District Attorney Ronald Pina:

"On the advice of my attorney I respectfully decline to answer that question put to me on the grounds that any answers which I may give may tend to incriminate me. This I do under the Fifth and Fourteenth amendments of the Constitution of the United States."

But on this hot August morning there would be no statements. Just a simple plea of "not guilty."

Each of the nurses pleaded "not guilty." In a moment it was over, and Anne was free to go. No bail was set. Anne couldn't believe that anything so important could happen so quickly.

"That's it?" she said to Elliott as they walked toward the door.

"I told you an arraignment was nothing," he said. "Now we wait for a trial date. It could take a while."

When they got outside and stood on the steps, Elliott patted Anne's arm. "You can be sure the D.A. is going to try this case in the newspapers," he said.

"So what do we do?"

"I think we should fight fire with fire," Elliott said. "I'll set up a press conference."

"Fine," Anne said. "I'm going to open a real can of worms."

Anne drove home from New Bedford thinking how ironic it was that she was being advised to make friends with the press. She had left the house that morning still raving to her family about what a bunch of heartless vultures reporters were.

"Ma could hardly stand to look at the papers even when they weren't using her name," Anne's daughter Meredith says. "Then after the indictment everybody knew her name. On the afternoon after the indictment came out . . . I guess it must have been about four o'clock . . . I looked out the window and there was this camera crew from Channel Six and there was a bunch of other reporters. Apparently they knew the street where we lived but didn't know which house and they were going along from house to house asking people where we lived. Then someone told them which house and I saw them coming; it was like a lynch mob or something.

It's the reporters, I said, and Ma and Susan and Lori and me all ducked down on the floor so they would think nobody was home. It was crazy, we were hiding behind furniture and crawling around on the carpet and all these newspeople were outside pounding on the door. And they were asking questions. I couldn't believe it. *They were actually asking questions through the door.* Finally Ma crawled around to the kitchen and she pulled down the phone and called Barry Vinton. He's the chief of police. He's really a super guy and he's a friend of my family. Barry came over and he drove around the house and came in the back door and said, 'What the hell is going on?' 'I'm up for murder,' Ma said. 'No shit?' Barry said, and he went to the front door and told everybody to get the hell out of there in a hurry or he'd arrest them. It was great."

Chapter Eight

Anne's press conference was held in David Elliott's office the day after the arraignment. Reporters from five newspapers, three radio stations, and two television stations crowded into the small room with videotape cameras, tape recorders, cameras, and notebooks. Before they arrived Anne had been wisecracking with Elliott. But now, startled by all the attention, she was struck shy, and when she stared wide-eyed and pale-faced into the cameras, she wore an expression of fright. She felt like a trapped animal.

She took a deep breath and began. She talked first about the ruinous effects that events were having on her family life. She decribed it as "a nightmare."

"I lost the job I loved," Anne said. She paused. She didn't know if she was supposed to give the reporters time to write in their notebooks. "I can handle it, I'm an adult," she said. "But my Meredith is not. She's just a kid." Anne's voice cracked. "Meredith is twelve and she likes to run for the phone and grab it first, the way kids do. And now we are afraid every time the phone rings. People call up and say horrible things. Meredith is in an awful emotional state because of what people have said. How would you feel if your twelve-year-old answered a telephone call from someone who said, 'Has your mother murdered anyone today?'"

Anne also told the reporters that she had been suspended from the nursing pool that had been giving her temporary assignments.

"I guess I'm too hot to handle," she told them. "Nursing is my life. It's all I ever wanted. Where do I go from here?"

Anne paused again to give the reporters time to write notes, and for the first time she really looked at their faces. She saw that they weren't monsters but people like herself. The thought came to her: *They're just trying to do their job.* She wondered if they had always dreamed of becoming reporters, the way she had always dreamed of becoming a nurse.

"Well," she said, smiling for the first time, "I guess I can't be a nurse anymore. I suppose I could become an airline pilot," and everybody laughed.

One reporter asked her if she would plea-bargain.

"I won't plead anything in this case except innocence," she said, feeling stronger now. "I have done nothing wrong. I was only following orders when I gave morphine to Norma Leanues. The doctor said, 'Give her anything she wants to make her comfortable.'"

Anne was asked to recall the specific conversation, and she told the press what she had told Costello. "Nancy Robbins asked him if he wanted his patient to have morphine by injection, and he said yes. I know because I was there, I heard him. The doctor told her that Mrs. Leanues had only twenty-four to forty-eight hours to live."

"Isn't a verbal order rather unusual?" one of the radio reporters asked.

"No," Anne snapped. She was angry, not with the reporters but with all the people who seemed to think she had done something far out of the ordinary at Morton.

"Verbal orders for medication are commonly given by doctors at Morton Hospital," Anne said. She described Morton as a place where harried doctors practically sprint through the wards all day long, casually calling out medication orders and not signing the written order form until hours later. Anne said that what she had done was routine procedure with terminally ill patients. When the reporters asked her how she knew Leanues was terminally ill, she repeated the "twenty-four to forty-eight hours to live" remark and said that after Hillier operated on Leanues's spine he told several staff members that the cancer was already growing before he closed the incision.

"Was it mercy killing?" someone said. The room grew tense, as if everybody expected Anne to break down or lose her temper.

Instead, she smiled. "You tell me," she said. "The nurses all kept accurate records. You certainly are not going to administer a narcotic and write down the orders if you're taking part in a mercy killing."

David Elliott, recognizing a point in Anne's favor, moved in and continued. "I don't think you'll find any case on record involving more than one person participating in a mercy killing," he said. "And no person has actually written down what was done. A classic mercy killing case involves a close relationship built up over a period of time between the defendant and the patient, the motive being love and compassion for the patient. In this case the relationships were brief between the nurses and the patient."

Anne's remarks created a sensation. A shadow fell across the reputation of Morton Hospital as Anne's comments about "routine procedure with terminal patients" and verbal medication orders were widely quoted.

When the story faded from the front page it became the peg for all sorts of euthanasia stories. People everywhere asked old questions and some new ones. Does a doctor have the right to play God? Is anybody ever terminal, or is a miracle always possible? Is it murder to withhold the "heroic measures" that can save lives? And if plugs are to be pulled on life-sustaining machines, who is to pull them, and when? Newspapers editorialized about euthanasia. Ministers sermonized. Television dramatized.

And a strange thing happened.

The real question, the one that had relentlessly grown for months in the corridors of Morton Hospital, was, "Did three nurses commit a mercy killing?" But in the public mind that question drifted into irrelevancy and was replaced by the more compelling, "Is mercy killing right or wrong?" Public sentiment for the three nurses was determined not by belief in their guilt or innocence, but by individual attitudes about mercy killing.

"Even now I find it strange," says Anne's daughter Susan, "that there were people who were for my mother and people who were against her, the people on both sides just sort of assumed that she committed a mercy killing. Some think she did it and she's a terrible person. Others think she did it and she's a wonderful person. But the idea that Ma didn't do it at all just doesn't seem to occur to most people."

The "Mercy Killing at Morton" story stayed alive in the newspapers for weeks after Anne's press conference. The Department of Public Health was investigating Morton, and their records were public. But, more important, somebody was leaking secret grand jury testimony to the press.

One of the earliest and most startling news leaks concerned the testimony of Dr. Robert Greene, the expert who had been hired by the commonwealth of Massachusetts. Dr. Greene had read the hospital records, and he had talked with Dr. Ambrose Keeley, who performed the Leanues autopsy. Greene told the jury, "there was no cancer in the brain, liver, or lungs. In general, Dr. Keeley's finding was there wasn't a tremendous amount of cancer in the patient's body. The patient was not loaded with cancer."

Though the primary site of Norma's cancer had never been found while she was alive, the autopsy revealed that it was the breast, which had been X-rayed and examined many times. Greene described the breast cancer as "much more treatable" and said, "With effective treatment it is possible she might have lived for years."

During the summer and fall of 1980 reporters called the Capute house daily. After a while Anne could not bear to talk to them. "This isn't Anne," she'd say, "this is her sister." It became a game. "Anne has gone to Montana," she'd say, or Anne has gone to Kansas, or Martha's Vineyard, or Tibet. Each day she'd see what she could get them to believe. Anne found it was easier to fool reporters than bill collectors. Once she told a reporter, "Anne has gotten a job as a stewardess with United Airlines. I know it sounds ridiculous, but you'd be surprised at how much weight she's lost. She looks great."

In fact, Anne had lost weight. After the interview in Costello's office she had started losing weight steadily, and by September she had dropped thirty pounds.

The Morton case became a leading topic of conversation in diners, barbershops, and taxicabs all over New England. Anne's daughters were aware of the talk but, for the most part, they were not hounded by embarrassing questions. Barbara, Susan, and Lori were not Caputes, so no one connected them with the story. Only Meredith was a Capute.

"It wasn't to bad for me in school," she says. "I found out who my real friends were, and they really stuck with me. A few kids said that my mother was a murderer, but there wasn't much of that. I was twelve years old then and most of the kids didn't know too much about what was going on in the newspapers."

The older girls all had experiences similar to Barbara's.

"I was working in a bank then and the story was in the paper a lot. One day I was in the lunchroom sitting near these two people I worked with. They had the newspaper and one of them was saying, 'Did you see this story about the nurse? She killed a woman,' and that type of thing. My first reaction was to get defensive, but I didn't say anything right away. I figured I'd let them hang themselves. I sat back and let them go on and when they were finished I said, 'Oh, yeah, I know about that. That's my mother.' They were so embarrassed, I was sorry I had said anything."

Charlie was also harassed from time to time. People were more curious than rude, and sometimes they would pull him aside and lower their voices and say, "So tell me, Charlie, did she do it?" Charlie was uncomfortable and somewhat embarrassed about the whole thing. He would ignore the question and mutter something like, "I'll tell you who's the problem here. It's that damn doctor, he's the one."

During this period, Anne was also harassed by old acquaintances. She refused to refer to them as "friends"—people who had been out of touch for years but now wanted to renew their connection with a celebrity.

"Ma had this one friend named Sue," Lori says. "Ma had actually met her years ago when Ma was in the hospital as a patient, and Sue was her nurse's aide. Just by coincidence they met again when both of them were going to nursing school at Shattuck. Sue dropped out and that was the last Ma saw of her. Then one night after Ma was in the papers a lot Sue showed up at our house with a tray of homemade lasagne. Ma was really annoyed. She thought it was kind of sick, these people trying to get to know her again because she was accused of murder. Ma went into her bedroom and wouldn't come out. Sue hung around for fifteen minutes, then finally left. At least she left the lasagne. We had it for dinner the next night. It was good."

During this time Anne saw little of her lawyer. David Elliott dropped by for a beer a few times and told Anne not to worry.

"Keep smiling," he said. "There is no way in the world a jury is going to convict three nurses for first-degree murder."

Anne wanted to laugh, but she couldn't forget that they had once thought there was no way in the world a grand jury would *indict* three nurses for first-degree murder. The idea of her being convicted for the murder of Norma Leanues had once seemed preposterous. Now it seemed real, and she was scared. She was beginning to have doubts about her lawyer. She was beginning to have doubts about everything, even her innocence.

Chapter Nine

Anne had a friend named Bonnie Dumalek. The two women had been friends for years. Bonnie would often drop by for coffee and conversation. And sometimes Bonnie and her husband, Ted, would go on hunting trips with Anne and Charlie. But lately, even before the Leanues case, Anne had sensed that she and Bonnie were drifting apart. They didn't call each other as much, and they drank less coffee together.

Still, Anne wanted to share something important with Bonnie, and perhaps recapture whatever it was that was fading from their relationship. So when Bonnie came over for coffee one autumn afternoon, Anne confessed to her that she had murdered Norma Leanues.

"Don't be ridiculous," Bonnie said. She stood by the kitchen table counting out supermarket discount coupons she was giving to Anne in return for some Anne had saved. Bonnie finished counting, then said, "You're starting to believe this junk in the papers about mercy killing. There never was a mercy killing."

"Wasn't there?" Anne said.

"Of course not," Bonnie said. She pushed aside the pile of coupons and sat down and sipped her coffee as if Anne had told her nothing important.

"The three of us were nurses, weren't we? We did inject all that morphine. Norma did die. Right?"

"Anne, you're being ridiculous," Bonnie said, and she stuck out her hand. "Manicure," she said. "My first one in years."

"Lovely," Anne said. She leaned back in her chair, slightly wounded. "Anyhow, I killed her."

"Anne, you didn't kill anyone. Mercy killing means there was an intention, doesn't it? You had to want to kill her."

"Well I think I did," Anne said. "I've been thinking about the way other people's pain affects me. You know how I get all upset when somebody else hurts. And Norma hurt—believe me, she hurt. So maybe I wanted to spare her all that, the way they say. You know, give her a boost into the celestial air force."

"Yes, but you weren't the only one," Bonnie said. "There were two other nurses."

"I gave the most morphine."

"It doesn't matter. Are you saying that all three of you could have decided independently to kill that woman?"

"Maybe," Anne said. "Nurses hate pain. That's why they're nurses."

"Sure," Bonnie said, "but don't they also hate death?"

"Yes. But Norma was already dying. At least that's what we were told." then Anne thought about it for a moment. "No," she said, "I don't think Judy Foley and Nancy Robbins were trying to dispatch Norma to the celestial air force. But I'm not so sure about myself. I think maybe the D.A.'s right, I did it. I really couldn't bear to hear that poor woman crying like that. She was in such pain."

"I know it's been rough on you," Bonnie said, "but you've got to push that kind of stuff from your mind." She sipped her coffee. "Is this Maxwell House?" she said.

"Hills Brothers," Anne said coldly.

"I thought it tasted different."

"You don't like it?"

"No, it's fine," Bonnie said.

Anne waited for Bonnie to return to the subject of Anne's guilt. But Bonnie didn't. Instead she told Anne about the incredible traffic jam when she was trying to get out of the K-Mart parking lot on Thursday night. Anne had nothing to say about that.

"Charlie's driving me bananas," Anne finally said when the silence was getting too long and awkward.

"Oh?" Bonnie said. Her eyes shone a little brighter. Marital problems was a subject Bonnie could always warm up to.

"It's this whole Morton thing," Anne said. "He's pretending it's not happening. He's burying his head in the sand. He won't deal with it. You know, he didn't even go to the arraignment with me."

"Did you ask him to?" Bonnie said.

"No," Anne said. Then defensively she added, "You think I should have sent out gold-engraved invitations?"

Bonnie didn't answer.

"Anyhow, I'm leaving him," Anne said.

"Every woman I know is leaving her husband," Bonnie said. "Most of them never do."

This led into a discussion of other people's bad marriages and then to children. Bonnie's kids were just entering their teenage years, and Anne had a lot of stories to tell about when her girls were that age. Bonnie mentioned that hamburger had gone up again and she was thinking of getting a bigger freezer. Anne said that was a good idea, and then she tuned Bonnie out and thought about Montana, all the time nodding her head while Bonnie went on about whole wheat bread and the kid down the street who played his radio so loud.

When Bonnie looked at her watch and said, "Got to go," Anne was relieved, but she offered the perfunctory resistance. "So soon?" she said. "What's up?"

"*General Hospital,*" Bonnie said. "I'll just have time to get home."

After Bonnie pulled out of the driveway, Anne went back into the kitchen, poured another cup of coffee, and lit a cigarette. She missed Bonnie. She missed the way it used to be, the way they could talk for hours, and laugh together, and sometimes cry. Bonnie had changed so much, Anne thought, talking all the time now about food sales and clothes for the kids. What happens to people? she wondered. And the more Anne thought about it, the more she realized she was wrong. Those were the things that Bonnie had always talked about. Bonnie hadn't changed at all. Anne had.

There is a time in a woman's life, Anne thought, when baby food and disposable diapers are where it's at. And there is a time for discount coupons and manicures. There is, she thought, a time when all the domestic details are important and worth talking about. But that time had passed for Anne. Her mind these days moved more to religious questions, and the nature of relationships, and sometimes even politics. And, as if to explain herself to the world, she spoke the words out loud in the empty kitchen: "I'm up for murder," she said. "I just can't get excited about the price of hamburger."

Two nights later, Anne and Charlie went out to dinner with some friends in Hanover. On the drive home Anne told Charlie about the visit with Bonnie. Anne explained her realization that Bonnie and she lived now in two different worlds, that they had grown apart because they care about different things.

"It's not a case of one of us being right and one of us being wrong," Anne said. "It's just that we're different. We're not right for each other."

After a moment of silence Anne added, "Like you and me, Charlie."

Charlie didn't respond. Anne had made comments like that before. Charlie usually ignored them, and Anne usually didn't pursue them.

"I guess you know I'll be leaving you," Anne said. She was surprised that she had found the strength to say it.

Charlie twitched. "I can understand your saying that," Charlie said.

Anne was annoyed. Charlie sounded more like a therapist than a husband. "You can understand that I'm leaving you?" she said.

Charlie forced a smile. He stared straight ahead at the dark highway. "Well, no, not that," he said. "I mean, I can understand that you feel that way. You've been under so much pressure, you probably want to run away from everything."

"You got it," Anne said.

"But when all this is over—"

"When all this is over I'll either be in prison or Montana," Anne said. "Or California. Or someplace else, as long as it's far away from here."

"Why do you say that?" Charlie asked. He sounded hurt.

"Charlie, our marriage was over a long time ago. You know that. We just live together. We're roommates."

"We don't fight," he said.

"I know we don't fight. If we did, I'd be gone yesterday. We don't fight because we don't care enough about each other to fight." Anne smiled. Now she was the one who sounded like a therapist.

"Well, I've been pretty busy lately," Charlie said. "It's the feast season and all."

"Charlie, let's cut the bullshit, okay? We're not talking months here, we're talking years. And I'm not blaming you. It's not just you. It's us. We're both wonderful people, okay? We're just not wonderful for each other. I read books every night while you watch TV. I'm a flaming liberal. You voted for Reagan. We're different, that's all."

"Well, I watch TV because I'm tired," Charlie said. "I work hard all day."

"Oh, for God's sake," Anne said. "I'm not saying you're wrong and I'm right. I'm not saying that, Charlie. I'm saying you're you and I'm me. It's just time for me to move on. You should be glad. At least you won't be married to a convict. You won't be—" she paused and honed a cutting edge onto the final word—"embarrassed."

"What does that mean?" Charlie said.

"Oh, come on. You know you've buried your head in the sand over this whole thing. You're an ostrich, Charlie. You don't want to know about it, you don't want to deal with it."

A moment passed. Anne knew that Charlie was looking for something to defend himself with.

"I helped you get through nursing school," he said.

"I know you did," she said, "and I appreciate that more than you can imagine. But it's just . . . over."

They didn't speak again that night.

Lawyers for Nancy Robbins and Judy Foley filed motions in New Bedford Superior Court for the severance of the cases. The motions were granted. The nurses would be tried separately. District Attorney Ronald Pina told the press he expected to schedule the first murder trial "sometime in March of 1981."

Though she had no regular contact with Nancy Robbins or Judy Foley, Anne had always felt as if the three of them were trapped on the same island. Now Nancy and Judy were floating away. The separation of the cases reinforced for Anne a terrible feeling that she had been abandoned by the nursing profession. The feeling had been growing ever since the night of the interrogation in Costello's office. After that, except for a few phone calls from Nancy Robbins, Anne had not heard from any nurse at Morton. She wanted someone to call her up and say, "How are you doing, Anne? We miss you, Anne." But the calls never came. And no letters or cards came from the women she had worked with. It hurt.

Anne knew she had never been one of the "in"

crowd at Morton, but certainly she had friends there. She was part of a group of four or five nurses who would often head off to The Irish Peddlar after work and have a few drinks and talk about patients and kid around. It was fun. Anne had always enjoyed the camaraderie of other nurses because they were people who understood her dream. Now she missed it.

Anne was not alone in her belief that she was dumped by the hospital. It appeared to many people that the hospital was totally disowning her as if she were some wicked child. The *Boston Globe* in an editorial described Anne as "an individual at the bottom of the hospital hierarchy cut adrift by the institution."

Anne told friends that Maureen Costello had warned the other nurses not to speak to her. The hospital denies it.

"It's absolutely untrue," says administrator Larry Ross. "At no time was anybody in the hospital advised one way or the other about talking to Anne."

Whether Anne was deliberately ostracized or not is arguable. But that's how she felt, and as winter approached, the belief that she had been abandoned by her sister nurses deepened Anne's despair. She had lost her job and her dream. Her marriage was a mess, her friendships were fading, and more and more she was convinced that "they," this powerful legal machinery that could so easily move her life around like a piece on a chessboard, were going to find her guilty of murder and lock her up. Anne decided to kill herself.

Chapter Ten

Warren Magee was the first person Anne told. She thought Warren would understand about suicide. He had been depressed often and had thought many times of ending his own life. One night when Charlie and the girls were out, Anne and Warren sat in the living room drinking wine. Warren sat on the couch, and Anne sat cross-legged on the floor in front of him, and she revealed her decision. If the jury found her guilty, she would commit suicide rather than go to prison.

Warren stared at Anne for a long time after she told him. Anne could see that he was upset by her decision; his pipe and the hand that held it trembled. This surprised Anne. She had naïvely believed that Warren would be calm and supportive about the whole thing. She watched his dark eyes move. She knew he was searching for the best response to her shocking statement. Finally Warren hunched forward, placed his hands on his knees, and said, "Well, I guess it's a little early for me to try to talk you out of it. We'll wait until we get there."

He leaned back then, as if the discussion were over. But after a moment he said, "How would you do it?"

"Charlie's shotgun," Anne said, tilting her head in the direction of Meredith's room, where the gun cabinet was kept.

Warren made a face. He knew nothing about guns, and he had always been uncomfortable with them, and a bit perplexed about why Anne and Charlie and the girls liked to shoot.

"You're really gun people, aren't you," he said.

"We're hunters," Anne said. "It's not so much the guns. It's the outdoors. I love the outdoors."

Warren shrugged. "Well, maybe it's just a personal prejudice," he said, "but I find it hard to imagine you, of all people, shooting animals."

"Well, that's the way it is, folks!" Anne said abruptly. Then she felt ridiculous. That was one of her defense mechanisms, and she knew she didn't need that sort of thing with Warren. "I'm sorry," she said. "It's just . . . it's nature's way. I wouldn't kill anything I didn't plan to eat."

Warren didn't reply.

"It's not the hunting, Warren," she said. "It's the freedom of being out there in the wide-open spaces. This one place we go to a lot is about twelve miles from the Canadian border. And it's so vast! It's like belonging to a special club. You can look for miles and not see anybody or anything. You sit around by the fire and play penny poker. You have a few beers, you clean your guns. Good friends, good food. No radio, no television, no outside world."

Anne sipped some more wine. "Besides," she said, "you're talking to the hunter who never shot a deer."

"What?"

"Me," Anne said. "Now, don't laugh. I never actually shot a deer."

"Why not?" Warren said. He was grinning now.

"Well, I love venison, Warren, I really do, and I'd love to shoot a deer."

"But you never saw one?" he said.

"No, that's not it. I run into deer every year. But I never get a shot off because the first thing that strikes me is a feeling of Wow, look at that! I'm in awe of the damn thing, and by the time the feeling is gone, so is the deer."

Warren laughed.

"Oh, but it is so beautiful out there," Anne said. "I remember one morning I woke up and there was a red squirrel sitting on my boot. So big deal, huh, a squirrel on my boot? But Warren, I thought that was one of the most beautiful things I ever saw."

"So you're telling me that in all these years of hunting you've never actually killed anything?"

"Once," Anne said. "A bear."

"A bear. You like bear meat, do you?"

"Somebody else had already shot it," Anne explained. "It was wounded and the guy's gun was jammed. So I shot the bear, you know, to put him out of his misery."

Warren studied Anne's face as if a question were written on it. "Mercy killing?" he said.

"Yes," Anne said.

They stared into each other's eyes as if each knew a secret about the other, and then Warren said, "So now you're thinking about another one."

"Another what?"

"Mercy killing," he said. "You're going to knock yourself off if it comes up 'guilty as charged.'"

"And?"

"Well, that's a mercy killing, isn't it? You'll shoot Anne to spare her the pain of going to prison."

"I guess it is," Anne said. "I never thought of it that way."

During the weeks that followed, Anne went from one extreme to the other. Her daughter Lori says, "I guess Ma was a little bit crazy during this period. She'd be very flippant one day, almost jolly, then depressed and suicidal the next. At first she talked about committing suicide if they found her guilty. But then she started feeling so helpless, and she started thinking that after the verdict it would be too late because they'd already have her, and she talked about committing suicide before the trial. Sometimes she talked about smashing her car into a tree or something so it wouldn't look like suicide. 'I might have an accident tonight,' she'd say, and sometimes she was kidding and sometimes she wasn't. My sisters and I were scared to death. We hid scissors and everything. And if we were out we'd call home every ten minutes to see what kind of a mood Ma was in. Then for a while we'd never all be out at the same time. Ma didn't look suicidal. She was still making jokes. She wasn't in the pits; she didn't dwell on it. It was more like she had an attitude of This is a decision I've made and that's how it is, folks. I hope you see my side, but if you don't, well, that's just too bad. The main thing was that she felt as if she didn't have any control over her own life."

"I guess we knew Ma's mind was made up when she divided up the cut glass," Susan says. "Ma's never really been into things, but she really loved this collection of cut glass, which had been handed down to her from her grandmother. It had been Ma's grandmother's wedding gifts, candy dishes, goblets, beautiful things, and a lot of silverware that went with it. One night Ma made a long list of everything she had and she divided it up among the four of us. It was important to her to give away her most valued possessions."

In December Anne went to visit friends in New Jersey. It was a normal visit in every way, but when she left, she told them good-bye; she didn't expect ever to see them again.

By January, with a trial date set for April 6, Anne was obsessed with getting control of her own life. Suicide was her way of controlling her fate if she were found guilty. But more and more she was unwilling just to let *them* decide. She was tired of feeling helpless. She needed to *do* something. She was convinced that her case had acquired enough notoriety for her to get a big-name lawyer to represent her. She called David Elliott. She thanked him for his work but she told him that her life was at stake and she just didn't feel he was experienced enough.

Charlie and Warren were out ice fishing. They often spent the morning at one of the local ponds. They came in at about eleven o'clock, rowdy as a couple of schoolboys who had played hooky and boasting about their catch.

"Warren," she said, "this Pisciwhatsie lawyer. Has he got a phone number?"

"Sure does," Warren said, and he started searching through his wallet for the number. "Here," he said, handing Anne a piece of paper with Piscitelli's phone number on it. He smiled. "Glad to see you've come to your senses," he said.

Chapter Eleven

The day after Anne Capute's press conference, Pat Piscitelli rushed out of his office shaking a newspaper at his longtime office manager, Donna Piscatelli (who, despite the similar name, was no relation).

"Listen to this," he said. "Capute says, 'I was only following orders.' Jesus, she's pleading her case in the newspapers. Why doesn't she just plead guilty and take a cab to the state prison and get it over with?"

Piscitelli paced back and forth in the hallway for a minute and then he threw up his hands. "Why don't those nurses come to me?" he said.

It was the first outburst of many. Almost every morning during the autumn of 1980 Pat Piscitelli arrived at his office, poured a cup of coffee, picked up his morning paper, and read something new about the "alleged mercy killing by three nurses at Morton Hospital." Often he grumbled about what he perceived as some mismanagement of the case by the district attorney, the hospital, or the nurses' lawyers. At other times he just tossed the paper onto his desk and shook his head. And at still other times he would walk out to the hall in front of his office, take two steps, cry, "Incredible, just incredible!" as if it were the last line from a play, then step back into his office and go to work.

Pat Piscitelli was frustrated. He wanted the case, but there was nothing he could do. Lawyers are not allowed to phone people and say, "I read about you in the papers, I'd like to represent you." The case would have to come to him, and there was little chance of that.

Piscitelli wanted the case because he craved new challenges and he knew this one could test him severely. Often he had described himself as a "frustrated doctor," and the medical aspects of the Morton case intrigued him. He was also a frustrated actor, and the publicity attracted him. Piscitelli had been on many radio and television shows in connection with other cases, and the public exposure had always given him an exciting shot of adrenaline, much as he imagined a round of applause would.

He was certain that he could win the case. He knew that District Attorney Ronald Pina was relatively inexperienced with murder trials but that Pina, politically ambitious and even more anxious for publicity, would probably try the case himself.

Piscitelli followed the Morton case closely, and as each new bit of information was revealed in the newspapers, he worked it into his imaginary defense. He knew what he would do if the case were his, and he often joked to friends that he could retire at fifty if someone would let him handle the nurses' civil suits.

"The successful criminal lawyer must have a monumental ego," Pat Piscitelli had often said, and this Morton case was tantalizing to his ego. But there was nothing to be done about it, and he thought he would have to stand by helplessly and watch three nurses march off to jail, and all the time he would know that he could have saved them.

Pat Piscitelli was not alone in his high opinion of himself. At forty-eight he was tall, handsome, and athletic—a lawyer who could have come directly from central casting—but he was much more than just good form in the courtroom. He was also well-tempered substance.

Pasquale "Pat" Piscitelli had grown up on the streets of Brockton, a city in southeastern Massachusetts. After he worked his way through Boston University he served simultaneously as assistant attorney general for the Commonwealth of Massachusetts and Brockton City solicitor. In the 1960s he began his private practice in Brockton, and he scored a remarkable series of acquittals in prison murder trials that helped forge his reputation as one of the best criminal lawyers in the nation. His fellow lawyers dubbed him the "Bailey of Brockton," a tip of the hat to Piscitelli's friend and colleague F. Lee Bailey.

By the time the Morton Hospital case started making headlines, Piscitelli's practice had expanded to include six full-time lawyers, two legal assistants, seven secretaries, and a client list that included corporation presidents concerned about trust funds, as well as street junkies up for murder one. But Piscitelli, well known in Massachusetts as a defender of the underdog, remained true to his first love, criminal law, and turned most of the civil work over to his associates.

Though he was now wearing suits that cost more than the cars he used to drive, Pat Piscitelli still regarded himself as a street kid, and he identified less with bankers and businessmen than he did with waiters and nurses. To him the three Morton nurses were hardworking people like his parents. They were the underdogs being bullied by a system that could destroy them.

Though Pat Piscitelli had the admiration of his brothers in the legal profession, he wanted more. He wanted a broader recognition. He wanted the general public to know him and his talents. Certainly there was a part of him that wanted to strut across a Broadway stage or peer into the lens of a movie camera, and he knew he would probably never do those things. But it was for a different reason that he yearned for that recognition. Whatever praise and attention was directed at him would go not just to him but also to the name Piscitelli, his father's name.

"My father came over from Italy," Piscitelli says. "He spoke English but with an Italian accent to it, and he was not clever with words. He ran for city councilor every chance he got for thirty-five years, but he never won. When I was a kid I would live and die with him as he ran for office, and I wanted to be what my father never became and show the world what he could have been if he had the gift of speech."

By early 1981 Pat Piscitelli had put aside his fantasy of defending one of the Morton nurses. He tried not to think about the case; he didn't want to stand by as a newspaper reader and watch some other lawyer botch the trial. There had been exciting cases in his past, and he knew that other exciting cases would come along. This would just have to be the one that got away.

He had no way of knowing that Anne's friend Warren Magee had been hounding her for months to call the Bailey of Brockton.

On January 16 Piscitelli came back to his office in the afternoon after trying a minor felony case in Dedham court. His secretary met him just inside the door.

"Guess who called?" she said before he even had a chance to take his coat off.

"Who?"

"Anne Capute."

Piscitelli smiled. "Well," he said, "it's about time."

Chapter Twelve

The drive from Anne's house in Plympton to Pat Piscitelli's office in Brockton takes about a half hour. Anne drove it for the first time on January 20. She brought along her friend Beth Whitehead for no

particular reason except that Anne didn't trust lawyers and felt better having a witness to the proceedings.

Piscitelli's law offices occupied all of a two-storied
converted ranch house about a mile from downtown
Brockton. While Anne and Beth waited in the lobby,
sipping coffee, Piscitelli came out once to hand some
papers to a secretary.

"He really is handsome, isn't he," Beth said.

Anne grunted. "I suppose some people would
say so," she said. "He's not my kind of handsome."
Piscitelli, with his dark complexion, three-piece suit
and brushed-back dark hair, was just a little too suave-
looking for Anne. "Rod Steiger is my kind of handsome."

A few minutes later, when the two women were
led into Pat's office and sat down facing his desk, the
lawyer was equally distressed by Anne's looks. Her
appearance would not be an asset in court, he
thought. She was overweight, her hair was too short,
and she was dressed too much like a man in slacks and
a plaid flannel shirt. She looks too tough to get a jury's
sympathy, he thought. Some changes will have to be
made.

Pat introduced his assistant Don Harwood. Harwood had finished law school and was waiting to take
the bar exam. He was twenty-three, good-looking,
well dressed. A future Piscitelli, Anne thought. She
glanced at him, thought she saw a look of disapproval
in his eyes, and decided that he also was not her type
of guy.

Pat Piscitelli had already begun a Capute file.
Now he sat behind his desk looking over the few
papers in his folder. Anne fidgeted in her seat. She
was uncomfortable with these lawyers in their suits.

And besides, the last time she'd sat in an office facing a desk was when this whole mess started.

"Look," she blurted out, "there's two things I won't do. I won't plead guilty, and I won't lie to you."

Pat looked up. He smiled. She had broken the ice. "I'll accept those terms," he said. He pulled out his wallet, removed a dollar bill, and handed it to Beth Whitehead. "You're now an investigator for this office," he said. "That's your salary."

Beth stared at him.

"It protects the attorney-client privilege," he explained.

Anne watched as Beth tucked the dollar bill into her pocketbook. "I hope you work as cheaply as her," Anne said to Pat. "Before we go on we might as well discuss money."

Pat was pleased but unnerved. It was never easy to tell clients about legal costs, but it was necessary. He took a deep breath.

"I'll need a twenty-thousand-dollar retainer," he said. "We'll worry about the rest later."

Anne winced. "That much, huh?"

Pat knew that most people could hardly imagine the reality of legal expenses for a case like this. "That's a drop in the bucket," he said. "I could use that up by tomorrow at this time, just hiring expert witnesses. By the time this case is over you could conceivably run up legal bills of a quarter of a million dollars."

"Well, that's a relief," Anne said. "Twenty thousand dollars I worry about. A quarter of a million dollars, that's too ridiculous to even think about."

"I agree," Pat said. "I don't want you to worry about money. I need you to be as sane as possible under the circumstances. Get what you can. I intend to win this case, and after that, maybe we can recover some of the money from other parties."

Pat, believing that a lawyer never can know too much about his client, then asked Anne to tell him about her childhood.

Don Harwood took notes while Anne described her life as a kid in Jamaica Plain. After she told Pat that she had dropped out of high school, Anne confessed she had used someone else's high school transcript to get into nursing school. Pat looked troubled, and he made a note about it on his own pad of paper, then told Anne to go on. She told him about her jobs, her marriages, her children.

When she told him about her conversion to Judaism, Pat stopped her.

"You observe the high holidays?" he said.

"Yes."

"If we go to trial I'll try to get you the most sympathetic jury possible," he said, "but realistically, considering where we are, it's going to be loaded with Catholics and a little short on Jews."

"So?"

"So you can't observe the Jewish holidays. We can't risk alienating anybody on the jury."

"I'm sorry," Anne said. "I can't do that. If they don't like my being Jewish, that's too bad."

Pat gave her a look. "Anne," he said, "there are two things we've got to get straight right now. One is that your life is at stake here. Your life, Anne. No less. And if we get to the point where principles are in conflict, then we have to go with the one that will keep you out of prison."

Anne nodded. She understood.

"What's the other thing?"

"I'm the boss," Pat said. "You're paying me a lot of money because I'm good at what I do. So let me do it. I want your opinions, your ideas, as we go along. But I will not compromise on anything that I think might reduce our chance of winning, no matter how small. I want absolute final word on everything. Do I have it?"

There was a long silence. "You got it," she said.

She described her volunteer work at Jordan Hospital, and she told him about the school bus incident. Pat smiled when he heard about the citation, and he made another note. He's keeping score, Anne thought. Points for me and points for them. Then she talked about her lifelong dream of being a nurse.

On the other side of the desk, Pat carefully studied Anne's demeanor, wondering how he would get the best out of her on a witness stand if it ever came to that. He saw that when Anne talked about her dream of being a nurse, her face softened. Her arms spread apart, she uncrossed her legs, and she seemed to glow. For a moment the music of her words transported him back to a dream of his own. He remembered a summer from his youth, spent in Onset, near Cape Cod. A woman had been strangled and dumped in a cranberry bog not far from where Pat worked as a pinboy in a bowling alley. The murder trial that followed was a sensation. It was the big story of the summer, and with a growing sense of excitement Pat followed it daily in the newspapers. Guilty or not guilty? What would the lawyers say? Would there be some new evidence? He was fascinated by the processes of law, and that summer of his thirteenth year he first dreamed of becoming a lawyer.

Now, as Anne talked about her dream of becoming a nurse, Pat found what he needed, a hook into the woman's soul. She had dreamed, and he had dreamed. And Pat knew from experience that the way to survive, to *continue to care* over the long and

exhausting months of a murder case was to find in the
client some part of himself. Anne was no longer just
some tough-looking gal who would have to grow her
hair longer and put on a skirt. She was what he
needed her to be, a street kid like himself.

When Anne talked about her year in nursing
school, Pat began to ask specific questions:

"Did you administer drugs in nursing school?"

"Oh, sure. Under hospital supervision."

"Morphine sulfate?"

"Yes."

Pat looked through his file folder and pulled out
a news clipping. An unnamed source had told a reporter that Anne Capute often bragged about putting
"two doses in one shot" and referring to it as "an old
trick at Shattuck." Pat asked Anne about the remark.

"I don't remember making the statement," Anne
said, "but I could have. The practice was not unusual.
You stick the patient with two doses at a time so
there's less pain. It's a way to prevent two separate
injections."

"Is that allowed?"

"Sure. It's everyday stuff at Morton. There's even
a chart on the wall showing which two drugs you
could mix together and which ones you couldn't. For
example, Valium couldn't be mixed with Demerol."

"What about Valium and morphine together?"

"You wouldn't actually mix them together," Anne
said. "Valium is a muscle relaxer. It can prolong or
enhance the effect of morphine.

Pat mulled this over. He was already envisioning
the courtroom. "Okay," he said, "so if you were on the
stand you'd simply say the Valium has an extended
effect, that it would not increase the power of the
morphine but simply prolong the effect."

"Sure."

Anne told Pat about the death and dying course

that had so excited her at Shattuck, and she revealed
that one of her dreams was someday to work with
Elisabeth Kübler-Ross. Anne told him that after she
graduated, she applied for work with terminal patients at Shattuck.

"Why?" he asked.

"They were just such poor, forgotten souls,"
Anne said. "There was this one particular man, this
was when I was still a student. He was a Chinese man
and he had metastasis of the brain and no one gave a
damn about him. He was covered with feces all over
his face and hands and he was even eating it and
nobody cared. A lot of times the nursing staff was
simply too shorthanded to clean up any basket cases
like this. I remember one time the night nurse didn't
even know if he was dead or alive. So I talked to an
instructor about it to see if I could be assigned to the
Chinese fellow, but she wouldn't assign me. I asked if
I could at least clean him up, and she wouldn't even
let me do that. The next day I cleaned him up
anyway. He was in a coma. I got very close to him
anyhow, and I was with him when he died. Nobody
should die alone."

"That's why you like to work with terminal
people, so they won't die alone?" Pat asked.

"Sure," Anne said. And when no one else spoke
she added, "And besides, I love them."

Pat asked Anne if she'd gotten in any trouble at
Shattuck and she told him about the sterile-water
incident with the needle-addicted patient. Again he
made a note.

He asked her about the different methods of
medicating. She told him about oral medication, and
IM, and IV, and s.c. He asked her about her job at
Morton, the nurses' schedules, the chain of com-
mand, the number of wards, employee morale, patients' charts, everything.

"Tell me about the doctor's order sheet," he said.

"It's filled out whenever a doctor orders medication," Anne said. "A doctor is supposed to countersign any order within twenty-four hours."

"But he can give it verbally to a nurse?" Pat said. "That's what you told the papers."

"Sure," Anne said. "Morton was more relaxed about that sort of thing than, say, Shattuck. Sometimes at Morton if the doctor wasn't around the head nurse on a floor would sign it."

Pat asked Anne about her relationship with Norma Leanues.

"I had her as a patient about five times," Anne said. "I never asked to have her specifically."

"When did you first see her?"

"In recovery. Probably around May sixth. It was her last operation. She was screaming something awful. She couldn't stand the pain. I heard one of the nurses say, 'Why didn't he leave her alone? She only has a month left.'"

"In other words, she was terminal?" Pat asked.

"Yes."

"What does 'terminal' mean to you?"

"Very limited time," Anne said. "Days to a few months."

"When did you learn that Norma Leanues was terminal?"

"The night Hillier gave the order," Anne said. "But there was a general feeling before that. The nurses on the ward knew that Norma was terminal."

"Who told you?"

"I don't know. She was just . . . just in so much pain, Mr. Piscitelli."

"Pat," he said. "Call me Pat."

"Pat," she said. "Okay, Pat. This woman was in so much pain that you couldn't even touch her. Once they called me to help Norma because she was in a circular bed and I knew how to work it right. Norma was lying on her bed screaming, 'Don't touch me!' It got very bad sometimes, very bad."

Pat asked Anne about the conversation with Dr. Hillier, and she described it as she had that night in Costello's office.

"Hillier was always moving in and out of the corridors real quick, so it was hard to slow him down. I had to grab him by the elbow so Nancy could talk to him. We tried to explain that Norma was in a lot of pain. Hillier said, 'Give her anything you want to make her comfortable.' Nancy said, 'Fine, give it by shot?' He said, 'Yes,' and Nancy said, 'Can anything else be done? She's in so much pain.' He said, 'Of course she is, she's only got twenty-four to forty-eight hours. In this pain, of course she'd be screaming and crying."

"Are you sure he said she's only got twenty-four to forty-eight hours to live?" Pat asked.

"Yes," Anne said. "I'm sure about that. Is it okay to smoke in here?"

Pat glanced at Don Harwood and Beth Whitehead to see if they objected. Neither did. "Sure, go ahead," he said. He didn't like smoking, but he wanted a happy client.

Anne lit a cigarette and stretched her legs in front of her. She was feeling more comfortable now. "Yes," she said, "Norma was definitely a prime candidate for the celestial air force."

Pat was reaching into a lower desk drawer for an ashtray, and he froze suddenly, as if someone had struck him.

"The celestial air force?" he said. He sat up and grabbed his pen.

"Yes," Anne said, "that's what we called it. We

used to joke about helping a terminal patient to join
the celestial air force."

"Who?"

"The nurses," Anne said.

Pat was stunned. "Are you telling me this sort of
thing went on before?"

"Well, I don't think anybody was turning out a
body a week," Anne said, "but . . ." Now Anne
leaned forward for the first time and looked Pat
straight in the eye. "Look," she said, "you have to
understand about nurses." She felt all her nurse pride
rising to the surface. "We don't make a lot of money,
but we're still willing to stick needles in people and
listen to a lot of people crying in pain. Sometimes we
have to look at children who have been burned or
battered by parents. We clean up excrement and
urine and blood and vomit and spit, and sometimes
we even hold a patient's hand while he's dying. Did
you ever feel the life leave a person's body? I'm not
trying to tell you that we're all the angels of mercy you
see on television. We're not. I've known plenty of
nurses who were real bitches. But we all have one
thing in common: We care. We really care about those
patients. You have to care, or you couldn't possibly do
the job. Some patients treat us awful; they hate being
in the hospital, and they take it out on us. Sometimes
doctors don't treat us so great, either. But we do the
job because we love the patients. Can you understand
that? We love them, even the nasty ones. We hate to
see them suffer, and when we know they are dying,
it's that much harder. It's not like listening to a woman
screaming in labor when you know that tomorrow
she's going to be happy because she's got a new baby.
It's someone who's going to suffer and then die. Do
you see what I'm saying? If you had to pick one group
of people more likely than any other to commit a

mercy killing, that group would be nurses. I'm not saying that Morton is different from any other hospital. I'm just saying that the *idea* of a nurse committing a mercy killing is not at all strange. It happens all the time."

The room was quiet. The nurse and the lawyer stared at each other as if no one else was present. Then Pat said, "But it didn't happen this time. Did it?"

"I don't know," Anne said.

"You don't know if you're innocent?"

"I thought I was," she said. "Now I think I'm guilty. I mean, everybody says I did it. And I did. I mean, I gave her all that morphine. I hated to hear her screaming. I knew she was dying. It just figures, doesn't it? I killed her."

"On the day after she died, did you think you killed her?"

"No."

"The night you went to Maureen Costello's office, did you think you killed her?"

"No. Well, I did for a couple of minutes, but that's all."

"When you were indicted for first-degree murder, did you think you killed her?"

Anne laughed. "I was beginning to have my doubts. I mean, who am I to contradict a whole grand jury?"

Pat leaned back and placed his hands on the desk. He and Don Harwood glanced at each other as if they both knew what was going on. Then Pat surprised Anne. He stood up and walked around the desk. He stood in front of her. He still looked very tall to her, though not as tall as when she had first seen him. Then he sat on the edge of his desk. He reached forward and took one of her hands and held it between his own. His hands felt warm, comforting, and his eyes, when he looked into hers, seemed almost loving. He does have nice eyes, she thought, not as nice as Neil Diamond's, but nice.

"Anne," he said, "I want to tell you about something that happened to me once. When I was thirteen years old—this was in the 1940s—I was walking home from church one Sunday morning and a police cruiser pulled up beside me and the cops told me to get in. They didn't tell me why. They took me down to the police station and they interrogated me for a long time. They asked me if I had talked to any woman on the way home. Did I have any sexual fantasies? What were my sexual inclinations? They asked me all sorts of questions about sexuality, and they weren't polite about it. I was really scared, Anne. Finally two more Brockton police officers showed up with a woman and she said, 'That's not him.' She had been molested on the way home, and the fellow who did it fit the same description as me. The police took me home in a cruiser. Naturally, my mother was upset."

Pat leaned forward a bit, held Anne's hand a little tighter, and said, "But the strange thing was, Anne, that all the time these two cops were badgering me, I didn't even know what crime had been committed. And I still felt guilty. I mean, everybody was acting as if I'd done something terrible, so I figured they must be right. I must have done something. That's how I felt. Do you know what I'm saying?"

"Yes," Anne said.

When the interview was over, Pat walked Anne to the door and told her to make another appointment with his secretary. "Don and I will get right to work on this," he said. "We've lost a lot of time. I'm going to want to know everything about you, Anne."

"I've got no secrets," Anne said.

Pat put his arm around her. "You know," he said, "that incident I told you about had a tremendous impact on me. It make me think, Boy, it could happen to anybody. You need someone to protect you. You can't be left at the mercy of only police officers alone."

"Or district attorneys?" Anne said.

Pat chuckled. "Especially district attorneys," he said.

When they got into the parking lot, Beth turned to Anne. "Well, my friend, there's only one reasonable thing to do at a time like this."

"A movie?" Anne said. Anne was rarely able to get Charlie into a movie theater, so Beth had become her moviegoing pal.

"At least one," Beth said. "Maybe two."

"You got it," Anne said. "But no trial pictures, okay?"

"You got it," Beth teased, and the two women spent the afternoon at the movies.

Chapter Thirteen

"I got Pat his twenty-thousand-dollar retainer," Anne announced as she sat at her kitchen table playing penny poker with Beth Whitehead and Warren Magee. The girls were doing homework, and Charlie was stretched out on the living-room couch watching *M*A*S*H*.

Warren was surprised. "The bank actually came up with the money?" he asked.

"Are you kidding?" Anne said. "I must have gone to sixteen banks looking for a second mortgage. For some strange reason nobody wants to lend twenty thousand bucks to an unemployed woman who's up for murder."

"So," Beth asked, "how did you get it?"

"Charlie's mother."

"Charlie's mother? Has she got that kind of money?"

"Oh, Charlie's parents are loaded," Anne said. "They hang on to money forever. The old lady bought a lumber company about a hundred years ago. Later she sold it, and since then it's been invest, invest, invest. Of course, Charlie doesn't have a cent of it."

"So you just asked her for the money?"

"Well, it wasn't quite that simple," Anne said. "See, there was this minor problem. Charlie's mother hates my guts."

"Oh."

"To tell you the truth, I don't care much for her guts, either."

"Nice to have mutuality," Warren said.

"Just to give you an idea of how happy the old lady is about our marriage," Anne said, ". . . Charlie's parents own ninety-five acres of land up in New York. They bought it for an investment. So a while back—this was long before I got my face in trouble—Charlie's mother calls up and says to him, 'We'll give you that land and set you up there if you'll just get out of that marriage you're in'"

"What is it they don't like about you?" Warren asked.

"They don't like my personality," Anne said. "They don't like the fact that I've been married before. They don't like the fact that I've got three other daughters."

"They sound like charming people," Warren said.

"So," Beth said, "Charlie had to ask for the money?"

"Come on, Beth, be serious. "Charlie is a lump. Lumps don't take action."

"He wouldn't help you?"

"No," Anne said abruptly. "He refused to ask his mother for the money."

"Why?"

"Why?" Anne said. She dropped her cards on the table and jerked her hands into the air in front of her. "Hey, that's just the way it is, folks," she said somewhat bitterly, momentarily shattering the jovial mood of the card game.

Beth and Warren said nothing. They knew that Anne was extremely angry with Charlie over his "ostrich routine." After a minute or two Anne was cheerful again, as if she had yanked a painful thorn from her side and was now relieved.

"So anyhow, I called Charlie's sister Meredith out in California," Anne said. "I figured she could get the old lady to part with a few bucks. It's kind of a crazy coincidence, but she and her husband are in the middle of financing a new business, and they had just asked the old lady for the same amount, twenty thousand. Do you know what Meredith did for me? She turned right around and told her mother to cancel their loan and give it to me instead. I was very touched by that. Meredith told the old lady that I needed the money more than she did. It took some doing, but the old lady gave me the second mortgage. I had to go down to the registry of deeds and all that, but I got the money. I didn't have it for long, though. It lasted all the way from this house to Pat's office."

They played five or six more poker hands and then Warren sank into his familiar melancholy. It was as if a huge, invisible hand reached out and crumpled him up in his chair. He pushed his cards to the center of the table. "Don't feel like playing anymore," he said.

"What's wrong, Warren?" Anne said.

"I don't know. It's just . . . it's just not fair, you know, you having to go through all this and spend all your money and go in debt just to defend yourself."

"Life isn't supposed to be fair," Anne said. "Life just is. There's a lot of people who are going through a lot worse than what I'm going through, and they didn't do anything wrong, either."

Warren did not answer, but Beth smiled and said, "Gee, Anne, you're turning into a philosopher."

"I know," Anne said. "Stop me if I get obnoxious. But the thing is, I do a lot of thinking these days. I just curl up on the couch and I put on the headphones and listen to music, and I think."

"What do you think about?"

"Everything," Anne said. "Just everything."

"Still planning suicide?" Beth asked cautiously.

"You bet," Anne said. She was serious. Then she added, "Of course, I might not have to. Somebody might save me the bother."

"What?"

"Oh, yes," Anne said. "I got some lovely fan mail today. It was a letter threatening to kill me and Judy and Nancy. This lunatic says we probably get our rocks off seeing babies killed. You know, there's some really sick people out there." Anne paused. "It really makes me wonder about Morton Hospital," she said. "I mean, the letter was written on yellow composition paper, right? No envelope, no stamp. It was just

stapled up and had the names Judy Foley, Anne
Capute, and Nancy Robbins written on it. Now, either
it came from inside the hospital, or some looney
dropped it off there. Anyhow, somebody inside the
hospital put the whole thing inside an envelope and
mailed it to me. *Me.* What were they thinking? It was
written to all three of us. My name wasn't even the
first one. So why me?"

Chapter Fourteen

"I wouldn't say absolutely that Anne is not guilty of
first-degree murder," Don Harwood says. "I'm still
not sure if all those doses were accidental, or if she
actually knew what she was doing. I do know that
Anne is one of my favorite people. And I know that
when we started preparing for her trial I didn't spend
a lot of time agonizing over whether or not she was
guilty.

      "Like Pat, I had been following the case for a
while before it came to us, but for a different reason.
My dad had recently died of cancer. He had cancer of
the colon for six years and he died at home, but he
went through terrible pain before he died. So when I
heard about the nurses being charged with mercy
killing I was, of course, sympathetic. I could see why a
nurse might do a thing like that."

      Harwood, who became Pat Piscitelli's right-hand
man on the Capute case, says he knew when he met
Anne that she didn't like him.

"Anne was kind of uncomfortable during the first interview," he says. "She didn't like me at all. She acted as if I had the plague. She told me later she thought I had a weak handshake. And, to tell you the truth, I didn't have a real good first impression of her, either. Who would have thought we'd become such close friends?"

After Anne's initial visit, Pat Piscitelli put Harwood to work on the case immediately, and for the next several months half of Harwood's professional time went to helping Piscitelli prepare Anne's defense.

"Preparing for a major murder trial involves an incredible amount of work and research," Harwood says. "It's really staggering. A person's life is at stake, and you can't overlook anything. Especially if you're working for Pat. Pat is so thorough he tends to fatigue everyone around him. I honestly don't believe there is a better criminal lawyer in the country. I don't know of one who puts as much time in on a case."

From the outset Pat made it clear to his assistants that the defense would take the point of view that Anne was just an L.P.N. at the bottom of the Morton totem pole, a victim of careless doctors and shabby supervision.

"For us," says Harwood, "it was a matter of breaking down all the hospital reports which we had. There were nursing notes, doctors' reports, investigation reports from the district attorney. We had to submit medical records to doctors to get opinions, interpretations. We wanted to get opinions from cardiologists on whether it was the morphine that killed Leanues or if her heart just gave out. We talked to pharmacologists. We talked to pathologists. Pat would not leave any stone unturned. We had to meet with all of these people and get crash courses in medicine. Of course, Pat already had a pretty substantial knowledge of medicine. He had done a lot of murder cases, and in a murder case you almost always have to deal with an autopsy report. But there was still a tremendous amount of medical information to be learned, and Pat was an intense student. It was as if he just dove into all this information and absorbed it through his pores.

"Then there was the grand jury testimony. We had to go over that. There were all sorts of hearings. And interviews almost daily. Pat interviewed everybody he could think of. He talked to six or seven nurses. He talked to Maureen Costello. He talked to Larry Ross. He talked to the D.A.'s expert witnesses as well as ours. He talked to anybody who might give him one more scrap of information, anything he might use, no matter how small. The only one who refused to talk was Hillier. On most of the interviews Pat would have me present as a witness to the conversation, in case the person told a different story when we got to court.

"Then there was the enormous amount of time spent with Anne. She practically had to move into the office, and we used to joke about it. 'Why don't you bring a cot, Anne?' and things like that. Some nights she and Pat would be in his office or in the law library until two in the morning going over her story again and again. Each time something new would come up—a word, an incident, whatever—and Pat would grab it like it was a piece of string and follow it with Anne until he knew every place it could possibly lead. And some nights it would be me and Pat burning the midnight oil, studying the transcripts from the grand jury testimony or the interviews Pat had done. Or some nights all three of us would be there long after everybody else had gone home, and Pat and I would take turns trying to trip Anne up. Anne wasn't comfortable with that. She was terrified of the idea of taking the witness stand, but she was gutsy and she hung in there.

"And there were nights—a lot of nights—when Anne was at home with her family, and I was home with my girlfriend, and it would be just Pat working at the office long after midnight, going over the records and reports and interviews until he knew them cold. He was obsessed with the case."

From this obsession Pat Piscitelli built a defense strategy that he thought about constantly and refined daily. He thought of it as his "four rings of defense," and the rings became as real to him as the objects in his office. He knew that if the district attorney could pierce all four rings that he, Pat, would have failed, and a woman who trusted him would spend the rest of her life in prison.

"I decided to build a defense like a system of concentric circles, or rings," Piscitelli says, "with Anne at the center. My outside ring would be the contention that Leanues died of cancer, not morphine. Pina would have to convince the jury that it was morphine that did it. If he broke through that ring, I'd try to prove that Leanues didn't die from the morphine that Anne injected. It was Nancy Robbins who injected the final forty-five milligrams the morning Leanues died. If he penetrated that ring, my next layer of defense would be that Anne was only following Dr. Hillier's orders, and I intended to keep the focus on Hillier and the hospital administration. I wanted the jury to see Anne as a scapegoat for a lot of mistakes, vague orders, and poor supervision. And if that didn't work, my final ring, my last hope for Anne, would be to convince the jury that no matter what the orders, no matter what the procedures, Anne was acting in the best interests of the patient."

To build this defense Pat had to follow many paths, some of them leading nowhere. He pursued to the end any idea that might be used to save Anne's life.

Within his larger strategy were many smaller ones. There was, for example, the contention that Norma Leanues might have died not of morphine overdose, but of a heart attack. The autopsy had revealed a 70 percent stenosis in the LDA, the left descending artery, which meant that Norma's arteries were dangerously narrow. In fact, Ambrose Keeley, who performed the autopsy, described Norma as "a prime candidate for heart bypass surgery." If an embolism had gotten lodged in the LDA it could have brought on a fatal heart attack.

But no embolism had been found during the autopsy, and Pat needed expert testimony to prove that there could have been one. It occurred to him that an obstruction might have gotten washed away when Norma's blood was drained and the preservative formaldehyde was pumped into her body. So Pat went to the embalmer to find out if formaldehyde was pumped in at high pressure.

The embalmer said the fluid was not pumped in at high pressure. Once in fact, he said, he had applied too much pressure with a corpse and the corpse's eyes had popped out.

So Piscitelli called a chemist at Dodge Chemical Company, manufacturers of the formaldehyde. "Could it dissolve a clot?" he asked. "No," she said, and he was back where he'd started.

Pat studied anatomy books and medical textbooks. He pored through dozens of legal journals in search of a similar case. Nothing. The closest he came was a New Hampshire case involving a doctor who was accused of mercy-killing a patient by injecting air into the veins. But there was nothing involving nurses, nothing like this.

Before the Capute case Pat Piscitelli had never met Ronald Pina, though he had seen him on TV often because Pina had been a Massachusetts representative for seven years before he ran for district attorney. So instead of sending for the records he needed, Pat decided to visit the D.A. in person. It was a chance to take the measure of the man.

They met at Pina's office, a penthouse suite just a few blocks from the New Bedford courthouse where Anne had been arraigned.

"Pat! Good to see you," Pina said when they met, greeting Piscitelli as if they were old friends and pumping his hand in the easy, effusive style of the seasoned politician.

Pina offered coffee. Pat declined.

"Well this is it," the D.A. said, proudly showing Pat around the office. Pat was impressed. The office was spacious and orderly.

Pina was in good humor and he tried at first to engage Pat in some verbal sparring. Ordinarily this would bring out the actor in Pat, but he remained quiet for now, hoping to reveal as little of his nature to Pina as possible.

"You know, Pat, I'm really glad Capute's got you," Pina said as he went about the office gathering the material Pat had come for. "It's best for her, I mean. This is a complicated case. It's going to take someone of your talents."

"Thank you," Pat said, though he knew the remark was not meant as flattery; it was an attempt to draw him into a discussion of the case.

"Of course, for myself I'm not so happy," Pina said. "I figure you're going to try to win this murder case the way you won all those others."

"I'll do my best," Pat said. He knew that Pina had been sizing him up.

Pat eyed his adversary carefully and wondered if Pina, who had never tried a murder case, would turn out to be a worthy opponent. Pina was tall, dark, and good-looking, a sharp dresser and smooth talker who would be impressive in the courtroom and on television.

Pat knew that the district attorney liked to play to the press, and that could be a weakness. Pina had once gotten trapped in controversy by telling a judge that the defendant in a murder-kidnapping case had confessed several times. The remark was made within earshot of several reporters, and afterward Pina had gone to them and asked them not to print the remark. But the papers had printed it, and now as Pat stood in the D.A.'s office studying the man, he recalled the newspaper quote of one defense attorney who said of Pina, "Someday it will become apparent to him that cases are won in the courtroom, not on the six-o'clock news."

Nonetheless, Ronald Pina had put together a good record in the Massachusetts legislature, and he was a popular political figure in New Bedford. He was not a man to be taken lightly.

"I've been doing my homework," Pina said, breaking into Pat's thoughts. Pina proudly motioned to a tall stack of thick notebooks.

"My notes on the Morton case," he explained.

Pat was impressed. And a little bit worried. It occurred to him that Pina's desire for publicity could also be a strength. His ambition would be the fuel to keep him going. Obviously Pina was pulling out all the stops on this one. He wanted to win it, and he had a ten-month head start on Piscitelli.

"I'm almost a year behind you," Pat said.

Pina smiled. "I know," he said. Then he added, "But judging by your reputation, I'd say that makes us just about even." He handed Pat a pile of papers. "That should be everything," he said.

Pina was friendly and helpful as he filled Pat in on the various documents. It had been Pat's experience that prosecutors and defense lawyers generally got along well early in a case. But the congenial spirit often eroded as the case moved closer to trial. He glanced at Pina, who was smiling. I hope he won't be smiling when it's over, Pat thought.

Among the papers were copies of letters of immunity that had been sent to Lorraine Hickey and Tom Bosanquet, and also to head nurse Fran Silva. Pat had wondered how Pina was getting so much cooperation from people at Morton. Now he knew. Pat was shocked, but he said nothing. He was being extra cautious, knowing that even an expression of attitude could be a tip that would indicate some of his defense strategy. These letters, he thought, could be extremely damaging to the prosecution. It gave the appearance that the commonwealth was handing out immunity wholesale to the upper-echelon people while trying to nail three nurses for murder.

Pat left Pina's office that day convinced more than ever that Anne Capute was the intended victim of a huge medical-legal-political monster that would not sleep well until she was in jail.

Pat contacted a lot of potential witnesses. He knew that many of them would never get to the courtroom, but he wanted them in reserve. He spoke, for example, to Helen Smith and Henry Butler, two people who had been patients on the ward with Norma Leanues. Smith and Butler both described Norma as a woman in agony, a woman who screamed. Smith and Butler would be good ammunition on that particular point if Pat needed it.

Pat also acquired the X rays that had been taken of Norma after her spine operation. He brought the X rays to a doctor for an opinion. Pat wanted to know how the spine curvature might have affected Norma's breathing. During this particular pursuit he discovered that the D.A. hadn't even gotten the X rays. It filled Pat with hope that Pina would not be as thorough as Pat had feared.

But such waves of optimism were often followed by small defeats that brought on pessimism. Pat, an ardent Boston Celtics fan, began to see his pursuit of information metaphorically as a hard-fought and extremely close basketball game. One day he'd go two or three points ahead, and the next, something would happen to make him feel as if he had fallen behind. A strong example of this was the strange case of Dr. Ambrose Keeley.

Dr. Keeley was the medical examiner who had performed the autopsy on Norma Leaunes. District Attorney Pina had never brought Keeley before the grand jury, so Pat suspected that Keeley had testimony that was not favorable to the prosecution's case.

In late January Pat went to see Keeley at Waltham Hospital, where Keeley was an associate pathologist.

"I've been expecting you for a long time," Keeley said.

He was a young man, forty-one, who had been a lieutenant commander in the Navy, and he had a long and impressive list of professional credits. Pat found him to be articulate and somewhat critical of the doctors who had treated Norma Leaunes.

Pat discussed the autopsy report with Keeley. At this point Keeley had not seen the nurses' notes concerning the morphine, and he told Pat that, in his opinion, Norma Leaunes had died of a heart attack.

Pat left Waltham that day excited and confident. He had jumped five points ahead. Keeley would be a very strong witness for him.

But on April 10 Pat went to see Keeley again. By now Keeley had examined the nurses' notes and other Leanues medical records. This time he told Pat that if he were put on the witness stand he would say that in his opinion Norma's death was consistent with morphine overdose.

Pat left that day knowing that things looked grim for the heart-attack theory. Again Pat had fallen behind.

But during the second week of May Pat picked up his morning paper and was shocked when he got to the obituary page.

Dr. Ambrose Keeley had died of a heart attack, leaving both the commonwealth and the defense without his potentially crucial testimony.

During these months of trial preparation, as Pat interviewed hundreds of experts, witnesses, and even friends who had valuable expertise, Anne became hopeful. Though she still intended to kill herself if convicted, her moments of despair became rare. She felt as if she had taken control of her life by hiring Piscitelli. And because in some strange way her case had become more important to Pat than it was even to her, she felt as if she were giving something. She felt needed.

Though Anne had at first regarded Piscitelli as "just another damn lawyer," one more of a despicable breed, it was not long before she was swept up by his energy and his excitement over the case. She began to speak highly of him—so highly, in fact, that many people, including Meredith Piscitelli, Pat's wife, believe that Anne fell in love with her lawyer.

Chapter Fifteen

"Did you ever shoot your husband on the stairs?" Pat asked Anne.

It was seven o'clock in the morning, and they stood in the small, square coffee room at Pat's law firm. It was the middle of March, and by this time the law office had become a comfort zone for Anne, a second home. Pat had given her a key, and she would often arrive before anyone else in the morning and make coffee for the staff.

"Did I what?" Anne said. She nearly spilled the coffee pot.

"Shoot your husband?" Pat said. "On the stairs." He had just come in, and hadn't yet put down his briefcase or taken off his coat.

"Which one?" Anne said.

Pat smiled. But he looked troubled. "How many have you shot?" he asked.

"None," she said. "What on earth are you talking about?"

"Meet me in my office when you're done," Pat said. "We need to do an interview."

"That will be the tenth one this week," Anne joked. "Are we going for the world record?"

But Pat didn't respond. He had already stepped into the hallway and was heading for his office.

During the first few weeks of their relationship Anne had felt hurt when Pat would cut the banter short like that and suddenly become silent and distant. But now she was used to it. Like everyone else in Pat's life, Anne had accepted the fact that Pat spent most of his time in an imaginary courtroom defending her against a charge of first-degree murder.

When Anne got to Pat's office, carrying coffee for both of them, Pat was sitting at his desk staring intently at a single typewritten sheet of paper. "Anne," he said, "this is from the material turned over to us by the D.A.'s office. The prosecution has got to give us anything that might be used against you. It's a list of naughty things people have said about you. Pina's been asking around, trying to get anything he can to discredit you. It looks like gossip mostly. But I don't want any surprises when we go to trial, so we've got to go over this carefully. One of the items on the list says, 'Anne said she shot her husband on the stairs.' What's that all about?"

Anne was baffled. "I have no idea," she said. "I can't imagine."

"You can't think of anything you might have said?"

"No."

"Something that might have been misunderstood?"

"No."

"Some combination of words that might sound like that?"

"Nothing," Anne said.

Pat studied his piece of paper again. He didn't speak for a while. Anne wondered if he believed her. Because she had grown to respect him so much, it was important to Anne that she have his respect. She was never quite sure of how Pat felt about her personally.

"Pat," she finally said.

"Huh?"

"You do believe me, don't you?"

"Sure," Pat said without looking up.

Then, perhaps sensing the importance of Anne's question, Pat returned his attention to her. He set his paper down and leaned forward at his desk. "Anne," he said, "I'll tell you something, and I have never said this to any other client. If you tell me something is true, then I would stake my life on it. And I mean that literally."

"Gee, thanks, fella," Anne said, shrugging off his words, but she felt a surprising wave of emotion roll up inside of her and press against her chest. Anne reached quickly for her coffee cup, hoping to hide her face behind it so that Pat would not see how moved she was.

Pat picked up the list again. "It says here that you stated that you could get three dollars for disposable Kellys."

"Oh I don't believe this," Anne said. "That is so absurd."

"What does it mean?"

"Okay," Anne said, "at one time we had a terrible overstock of major surgical kits. You use them once and throw them away. Inside there were these Kelly clamps, and the ones that weren't touched would be thrown in a drawer in the utility room. Some girl came along and she was stealing clamps because they can be used as roach clips. So one day we were all kidding around at the nurses' station and someone was saying, 'What the hell can you do with all those Kelly clamps?' and I said, 'I heard you can get three bucks for them out on the street.' It was just a joke! You mean somebody's made a big deal over that?"

Pat went on. "It also says here you like to kill animals."

"Oh, Christ! So I go hunting once in a while.

They make it sound like I'm out on the street shooting people's pets. The only reason they know about that is once in a while we'd get a fellow on the ward who liked to hunt or fish and I'd strike up a conversation. Big crime!"

Pat smiled. "How about this one? 'Anne stated that she had someone else take her entrance exam'?"

"No one took my entrance exam," Anne said. She was getting angry. "I took my own entrance exam. A lot of people at the hospital knew I had gone into nursing school under someone else's papers. Why do they distort it like that?"

"How about, 'She was called "Pat" by a member of the staff'?"

"Oh, God," Anne said. She made a face. "A lot of times we'd have temporary nurses from Staff Builders—it's a rent-a-nurse group. And one day they sent over a woman I had known before I went to nursing school. My middle name is Patricia, and a lot of people in the past knew me as 'Pat.' She was one of them, that's all. Besides, if that's a crime, you should go to jail. You're always being called 'Pat' by members of the staff."

Piscitelli remained serious. "Anne, I'm very worried about that name change," he said. "If I have to put you on the stand you'll be under oath and you'll have to give your real name."

"That's a problem?"

"Yes," Pat said. "Then the jury will know you lied at least once. They might not trust you after that."

"Then don't put me on the stand," Anne said. She grinned as she said it, because she had been begging Pat to find a way to keep her off the witness stand.

"I don't know if I can avoid it," Pat said somberly. "We'll see." He looked at the list once more. "Hang in there, Anne. Just one more. You're quoted as saying, 'Boy, I really medicated Mrs. Leanues heavily. I mean, I *really* medicated her.'"

"Yes, I said that. I talked about the medication pretty freely with my head nurse after Norma died. Everybody was a little bit uptight about the Joint Commission coming, and I was wondering if they would look at drug charts. I said to my head nurse, 'Gee, I really gave Norma a lot of morphine,' and she said, 'Don't worry about it.'"

"Okay," Pat said. "That's all."

"For now," Anne snapped.

"Yes," Pat said. "For now."

"But there will be more," Anne said.

"There's always more."

"You're damn right, there's always more," Anne said. "They'll keep coming back at me, won't they? They'll keep coming up with some joke I made once, or the way I comb my hair, or they think I'm too fat or too blunt or too something. Am I right?" Anne could feel the rage swirling inside her.

Pat looked helpless. "Yes, Anne, you're right."

"And these juicy bits of gossip," Anne said, edging closer to what was bothering her the most. "Where do you suppose they came from?"

"People at the hospital," Pat said.

"People? You mean nurses, don't you? All this shit came from nurses." Anne felt betrayed by her sister nurses, and it cut her to the heart.

"Some of it," Pat said.

The idea of women in white dishing dirt about her to the district attorney was just too much. "Why are they all saying these things?" she cried. "I didn't do anything to them." Her voice boomed, but there were tears pressing at her eyes.

Anne had cried a few times since that night in

Costello's office, but now, for the first time, Anne broke down and truly sobbed. Wails of sorrow broke out of her, and her whole body shook as the tears flowed from her eyes. She tipped her head forward into her hands.

In her sadness she felt like a little girl.

For a long time Pat let Anne cry alone. And when she was almost all cried out and sat in front of his desk weeping softly and dabbing at her eyes with the handkerchief he had given her, Pat stood up and walked around the desk to her as he had on their first meeting. He leaned his tall frame over her and slipped his arms around her shoulders.

"Anne," he said, speaking so softly that he was almost whispering, "I know this hurts. But I want you to remember something important. All the things on that list I read to you didn't come from a lot of people. Most likely they came from one or two busybodies. The nurses are with you on this thing, Anne. They are, I'm sure of it. Not just nurses at Morton, but nurses everywhere. They support you. They're rooting for you. Just remember that when a nurse stands up for you, when she says that you were right, that's not going to show up on the district attorney's list. He can't use that."

Anne clutched Pat's arm and held it tightly as if it were a rope that could pull her back to safety.

"Thank you," she said. But when she left his office that morning she wasn't at all sure he was right.

Pat and Anne went to court often during the winter and spring of 1981. Pat asked to have the trial rescheduled. April 6 was too soon, he argued, claiming that because of the switch in lawyers it didn't give him enough time to prepare. The district attorney did not object, and the judge granted the delay. The trial was rescheduled for July. After Ambrose

Keeley's death the trial was moved up to September. The trial dates for Nancy Robbins and Judy Foley were also moved up. Pina had committed himself to trying Anne first. She had given the most morphine, she had made several incriminating statements, she was the low person on the totem pole, and she would be, it seemed, the easiest one to convict.

Piscitelli also tried to get the case moved out of Bristol County. There had been too much adverse publicity, he said, and he also objected to the county's system of jury selection. He was turned down. The court ruled that much of the bad publicity was Anne's own fault because she had chosen to talk to the press.

Early in May, Anne and Pat went to court on a "motion to suppress." Pat asked the court to disallow from the trial any statements Anne had made in Costello's office. He argued that Anne was acting as an employee of the business at the time and that her statements should have been regarded as confidential.

"We'll probably lose this one," he explained to Anne in the car on the way to court. "But the people who were in the office that night will have to testify, and that will at least give us a shot at some conflicting testimony later on."

On the third day of that hearing Anne and Pat arrived back in Brockton in the late afternoon. Anne climbed out of Pat's Mercedes and went directly to her car instead of stopping at the office for coffee and small talk with Don Harwood and Donna Piscatelli, the way Anne usually did. Anne was anxious to get home because Lori had been badly sunburned the day before and had stayed home from school.

But when Anne pulled into her driveway and shut off the ignition at about four forty-five, she didn't get out of the car right away. She took a deep breath and closed her eyes and let the tension drain from her body. She was glad the day was over. It had been just about a year ago that Norma Leanues had died. A hell of a year, Anne thought. No wonder I'm exhausted.

"Oh, Anne, Anne, Anne!" she heard. It was Beth Whitehead running across the yard, waving her arms, looking half crazy. "Anne!" Beth cried, looking at Anne through the car window. There was wildness in her eyes. "Warren is dead!" Beth said. "He's dead, he's dead! He killed himself! In your house!"

Anne threw open the door and bolted from the car.

"My Lori!" she cried as she rushed past Beth. "My Lori is in there!"

Chapter Sixteen

At eleven o'clock that morning Barry Vinton, the Plympton police chief, had responded to a call to go to 36 Maple Street. Vinton knew the address well. He was a friend to all the Caputes. Vinton had come over and chased away the TV news reporters in August.

"This time the call had come from Lori," he says. "She had been sleeping, and the gunshot woke her up. She rushed into Meredith's room and found Warren's body. Then she called the police station, but she doesn't remember any of that now. When I got to the house that day, Lori was hysterical. I think seeing me calmed her down a bit, not because I was the police, but because I was a familiar face. I've been to the house for supper many times.

"After Lori was calm I went into Meredith's room. Warren's body was in there. That's where the gun cabinet was. He had just walked into the house. Anne never locks the door. Of course, Warren thought the house was empty; he didn't know Lori was home from school. He had jimmied open the gun cabinet. There were rifles and shells all over the place. Warren didn't know anything about guns, and he had apparently spent some time trying to figure out which shell went with which rifle. He ended up jamming a forty-four magnum shell into a two-seventy Enfield rifle, and he shot himself in the right temple. I called the medical examiner and had the body taken away."

When Anne got into the house that evening she found Charlie in the living room talking softly to Lori. But Lori was not answering. Lori, sitting cross-legged on the living room floor, had fallen lifeless and limp into a catatoniclike stupor. She was pale, still, mute. Her eyes stared straight ahead but focused on nothing.

"Oh . . . Lori . . . honey," Anne cried, rushing to her daughter.

Anne fell to her knees and wrapped her arms around Lori. Beth came in behind Anne and paced helplessly about the room, wringing her hands. "Oh, my baby," Anne cried. "It will be all right, it will be all right."

Charlie told Anne what had happened. He told her, too, that Meredith had come home but had refused to enter the house.

"Just then my wife didn't give a damn about Warren," Charles Capute says. "I guess that sounds cold, but only one thing mattered to Anne, and that was Lori. Anne's mother instinct blocked out everything else. Anne is, more than anything else, a mother. She would do anything for those girls. Taking care of her daughters is even more important than being a nurse, though I guess you could say the two things are related.

"Of course, she was mad as hell at Warren for killing himself with Lori in the house. But Anne told me once that she only stayed mad with Warren for about half an hour. Then of course there was just . . . grief.

"Lori was a vegetable for a couple of days, just staring off into space. Then after she came out of it she had to go to therapy for a while. Today she's the most together person I know, but back then she was an emotional wreck.

"All of us went through a hard time about Warren's death. Warren was a super guy and we were all close to him. I mean, it would have been awful to have him die under any circumstances. But to kill himself in our house. That was too much.

"After Meredith finally came home she had a lot of nightmares and she wouldn't go into her room. Can't blame her, the poor kid . . . Warren had died on her bed. Finally, after four or five weeks we told Meredith she could have her room decorated any way she wanted. She wanted rainbows. Meredith loves rainbows. So I got out my paints—I went to art school years ago—and I painted a huge rainbow across one wall. Then we all pitched in and got Meredith rainbow cards and rainbow stickers and rainbow everything. She went back into her room."

Shortly after Warren's death, Anne suffered another misfortune. Her floundering friendship with Bonnie Dumalek ended. The strange thing, from Anne's point of view, was that the final break came because of money.

Bonnie had inherited $9,000 from the death of

an aunt and she showed up at Anne's door flashing
some bills. "Come on," Bonnie said, "we're cele-
brating."

Bonnie took Anne to a fine restaurant in Plym-
outh and bought her an expensive lunch. While she
and Anne were eating dessert Bonnie playfully rolled
up a fifty-dollar bill and tossed it across the table to
Anne. "There's some pin money," she said.

Anne thanked Bonnie and smiled. "Fifty bucks,
huh?" she said. "If you think you're going to get off
that easy you're crazy."

Bonnie's face grew tight, but Anne continued.

"Bonnie, you know I don't like to beat around
the bush. So I'll just say it. I need a loan."

"A loan?" Bonnie seemed to be upset. Her eyes
started moving as if she thought something might
come at her.

"Yes," Anne said. "Twelve hundred bucks.
They're about to foreclose on me."

"Oh," Bonnie said. Her voice sounded hollow.

"I'll give you my car as collateral," Anne said,
though she had expected Bonnie to pull out her
checkbook right there and say that collateral was for
strangers, not friends.

There was silence. And then Bonnie began to
tremble.

"Anne . . . I can't," she said.

"Oh. Well, that's okay," Anne said. She was hurt
but she tried not to show it. "I just thought,
since . . ."

"I just can't," Bonnie insisted.

"Okay, fine," Anne said.

"I can't do it," Bonnie said. Her voice was getting
louder. She had picked up a fork and was holding it
tightly with two hands. "I mean I can't."

"It's okay, Bonnie," Anne said, trying to calm her.
"You want to order some more coffee?"

"I can't lend you the money," Bonnie said. "I wish you wouldn't pressure me this way."

"Who's pressuring you? Am I pressuring you? I said forget it."

"Well it sounds like pressure," Bonnie said.

"Well forget it," Anne snapped. "Just forget I ever brought it up, okay?"

The rest of the meal was tense, and the two women exchanged few words on the drive back to Anne's house. Bonnie seemed to be obsessed about Anne's request. "You're putting me in a terrible position," Bonnie said when they got to Anne's driveway. But Anne did not reply. "See you, Bonnie," she said, and she got out of the car, shaking her head and wondering what else could possibly go wrong in her life. After Bonnie pulled out Anne sat on her back steps for a few minutes, thinking about everything that was happening to her. "Jesus!" she said out loud and it all seemed so preposterous that she started laughing. Then she went into the house and treated herself to a hot bath and a Neil Diamond album.

Bonnie called a week later. She told Anne she had bought a new car, so would be unable to lend Anne the twelve hundred dollars. Anne and Bonnie didn't see each other after that.

Anne had always thought of Bonnie as the most generous person she had ever known, and Anne knew that whatever was making Bonnie act so strangely, it certainly wasn't the money. Anne concluded that Bonnie needed to sabotage the relationship for some reason that only a psychiatrist could pry out of her. And Anne had too many other things on her mind to spend time trying to figure Bonnie out or fix up the relationship.

Anne remained surprisingly forgiving of people

at this time. Once when she talked to Donna Piscatelli about Bonnie, Anne said, "I'm not angry with Bonnie. I feel sorry for her. Life is too short for me to be angry with everybody." And so it was with other people who were bringing pain into Anne's life. Friends asked her if she hated District Attorney Pina, or Maureen Costello or Dr. Hillier. "I don't hate anybody," Anne would say. "Hating people is bullshit. I don't want to waste my time hating people. Life is too precious."

The idea of life's preciousness, and life's shortness, was very much on Anne's mind. At first she had taken Warren's death as a sign that she should not kill herself. But gradually she began to see it differently. Everybody she loved had survived Warren's suicide and she knew they could survive hers if that's how it had to be. She would rather have her daughters experience the suicide of their mother than have to visit their mother in prison.

Anne also saw less and less of Beth Whitehead, and a few other friends who seemed to be part of another life which Anne had left behind. She had outgrown many people, and to the people who were still in her life Anne often said what she had once said to herself in the kitchen. "I'm up for murder. I just can't get excited about the price of hamburger."

By the time Anne Capute went on trial for first-degree murder she had lost her job, her savings, and three close friends. Her marriage was doomed, she had gone forty thousand dollars in debt, and her daughters had been pushed close to their emotional limits. But she began to feel that she was getting something in return for all her strife. She just wasn't sure what it was.

Chapter Seventeen

The first-degree murder trial of Anne Capute began on September 9, 1981, at the Superior Courthouse in Fall River, Massachusetts, an industrial city known for textile mills and granite quarries. The courthouse, built of local granite, is a venerable and magnificent-looking building that had once drawn the eyes of the nation to a woman on trial for murder. In 1892 Lizzie Borden was tried for the murder of her father and stepmother.

As Anne followed Pat Piscitelli and Don Harwood along the courthouse path that sunny morning, she trembled inside. She felt as if the courthouse were a huge granite monster waiting to gobble her up. She stopped twice just to stare at the building, as if she could chase it off with an evil look. The building was frightening. But then, she thought, everything is frightening. Even Pat, walking ahead of her in lively steps, as if he were on his way to accept an award. He was frightening. Certainly Anne drew from him a sense of security, a feeling of "Daddy will take care of everything." But with his expensive three-piece suit and his cool demeanor, Pat also seemed to be one of "them," and that's what scared her. Don, too, she thought, though a little less so, because Don was younger and often whimsical and just didn't exude as much power. An expensive-looking briefcase hung from Pat's hand, and it reminded Anne of the man

119

who follows the President around, carrying a case handcuffed to his wrist. The secrets of the bomb are in Pat's briefcase, Anne thought, and she wondered who would win the war.

Anne, wearing a light blue blouse and a dark blue skirt, felt awkward, as if she had put on someone else's clothes. She had gotten used to comfortable slacks and oversized men's shirts and flat shoes. But Pat had ordered her to get some clothes for the trial. "Modest but feminine," he had told her, and he had even offered her the money to buy some things. Anne, feeling proud, had turned it down, then gone out and bought three outfits she couldn't afford. On the way back from Filene's basement that day she had stopped in at Pat's office to show off what she'd bought. "Perfect," Pat told her, "just the thing. We want the jury to realize nurses don't make much money." And Anne had gone home, pleased with herself because she had gotten Pat's approval and she had been able to do at least one little thing toward saving her own life.

Despite the unfamiliar clothing, Anne felt good about her appearance as they approached the courthouse. Her hair had grown long, and she had lost ninety pounds since that night in Costello's office. She knew nobody would mistake her for Bo Derek, but she thought she looked just fine.

"Goddamn shoes!" she said out loud. Don turned around.

"The shoes," she said. Who the hell wears heels these days? They hurt my feet."

Don smiled. "It's all part of the million-dollar defense," he said. It had become a joke around the office that expenses were running so high on Anne's case that Pat was building a million-dollar defense for her.

"Wonderful," Anne said sarcastically.

They went through the main door and walked upstairs to the courtroom, the same room in which Lizzie Borden had been tried. So this is it, Anne thought. It was a squarish room with a high, impressive ceiling. Four tall windows on each side admitted the daylight. But the windows were narrow, and much of the light was absorbed by the dark fixtures of the courtroom, so it felt to Anne like three in the afternoon, not ten in the morning. A spirit of reverence pervaded the room, as if the space were sacred. It smelled of ancient wood and lemon oil. Though Anne had imagined a room the size of Kansas, this one was no bigger than a small New England church.

It feels like a temple, she thought, remembering that the Jewish high holy days were coming up. Anne had been disappointed when Pat had told her she couldn't observe the high holy days during the trial. Now it didn't matter. Her religion, like everything else, had been re-examined during this life-threatening crisis, and she felt no more Jewish now than anything else. Her religion now was one of questions, not of answers.

A few people were mingling at the front of the courtroom. Don went up front to talk with Pina and Pina's assistant Dave Turcotte. Pat stayed with Anne at the back of the courtroom, explaining.

"That's the jury box on the left," Pat said, pointing to the front of the courtroom. Anne gazed beyond the rows of spectator benches that looked like pews. "You see that rail in front?" Pat asked. "You'll see me leaning on that rail a lot. I like to get as close to the jury as possible as often as possible. I want to poke my face right into their lives so they'll see me as a person, not a lawyer. If I could, I'd sit you in there with the jurors, but judges get touchy about that sort of thing."

Anne looked at Pat's face. He looked somber, businesslike. She was learning that most of his humorous remarks came without a grin. She liked that, but it often took her by surprise.

Pat moved his hand to the right. "That's the witness stand," he said, pointing to a lectern. There was a long silvery microphone attached to the front, and a small wooden platform on the floor behind. "Everybody who testifies will stand there."

"Stand?" Anne said. "In the movies they always sit down."

"I know," Pat said. "In the movies they always have surprise witnesses, too. There're no surprise witnesses in a real trial. Anyhow, witnesses can sit down if they want to. The judge will order a chair. But you'll probably see most of them standing when they testify."

Dominating the front of the courtroom was the judge's bench. It looked like a great oak desk that had been built for a giant, and it was a clear indicator to any spectator that the person who sat behind it was in charge.

Pat's hand moved past the judge's bench to the right side of the room. "Those long tables up front are where we'll sit," he said. "One is for the defense and one is . . ." He paused in midsentence. A look of annoyance crossed his face. He gave Anne a quick pat, then rushed to the front of the courtroom.

For a moment Anne fantasized about making a run for it. She could just dash out the doorway and head for Montana. She smiled, thinking about what people would say. But she stayed put at the back of the courtroom, transfixed by the sight of Pat and the district attorney engaged in a subtle sort of combat.

She couldn't quite hear what they were saying, but from the animation of their hands and bodies she gathered that Pina had moved the tables around to suit his own purposes and that Pat wanted them back where they had been. Tension seemed to crackle between the two men. Gladiators before the battle, she thought. They were kidding each other good-naturedly, but the friendliness was shallow, Anne could see, and it seemed to her that it wouldn't take much to bring the men to blows.

In fact, Pina had moved the tables. The two lawyers, unable to settle their squabble, ended up paying a visit in chambers to Judge Robert S. Prince, who would preside at the trial. Pat and Pina returned like two scolded schoolboys with a judicial edict about the placement of tables. The tables were placed to the judge's left with the prosecution table closer to the front, and the defense table directly behind. As it turned out, this placement made it possible for Anne to overhear a good deal of what was said throughout the trial when Pina, Pat, and Judge Prince huddled for bench conferences.

The first week of the trial was taken up by jury selection. A pool of 165 potential jurors had been assembled, and each side had been granted 32 arbitrary challenges instead of the normal 16, which meant that as many as 64 of the potential jurors could be challenged and turned away without a reason being given.

Pat, along with lawyers for Nancy Robbins and Judy Foley, had hired Decision Research Corporation of Lexington to conduct a juror profile survey. The company made over 1,500 random phone calls in Bristol County and asked questions about age, sex, race, religion, occupation, and attitudes about nurses, doctors, and mercy killing. Their goal: to find the types of jurors most favorable to Anne.

Decision Research found that prevailing attitudes, at least in Bristol County, favored nurses and doctors, hospitals, and what they called the "blessing defense." The "blessing defense" meant that a jury would probably view favorably a passive response to a pain-ridden and terminally ill patient. In other words, it was okay to *allow* such a person to die. But the survey found negative attitudes toward an *active* response—that is, taking action to put someone out of his or her pain. The message was that people thought nurses and doctors shouldn't play God. The survey found negative attitudes about nurses going against doctors' orders. The company also discovered that nurses and doctors were held in equally high esteem.

The company concluded that the best juror for Anne was a blue-collar male between fifty and sixty years old who had not gone past high school and was not religious. They concluded that the worst juror for Anne was a highly educated, white-collar, nurturing person who was over sixty and very religious, especially Roman Catholic.

Though the survey was supposed to be kept secret from the district attorney, Pina found out about it through an ironic fluke: One of the random calls from the research outfit was made to a member of the D.A.'s staff.

Sixteen jurors would be needed, including four alternates. By the third day of the trial not even half that number had been picked. Anne listened carefully as each potential juror was interviewed by the judge. Many were dismissed either because they had pressing personal reasons to be excused or because they could not be regarded as impartial. Prospective jurors who had gotten the judge's approval were then assessed by Pina's people and Pat's team. Two women advisers from the research firm sat behind the defense table, thumbing through the full report. They helped Pat and Don decide who to challenge and who to accept. Anne envied the women. They had professions. They were good at it, and nobody was trying to kick them out of it.

Anne went along with Pat and Don's jury choices, with one exception. The judge interviewed a young black woman who told him that she was a nurse's aide. When Pat and Don and the women from Decision Research went into their huddle, Anne edged down to the end of the table, leaned into the group, and said, "Not the black girl."

"Huh?" Pat and Don were both stunned. They thought Anne would be pleased to have a black juror, since Anne abhorred racism more than almost anything else.

"We can't trust her," Anne said. "She's a nurse's aide."

"That's great," Pat said. "She knows what nurses have to put up with, she knows what it's like when you're right there with the patient and the doctor's not around most of the time."

Anne nodded to acknowledge Pat's point. "Yes," she said. "But look, the idea is all these blue-collar people are going to see me as the lowly L.P.N., someone just like them getting pushed around by the bosses, right?"

"Yes."

"Well, there's one thing lower than an L.P.N. in a hospital, and that's a nurse's aide. And believe me, they take a lot of crap from the nurses. To her I *am* the bosses."

Don and Pat looked at each other. "Okay," Pat said, "we'll challenge. And Anne," he added before he challenged selection of the nurse's aide, "if you can't get back into nursing, maybe you could become a lawyer."

By the afternoon recess of the following Tuesday it was clear that only one more day would be needed for jury selection, and Pat began looking forward to Thursday, when the impaneled jury would be taken to Morton Hospital to view "the scene of the crime."

There was a spare jury room behind the courtroom, a small room furnished only with chairs and ashtrays and a long wooden conference table. It was used by defense counsel for private meetings, and Anne liked to go there during breaks so she could smoke and stare out the window down at North Main Street. On the Tuesday afternoon break she sat by the window. Pat sat at the end of the conference table jotting notes on some of the hundreds of documents that he and Don carried to court every day.

"Oh, by the way," Pat said without looking up, "I want you to go to the hospital with me."

"Feeling sick, Pat?" Anne said, pretending not to know what he was talking about. "I hear they've got a nice hospital right here in Fall River."

"We'll go with the jury," Pat said. "They'll be shown around, the medication closet, Norma's room, the corridor where you talked to Hillier. . . ."

"Does the law say I have to go?" Anne asked.

"No."

"Then there's no way I'm going," Anne said. Her voice echoed softly in the small room.

Five or six silent seconds passed, and then Pat lifted his head and looked at her.

"You're going," he said.

"Pat," Anne said, waving her cigarette at him and smiling, "up yours!"

Now Pat rose slowly from his chair, like an exasperated parent, and he walked toward her. "Anne," he said, "I want you to mingle with that jury, and this is our only chance. You can't talk to them, but you sure as hell can get within their reach. I want them to see you as a person, not a defendant, nor a murderer. A person. I want them to smell you and hear your breathing. The more you're a person to them, the harder it will be for them to convict you."

"Oh, sure," Anne said. "Maybe we can all have tea before they hang me."

"Anne!"

"I can't go," she said.

"You can."

"I can't," she said. "Don't you understand? I'd be humiliated. All those nurses staring at me. 'Look at her, she's the one who murdered that poor woman!' You're asking too much."

Now Pat looked really irate. He started pacing up and down alongside the table. Anne could feel him bristling. He was a big man who seemed to get bigger when he was angry. She could easily imagine Pat getting in scraps as a kid on the streets of Brockton. It's his Italian blood, she thought.

"Anne," Pat said, his voice booming now.

"Pat, I am not going," Anne said. "Get it through your thick Italian head. Those people. I'd die."

Unexpectedly, Pat slammed his hand down on the conference table. "Damn it, Anne, do you want your life, or don't you?"

His words hung in the air, unanswerable.

He was right, Anne knew. So instead of replying, she turned her back to him and once more stared intently out the window at the traffic down below. The idea of going back to Morton with the jury made her feel like a scared little girl. But she remembered that she had promised Pat she would do whatever he said.

After a minute she crushed out her cigarette and glanced at Pat. He caught her look. "You're going," he said. It was not an order; it was an observation. He was getting very good at reading her expressions.

"Yes, massa," Anne said. That, too, had become a joke around the office. Pat was the master.

Chapter Eighteen

"That woman murdered Norma Leanues," Ronald Pina said, dramatically pointing his finger at Anne.

For an instant every eye in the packed courtroom turned to Anne. She remained tight-lipped and stared straight ahead, focusing on nothing. Then the finger was gone, and the district attorney continued with his opening statement to the jury.

Anne had spent the morning at Morton Hospital, and when she arrived at court after lunch she saw that Pina had pushed the prosecution table way over to the right-hand wall to open up as much space as possible at the front of the courtroom.

"Jesus, he's sending his assistant to Siberia," Pat had quipped.

Now Anne watched from her seat at the defense table as Pina used the space to strut and emote and make sweeping dramatic gestures as he revealed to the jury virtually everything he would try to tell them in the coming weeks. It looked to Anne as if his every step had been carefully choreographed.

"Norma Leanues was not dying of cancer," Pina

announced. "Dr. Robert Hillier had plans for more radiation treatments for Norma at Rhode Island Hospital. Norma Leanues had a future. But Anne Capute took away Norma's future. Anne Capute intentionally and deliberately violated doctor's orders."

Pina was as graceful as a tiger on the stage he had created. He was immaculately dressed. Anne could see that Ron Pina, like Pat, was a man most people would call attractive and charismatic, though she personally would still prefer Rod Steiger to either one of them. Once she was sure that people were no longer staring at her, she turned and glanced over her left shoulder to the source of Pina's energy and the reason he had pushed his own table and assistant prosecuter into "Siberia." It was a television camera. Anne wanted to wave at it, or stick out her tongue, or something, but she knew that Pat would consider that "communicating with the press," which he had forbidden her to do.

The trial of Anne Capute occurred during the commonwealth of Massachusetts's "camera in the courtroom" experiment, a two-year test to see if cameras could be allowed in courtrooms on a regular basis without disrupting the judicial process. Under the commonwealth's guidelines one stationary, mechanically silent videotape camera could be placed and operated in the courtroom. The camera was a pool camera, and its film was available to several local television stations, which would take what they wanted each day and air it on the news.

Despite the fact that some of each day's proceedings would show up on television right after supper, Judge Prince had decided not to sequester the jury because an unusually long trial was anticipated. His decision proved to be wise. The Capute trial turned out to be the longest trial in the history of the county.

While the district attorney continued to assault the jury with his outline of the commonwealth's case against Anne Capute, Anne studied the faces of the jurors for the first time. What did they think, what did they feel, when they heard Pina call her a murderer? Their faces were intent, enraptured, but revealed nothing.

Pat had gotten much of what he wanted in a jury, but still there was cause for concern. There were ten men and six women. Most of the jurors were blue-collar workers over forty, and only four had even had one year of college. The weak spot was religion. Ten of the jurors were Catholic. Among the jurors were a man whose sister-in-law had worked as a nurse at Morton Hospital, a woman whose daughter was a medical secretary, a man whose wife was a nurse, and a man who, after he was selected, found out that his mother rented an apartment to Norma Leanues's mother. There was another odd coincidence: Two old friends, lost to each other for years, were selected as jurors, and they renewed their friendship.

Even though the Bristol County district attorney was strutting back and forth like a rooster in a barnyard and telling the world that she was a murderer, Anne felt less tense than she had that morning. The jury visit to Morton Hospital had been, for her, like an hour in a dentist's chair waiting for the dentist to strike a raw nerve. No nerve had been struck, but Anne had been fidgety throughout. The jury had been taken by bus to Morton and brought to ward S-2. They had been taken to the narcotics closet, the nurses' station, Norma Leanues's room, and the corridor where Anne had talked to Dr. Hillier. Finally they were led down the stairs and out the back door to the administration building, following the same path Anne and Lorraine Hickey had taken on the night of

Anne's interrogation in Costello's office. There was no testimony at the hospital. The jurors were not told the significance of anything they saw. They were merely asked to observe and remember.

As they walked along the corridors of Morton Hospital, Anne had tried to keep herself always within reach of at least a few jurors, just as Pat had told her. But mostly she had tried to stay close to James Morton. He was her security blanket.

James Morton was a handsome young black man who, like Don Harwood, was a law assistant waiting for the results of his bar exam. Though Morton had not been deeply involved in the pretrial work, Pat had added him to the defense team after the trial began. Even more than the others, James was able to keep Anne calm. He listened to her when she spoke, no matter what she spoke about, and she found she could confide in him easily. Morton had driven Anne to the hospital for the jury visit. Pat, not wanting to isolate himself from the jury, had gone on the bus. During the drive over, James had told Anne not to worry, he would stay close to her. And he had.

Now, as Ronald Pina continued with his opening statement, Anne glanced at James, who sat next to her. James stared straight ahead, his wide eyes full of excitement. He reminded her somehow of Warren, though being black and very bright were about all the two men had in common. Anne knew that being black had played at least a part in the turmoil of Warren's life. How many pain points do we have to pile up before we kill ourselves? she wondered. And if Warren had been white, how many pain points would have been subtracted? More and more these days her mind grappled with such perplexing questions. Well, they won't get this one, she thought, smiling at James. He's going to be a good lawyer. Anne had been deeply touched by James's offer to drive her, instead of letting her go to Morton alone. She wanted to reach out now and pat his shoulder. But she didn't know him well enough yet. So she took the notebook Pat had given her. "Thanks," she wrote, and she ripped off the paper and slipped it under his hand.

"Anne Capute told employees of Morton Hospital that she knew she had killed Norma Leanues," Ronald Pina was saying. "She knew the morphine was doing her in, but she told them she only wanted to end Norma's suffering. She admitted that she gave Norma Leanues enough morphine to kill an elephant."

Chapter Nineteen

Pat Piscitelli was ready. It was Friday, September 18, the first day of testimony. He had been up until 3:00 A.M., but he felt rested. He felt like a bolt of lightning ready to strike. Strangely, what pleased Pat the most that morning as he and Donny and James and Anne set up their table for the day was that Ron Pina had done such a good job with the opening statement. Pina's fifty-minute presentation had been thorough, convincing, dramatic, and well staged. It was, Pat had to admit, a virtuoso performance. In fact, Pina's opening had been so good that Pat had given an opening statement, though he hadn't planned to. Unlike Pina, Pat did not throw everything he had at the jury on the first day. His presentation was

relatively subdued, primarily intended to take the
edge off Pina's performance and remind the jury to
withhold judgment until the evidence was in. Still, he
was glad that Pina had done such a good job, because
all along Pat had worried that he might underesti-
mate Pina, he might let down because Pina was
inexperienced in murder trials. Now Pat realized just
how hungry Pina was for this conviction. The TV
cameras, the publicity, the notoriety of the case. This,
Pat knew, was Pina's best shot at a seat in Congress,
and he would not give it up easily. And because of
that, Pat could take nothing for granted.

The day began with a bench conference, a
private discussion among Pina, Piscitelli, and Judge
Prince out of the jury's hearing. Pat wanted to get an
objection on the record. He wanted Linda Lawrence,
Norma Leanues's daughter, barred from the courtroom.

"I'm told that she's a very emotional person," Pat
said to Judge Prince. "I'm afraid she might end up
sobbing and have to leave court. The impact on the
jury would hurt my client."

Pat was turned down, but the objection was
saved, which meant there would be one more point
on which to base an appeal later.

The clerk called out the name of each juror, and
each one replied with a resounding "Present." Then
sixty-three-year-old Judge Prince outlined to the jury
what he would say every day for the rest of the trial.

"Ladies and gentlemen, I now ask you whether
or not during the recess from yesterday until this
moment anything has occurred orally or as a result of
anything you've seen, read, or heard, to make you
doubt your ability to decide this case in a fair and
impartial manner, and if anyone has made any effort
that you would have reason to believe was an effort to

affect your judgment. If in any way you feel that your impartiality has been compromised, would you please indicate now by standing."

The judge's words each day were a reminder to everybody that this murder trial was getting more publicity than any case in the history of the commonwealth.

"It was a very exciting time," says Don Harwood. "It was the kind of thing where you'd work hard all day, then rush back to the office to see yourself on television."

The prosecution's first witness was Edward Leanues. Leanues was a small man, bearded and pale. Pat watched carefully as the D.A. led the frail and pathetic-looking widower through the questions about Norma's fall, her visits to Hillier, her hospitalization. Mr. Leanues would certainly capture the jury's sympathy, and Pat knew he would have to treat him gently.

"And she finally just stopped breathing," Edward Leanues said after he described Norma's last night when he had sat by her bed and wept. And now Edward Leanues wept again, in front of the jury. Pat glanced at Anne. He could see the tears forming in her eyes. He knew that she felt terribly sorry for Mr. Leanues and for months had wanted to speak to him. Anne looked at Pat as if to plead for permission. Pat shook his head "No."

The D.A.'s direct examination of Leanues was not expected to be provocative, merely informative. Certainly everybody agreed that Norma did fall, she did see the doctor, she did die. But when Pat heard Pina ask, "Mr. Leanues, did you ever have a conversation with Anne Capute?" Pat leaned forward and glanced at Don Harwood to be sure he was taking notes.

"Yes," Leanues told the court, "I spoke to Mrs. Capute."

Pina dropped the subject of the conversation as quickly as he'd brought it up. He's trying to make the jury think that Anne had a special relationship with Norma, Pat thought. He objected, and the two attorneys met by the bench.

"Your Honor, I had not been notified that there was any conversation with Anne Capute," Pat said. "I'd like to know what it was."

Pina was smiling, as if he'd scored some points. "I'd object to the hearsay aspect of the conversation," he said.

"My client's statement?" Pat shot back. "You were supposed to give me that a long time ago, Mr. D.A."

Judge Prince looked at Pina. "If you're aware of any conversation . . ."

"I'm not," Pina said. He paused. "Nothing of substance."

"Then you won't mind telling me what it is," Pat said. "I can't imagine why you couldn't give it to me before."

"Fine," Pina said.

"Well? What is it?"

"Do you want me to ask Leanues?"

"No, I don't want you to ask Leanues! I want you to tell me. I want to know what it is in case I want to ask him."

"Well I'm not going to speak for the witness," Pina said.

Pat threw his hands in the air. "I've never heard of such a thing," he said.

"You're going to hear of it now," Pina said. The men glared at each other.

"Your Honor, I filed a motion to get my client's statements."

"And you got everything," Pina said.

"I did not. This is new."

"Mr. Leanues spoke to the grand jury, you know."

Pat had read the grand jury transcript several times. He knew Pina was bluffing. "At the grand jury Leanues said he never spoke to my client. Now he says he did."

"Well, I know what he said."

"Tell me."

Pina looked to the judge and saw that both men were waiting for an answer. Pina smirked, as if he were about to reveal the last line of some marvelous joke. "He said 'Hi' to her. He has talked to her."

Pat was not amused. "What else?"

"That's it."

"That's all the conversation?"

"That's all that I know of," Pina said. "I'm telling you this in good faith."

"Horseshit!" Pat muttered and he stalked back to the defense table.

The courtroom was filled that morning, and certainly most of the spectators and reporters who watched this exchange saw a Pat Piscitelli who was annoyed, upset, angry. But what they really saw was Piscitelli the actor putting on a performance, as he often would throughout the trial. In fact, Pat was delighted. He winked at Anne as he moved back toward the defense table, and when he sat down he whispered in her ear. "I'm going to move for a mistrial." He knew that Anne had said more than "Hi" to Edward Leanues, and he knew how to use it.

When Pat cross-examined Leanues he covered much of the same ground. But in his questions Pat underlined the pain of Norma Leanues.

"Did she at times say to you, 'God help me, God help me, the pain'?" he asked.

"Yes," Edward Leanues said.

"And did you go to Dr. Hillier because your wife was in such a tremendous amount of pain?"

"Yes."

"And did your wife tell you that whenever they tried to turn her on her side, that she experienced a great amount of pain?"

"Yes."

Pat continued to hammer away at the pain aspect, driving the words, "pain" and "suffering" deep into the jury's collective mind. These were all bricks for the final wall of defense, if he should need it, the "blessing defense" that said that despite everything else, Norma's death was for the best because of the agony she was in. But Pat knew this wall of defense would work only if he convinced the jury that Norma Leanues was doomed.

"Did Dr. Hillier tell you that your wife was terminally ill and would die within a matter of weeks?"

"He said a couple of months," Leanues replied.

"Okay, months," Pat said. He stood quietly, letting the jury absorb the testimony. He felt he had fortified the last wall of defense. He was pleased. He intended to spend the entire trial rushing from wall to wall, piling up the bricks, patching up the holes. Take nothing for granted, he told himself, build as many defenses as you can. Now, with one "pain" brick firmly in place, he moved to the point on which he planned to seek a mistrial, though he knew it was a long shot.

"Mr. Leanues," he said, "do you recall someone coming in and placing her hand on your shoulder and saying, 'It will be okay now, Mr. Leanues. We have a change in medication. Your wife won't suffer anymore'?"

Leanues looked lost for a moment, then he said, "I remember her . . . Mrs. Capute . . . saying that shortly after the operation."

Pat was pleased. After he finished up with Leanues he went to the bench and made a motion for a mistrial.

"That conversation must have been known to the D.A.," Pat told Judge Prince. "I'm amazed he says he doesn't know about it." In effect, Pat was calling Pina a liar for saying that "Hi" was the only conversation known to him.

Pat argued that the conversation was exculpatory information, meaning information that could help his client and that cannot legally be withheld by the prosecutor.

Pina simply denied knowing anything about the "she won't suffer" conversation, and that was the end of it. Motion denied.

Pat walked back to the defense table shaking his head like a kid who had missed an easy shot. In fact, it was a hard shot, and Pat knew it; it was one small point among many. But he hated every loss, no matter how small. After he sat down he analyzed the issue and the exchange, turning it around in his mind like a strange new object. He would do this with each witness, each question, each word. Each piece of the trial would become tangible to him, and he would peer into it from every angle to see what he had lost and what he had gained from it. From the Edward Leanues testimony, Pat concluded, he had gained knowledge of his adversary. He understood Ronald Pina a little better and how the game would be played. Ron Pina was obviously determined to do everything he could to put Anne in prison for the rest of her life. So it was not to be a game at all. It was to be a war.

The next witness was Larry Ross, the hospital

administrator. Pina used Ross primarily to identify several medical documents that were being entered as exhibits. But since Ross was on the stand, Piscitelli had a shot at him, and he used it to plant two important ideas in the minds of the jurors: "no limit" orders as common practice at Morton; and Anne as victim, the expendable "low man on the totem pole."

MR. PISCITELLI: The L.P.N. is kind of a low man on the totem pole, isn't she, in the hierarchy of nursing?"

MR. ROSS: That's correct.

MR. PISCITELLI: Do you know the policy that allows—the policy of the hospital that allows doctors to give narcotic orders prn, as necessary, allowing a nurse to exercise her own discretion as to how much to give?

MR. PINA: Objection, Your Honor.

THE COURT: Objection sustained.

MR. PISCITELLI: Are you aware that Morton Hospital has engaged in that policy for the last few years?

MR. PINA: Objection. He is testifying.

THE COURT: Objection sustained.

MR. PISCITELLI: That's all. Thank you.

Chapter Twenty

On Monday morning, as Dr. Robert Hillier was walking to the witness stand, Anne did something she had been wanting to do for days: She took off her shoes. The high heels were killing her feet, and she couldn't bear to sit through another day with them. So she kicked off the heels and propped her feet on Pat's briefcase, which was under the table.

Pat had told Anne that Hillier probably would be on the witness stand for two or three days. She was beginning to understand how slow, precise, and thorough a murder trial could be. Each idea had to be broken down into several questions for clarity. Still, there were plenty of objections, and Judge Prince had to rule often on whether a question was appropriate or an answer admissible. Though court was in session from ten in the morning to four in the afternoon each day, Anne had figured out that after you subtract morning recess, lunchtime, afternoon recess, and all the bench conferences, you end up with no more than three hours of actual testimony per day. So she'd be looking at Hillier's face for a while. She hated it.

Hillier was a large, fleshy man. He reminded Anne of one of Rubens's angels, but her name for him was drawn from a lesser form of art. She called him Baby Huey. Hillier was a product of Harvard Medical School, and it showed, she thought. Her impression of him was that he spoke as if everything

he said was an explanation to an idiot, and his firm
and certain tone implied that he had never been
wrong about anything. It seemed to her that Hillier
and the blue-collar people on the jury could well have
come from different planets.

As she listened to Hillier respond to the D.A.'s
questions about medical terms and procedures, Anne
glanced from time to time at Pat, who sat next to her
on the left. Pat's expressions had become Anne's
barometer of how things were going. Pat was smiling.
After the doctor had been testifying for ten minutes,
Pat leaned over and said to Anne, "The man is a
bubble of pomposity waiting to be burst. He's perfect."

"A perfect asshole," Anne said.

"Doctor, who prescribes medicine at Morton
Hospital?" Pina was asking the witness. Anne noticed
that Pina managed to get the word 'doctor' into
virtually every question.

"The doctors do," Hillier said.

"Anyone else?"

"No."

"Who has access to the medication charts?"

"The doctors do," Hillier said, "and the nurses,
physical therapists, dieticians, anyone involved in the
care of the patient."

"I see," said Pina. "And Doctor, who else can
write on the medication order forms?" Pina had
already introduced the order form into evidence and
had put it into Hillier's hand.

"Nurses."

"How can they write on the form?"

"They can write on the form if the order is given
verbally by the doctor."

"Does a doctor have a responsibility after the
nurse writes on it, to review the form?"

"Yes," Hillier said.

"When?"

"Well, the next day . . . usually the next day," Hillier said.

After questioning Hillier about the different ways that morphine could be introduced into the body, Pina asked about the side effects of morphine. Anne was impressed. She had expected the district attorney to be all flash and no substance, but it seemed to her that he had prepared well. She respected that.

"Morphine is a respiratory depressant," Hillier said.

"What does that mean, Doctor?" Pina asked.

"It affects the breathing center in the brain. It can cause you to breathe slowly."

"Are there any side effects from giving morphine to an individual who is asleep?" Pina asked.

"Yes."

"What are they?"

"Problems with breathing. There is the possibility that the previous dose of morphine is still working, and you run the risk of having more side effects, such as respiratory depression."

"I see," Pina said. He strode across the front of the courtroom, his face somber, as if he had just received terrible news and was now obliged to pass it on to someone else. He paused dramatically, swung around, and faced the witness. He's ready to pounce, Anne thought.

"Doctor," he said, "on the sixteenth of May, did you change Norma Leanues's medication chart?"

"Yes," Hillier said, "around five o'clock."

"What did you change the order to, Doctor?"

"I changed it to fifteen milligrams of morphine, IM, every three hours, as needed for pain, prn. To be given in addition to the morphine solution if that wasn't effective."

"And is that the order recorded on the doctor's order form in front of you?"

"No."

"Would you tell us, Doctor, what is recorded on that order form."

"It says give morphine, fifteen milligrams, sub-cu., prn, no time limit. Make her comfortable. Give Valium, IM. And then it says 'Dr. Hillier.'"

"Did you sign that?" Pina asked.

"No."

"Who signed it?"

"Nurse Robbins."

"Is that the order you gave, Doctor?"

"It's not."

The crowded courtroom buzzed. Anne was reminded that even though the defense and prosecution teams knew pretty much what every witness was going to say, most of this was new to the spectators, the press, and the jury.

Pina let the crowd's reaction drift away, and then he spoke again. "Doctor, how does that order differ from the order you gave?"

Hillier did not look at the order in his hand. He had memorized it. "The order I gave was an order for morphine, fifteen milligrams. The correct dose. But IM rather than subcu. I have never written an order that way."

"What would subcu. mean, Doctor?"

"By shot under the skin, rather than in the muscle."

"So there's a difference there," Pina said, glancing at the jury. "What else?"

"Prn."

"And 'prn,' you've testified, means 'as needed.'"

"Yes," Hillier said. "The problem is orders are always given with a frequency such as every two hours, every three hours, every four hours. So the frequency is not there. Prn is correct."

"And the phrase 'no time limit'?"

"That is not an order that I give."

"Have you ever given a 'no time limit' order?"

"I have not, no."

"What else, Doctor, that differs from your order?"

"'Make her comfortable.' I have never used that."

"Does that mean something in medical terms?"

"Not that I know of."

"What else?" Pina asked, again turning to the jury as if he were tossing them balls and wanted to make sure they were catching them.

"Give Valium, IM, which means to give the Valium by shot rather than by pill."

"Did you order Valium by shot?"

"No, I did not."

"Doctor, did you sign that order?"

"No," said Hillier. "I did not sign it."

Pina asked Hillier to describe the conversation in which the medication order was given. Hillier said that he talked to Anne Capute and Nancy Robbins around five o'clock on the sixteenth of May near the nurses' station on S-2. He told the jury that the change in medication was Anne's idea, because Norma Leanues was still in a lot of pain despite the morphine solution she was taking. Hillier said he then gave the medication order he had just described to the court.

"The shot was to be used only if oral medication was not working," he said, "and only at a frequency of every three hours, no shorter than that."

"Goddamn liar," Anne muttered. Pat, Don, and James were all taking notes. James looked up and winked at her. "Give 'em hell, Anne," he whispered.

"And did Anne Capute say anything else to you?" Pina was asking.

"Yes," the witness said. "She said, 'Don't worry, Dr. Hillier, we will take good care of Mrs. Leanues.'"

All morning long the district attorney relentlessly brought forth a series of facts intended to portray Anne as a woman who had planned and carried out the murder of a patient. Pat made occasional objections, but Pina did not often stray from the rules of a trial. Anne could see that Pat was frustrated. He needed some action. He had once told her that the worst part of a trial was sitting back and letting the prosecutor beat the hell out of you while you waited your turn. Now she could see that the muscles in Pat's face gradually grew tighter and his hands and feet became restless. By the time Pina brought out the medication chart for Friday the sixteenth, Pat looked like he was ready to explode.

The morphine injections on Friday were for fifteen milligrams, but Pina wanted to show that they were being given every two hours, not every three. After each entry, which Hillier read, Pina would ask, "Is it initialed?"

"Yes," Hillier would reply. "A.C."

"And who is A.C?" Pina would ask.

"Anne Capute," the doctor would reply.

By the time they got to the shot for one-fifteen on Saturday morning the shift had changed, and different initials were showing up. Pat was rapping his fingers on his notebook and occasionally tugging at his collar.

"The initial for one-fifteen?" Pina asked.

"It looks like Judith Foley, J.F." Hillier said, "but it's not clear."

"What is the next notation?"

"Four-fifteen," Hillier said, "and there is an initial, P.C. I can't make out who P.C. is."

"Okay, go on," Pina said, making no attempt to identify "P.C."

"NO!" Pat shouted. He jumped to his feet. Anne felt as if a bomb had gone off beside her. "It's not okay," Pat said. Piscitelli knew that "P.C." stood for Pat Courcey. Courcey had been suspended along with the others, but she had been reinstated. Pat wanted the jury to hear all the names and see Anne as someone who hadn't done anything that others weren't doing.

"Do you mind?" Pina said. "He's testifying."

"I do mind," Pat roared.

The crowd grew noisy. They want some action, too, Anne thought.

Then Judge Prince got into the act. He slammed down his gavel. "I will make the rulings here," he warned, and he glared at both men.

Pat sat down. His face looked calmer, and his hands were no longer fidgeting. "Just needed to shout something," he said. Anne could see that he felt better.

The next time Pat stood up was when Pina handed Hillier the nurses' notes for Saturday, the seventeenth. Pina would try to get Hillier to go through each medication, and Pat did not want the jury continuously reminded that the doses were thirty or forty-five milligrams instead of fifteen and that they were given every hour or so instead of every three hours.

"Your Honor," Pat said, "the defense agrees that the initials 'A.C.' appear throughout. The medication chart is the best evidence. Perhaps the jury can look at it. There is no dispute. We will agree, instead of wasting time going over the entries one by one."

Judge Prince was not convinced, however, and Pina was allowed to continue.

The D.A. led Hillier along carefully, reading from the nurses' notes.

"And what about ten-fifteen?" Pina asked. "What is the dosage there?"

"That's also thirty milligrams," Hillier said.

"And is that your order, Doctor?"

"No."

"Would you read us the vital signs written there."

"Temperature one hundred one, pulse one-twelve, blood pressure ninety over sixty, respiratory rate fourteen, and apnea ten seconds in duration."

"That means," said Pina, "that she was going ten seconds at a time without breathing."

"Yes."

"I see. And what about the pulse rate, Doctor? What does that indicate?"

"Distress. The heart is beating faster."

"I see. What is the dosage for eleven-fifteen, Doctor?"

"Forty-five milligrams."

"Is that your order?"

"No."

"Is anything else recorded there, Doctor?"

"Apnea ten to fifteen seconds in duration," Hillier read from Anne's notes. "Nail beds are bluish. Not responding. Condition very poor."

"And bluish nails, Doctor, you have told us indicate that the patient is not breathing properly."

"That's right."

"Do you give morphine to a patient when they have bluish nails?"

"No."

"What do you do?"

"You call the doctor."

"Did you get called?"

"No."

"And do you give a patient morphine when they are not responding?" Pina asked, turning to the jury in midquestion as if to say, "We all know the answer to that one, don't we?"

"No," Hillier said. "You stop all medication and inform the physician."

"Were you informed?"

"No."

And Doctor, when a patient is not breathing for ten to fifteen seconds at a time . . . do you give them morphine?"

"No." Hillier said.

"Doctor, would you total from five o'clock to eleven o'clock the amount of morphine given to your patient."

Hillier stared down at the sheets, adding the amounts in his mind. He looked up. "One hundred and ninety-five milligrams of morphine," he said.

"And whose signature is there at eleven-fifteen?" Pina asked.

"Anne Capute."

Pina brought Hillier's testimony through the one-fifteen notation that Norma Leanues had died, and at two-fifteen the last notation, "patient discharged to morgue." Pina was done with Hillier.

Anne searched the jurors' faces for some sign of how all this had affected them, but she could not tell. It was quarter to one, and the judge offered Pat the option of starting his cross-examination now and getting in fifteen minutes before lunch, or beginning the lunch recess early. Pat, seeing a chance to score one small point with the jury by giving them an extra fifteen minutes for lunch, said, "I would rather proceed at two o'clock."

Anne followed Pat out of the courtroom. She was in a kind of shock and had no appetite for lunch. Her feet felt like bricks. God, it's really happening, she thought. They are really trying to pin a murder rap on me. It's not make-believe. Her whole body felt numb. And her throat felt dry and tight, as if somebody were trying to slip a noose around her neck.

Chapter Twenty-one

Anne rose slightly from her chair in the crowded courtroom, leaned across to the end of the defense table, and pressed her head close to Don's.

"Donny," she whispered. "I have to ask you something very important."

"What?" he whispered.

"Was Baby Huey a person or a bird?"

Don grinned, and his eyes seemed to sparkle. He and Anne were growing close, learning that they shared the same absurd sense of humor. He pursed his lips as if to give the matter some serious thought.

"Gee, I don't know," he said. "And I usually keep track of important stuff like that."

"I'm trying to remember," Anne said. "I think Baby Huey was a bird. I think he was a big bird with a diaper."

"Yeah, I think you're right. Why?"

"Well, look at him now," Anne said, pointing to Hillier, who was on the witness stand. "He looks like a chicken, doesn't he?" A chicken being circled by a hawk."

"You're right," Donny said, and he gave her a poke.

Anne settled back in her chair and watched the hawk, Pat Piscitelli, close in on the chicken.

The tension between the two men was so real she felt as if she could almost reach out and grab it. Pat eyed the doctor as if Hillier were the one who should be on trial. And Hillier stared back suspiciously, as if he expected Pat to pull a gun on him.

For more than an hour Pat questioned Dr. Hillier about Norma's illness, her operations, her pain, and her medicine, and during the cross-examination Pat revealed to the jury his own remarkable accumulation of medical knowledge. He knew that if there was one thing that would impress a jury more than a doctor who knew a lot about medicine, it was a lawyer who knew a lot about medicine. He wanted to free the jury from any idealistic ideas they had about doctors.

While Pat cross-examined, Anne held her pen close to her notebook. Pat had asked her to write down anything that occurred to her that might be helpful. Across the top of the first page he had written a list of target areas he would cover with Hillier. "Areas of vulnerability," he called them. The list read: Norma terminal, vital signs, Hillier's character, medication, Norma's pain, no limit, Hillier's motivation.

In direct examination it had come out that Hillier had made plans to send Norma back to Rhode Island Hospital for more radiation treatments. Pat was afraid that this gave the jury the impression that Hillier did not regard Norma as a terminal patient. Pat needed to prove otherwise.

"Now, Doctor," he said, "you sent Norma Leanues to a psychologist because you wanted to prepare her for dying, didn't you?"

Anne, Pat, and Don Harwood leaving New
Bedford Superior Court during pre-trial hearing.

Anne at counsel table
during trial,
looking over notes.

Pat arguing
to jury.

Jurors examining
exhibits (needles and
syringes) during trial.

Anne and Pat at counsel table during trial.

Mr. Leanues and daughter in courtroom listening to testimony during trial.

District Attorney Pina
addressing jurors
during trial.

Anne at counsel table
during trial.

Maureen Costello and Judge
Prince during Ms. Costello's
testimony at trial.

Dr. Robert Hillier and Judge Prince during Dr. Hillier's testimony at trial.

Pat, Anne, and two of her daughters at a recess during trial.

Jurors listening to evidence during trial.

Pat, James Morton, and Anne conferring during break in trial proceedings.

District Attorney Pina, Judge Prince, Larry Ross, and Pat outside entrance to Morton Hospital during jury view.

A court officer, reporter Shelby Scott (Eyewitness News, NBC-TV), another court officer and a juror during jury view at Morton Hospital.

Pat, Anne, Don Harwood, and unidentified person during jury view at Morton Hospital.

Anne giving her unsworn statement to the jury.

Pat during closing argument to jury.

Photographers and press outside Fall River Superior Court awaiting verdict.

"No."

"Didn't you send her to him so that he could better psychologically orient her to the prospect of dying very soon?"

"I did not."

"Did you make the statement to anybody that you sent her to him to prepare her for what you thought was going to be an eventual death because of the metastasized bone?"

"No."

Hillier continued to deny and Pat, having planted the idea in the jury's mind, abandoned the issue for the time being. Pat moved on to his next target: vital signs. Pina had spent a lot of time discussing Norma's vital signs; he had tried to convince the jury that Norma Leanues was obviously in no condition to be given large doses of morphine. Pina had probably convinced the jury, Pat thought, and now he had to unconvince them.

"Now, Doctor," Pat said, "does a person sleeping in fact have apnea of ten to fifteen seconds?"

"Yes."

"Ten to fifteen seconds at a time without breathing?"

"Yes."

"And doesn't a normal person, when he is sleeping, have a respiration rate of ten to fifteen per minute?"

"Sometimes, yes."

"So that having a respiration rate of ten to twelve with periods of apnea of ten to fifteen seconds is not unusual, is it?"

"In certain forms of sleep it is not, no," Hillier said. He sounded defensive.

"I see," Pat said. "And the average person, when he is awake, has a breathing rate of sixteen to twenty-

five. And apnea of five seconds is not uncommon, is
it?"

"No," Hillier said grudgingly.

Piscitelli then described Norma Leanues's years
of heavy smoking and her curvature of the spine. He
got Hillier to acknowledge that both of these things
could lead to respiratory problems. Again he had
planted an idea in the jury's mind, and he left it for a
while.

He moved on to another target: Hillier, the man.
Pat wanted to portray Dr. Hillier as a somewhat
haughty individual who just couldn't be bothered
with the details of nursing procedures. Pat asked him
about nurses' notes. Hillier said he was not in the
habit of reading them. Pat asked about the tape-
recorded patient reports that nurses on one shift
leave for those on the next. Hillier said he didn't
know anything about those reports. Pat asked about
the Kardex system the nurses used. Hillier said he
never looked at it. Pat asked who carried the keys to
the narcotics closet. Hillier said he didn't know. It was
relatively minor and peripheral material, but the
questions kept coming, and they gathered enough
force to shatter the stereotype of the all-knowing,
infallible physician. Even Anne, with an already low
opinion of Hillier, was shocked that a doctor could
allow himself to be so ignorant of nursing procedures. Pat was delighted with Hillier's ignorance. Pat
wanted the jury to believe that this was a man who was
capable of making a serious mistake in judgment.

Court adjourned at four o'clock, but Piscitelli was
nowhere near the end of his cross-examination.
Hillier returned to the witness stand the following
morning.

The hostility between the men was unmistakable.
Throughout the morning session Hillier attempted to

elaborate on his answers, and Pat continually cut him short with, "Doctor, just answer my question, please. Yes or no, Doctor, Is it yes, or is it no?" And Hillier would flinch as if he had been slapped in the face.

On several occasions Pat listened patiently to the doctor's answer, then strode triumphantly to the defense table to snatch up a volume of grand jury testimony that Don Harwood always had ready. Back to the witness stand Pat would go and he would read Hillier's grand jury statements contradicting what the doctor had just said. After this happened two or three times Hillier got gun-shy and developed the habit of glancing at Pat before every answer, to see if Piscitelli was edging toward the defense table.

Pat often hovered over Hillier, browbeating him like a detective interrogating a street punk. Several times Judge Prince had to warn Pat to lower his voice and move away from the witness.

Anne knew that her life could depend on the degree to which Pat was able to discredit Dr. Hillier. But even knowing that, she couldn't believe how merciless Pat was with the doctor. Pat had told her that each witness required different treatment. Some you go easy on. Some you intimidate. She had seen Pat handle Edward Leanues with such gentleness, and now she could hardly believe it was the same man questioning Hillier with such brutality that Baby Huey seemed more than ever like a helpless chicken impaled by the talons of a hawk, flapping his wings and legs but unable to get away. She wrote a note to James and slipped it across the table.

"James," it said, "call Hollywood. Tell them to polish up an Academy Award. P.J.'s a shoo-in."

". . . and soon after the operation," Pat was saying, "because the pain was so intense, you gave her thirty milligrams of morphine orally, prn, around the clock?"

"Yes," Hillier said.

"And later in the week the original ten milligrams was quadrupled to forty?"

"Yes."

"And again," Pat said, "that was because she was suffering excruciating, unbearable pain, Doctor?"

"Yes."

Pat moved to the defense table. He paused. Slowly he picked up a glass of water, sipped from it, and slowly he put it down. Then, returning to the witness, he said, "Doctor, isn't it true that Norma Leanues's respiration rate was lower about twenty-four hours before than it was when Anne Capute gave that thirty milligrams at ten-fifteen on the seventeenth?"

"Yes."

"And the apnea, Doctor, twenty-four hours before, that was also more than the apnea which Anne Capute observed the next evening. Right, Doctor?"

"Yes."

"So," Pat said, glancing at the jury, "Norma Leanues looked to be, by these records, in worse condition twenty-four hours before than she was on the night she died, right?"

"Not necessarily," Hillier replied.

Pat smiled. Here comes the sarcasm, Anne thought.

"I see," Pat said. "You're saying that going fifteen seconds without breathing is better than going only ten seconds without breathing."

"No, not necessarily. Based on just respiration rate and apnea—"

"Doctor, it calls for a yes or no, based on vital signs."

"Not necessarily."

"You are saying that to have twelve respirations per minute is better than having fourteen, Doctor?"

"No," Hillier said, "I'm not saying that."

Like many issues throughout the trial, this one was belabored to the point where the question became more important than the answer. Finally Judge Prince ruled that the witness had answered the question, and Pat was obliged to move on to something else.

Another area of vulnerability was Hillier's failure to sign the narcotics order for Norma Leanues. Hillier admitted that the order should be signed within a "reasonable" amount of time but would not agree that it should be signed within twenty-four hours.

"Oh," Pat said, verbally winking at the jury, "then I guess you mean a reasonable amount of time as interpreted by the doctor, don't you, Doctor. In other words if you thought it was reasonable, Doctor, not to sign a narcotics order for three weeks, that's okay, right? Is that what you're saying?"

Again, the question was never successfully answered, but the point had been made. Pat was satisfied.

All day long the defense team worked like a well-oiled machine. Don Harwood was custodian of the grand jury transcript and the transcripts of various interviews that had been conducted at Morton Hospital. Harwood continually scanned the material so that when Pat spotted a contradiction in Hillier's testimony he could walk toward the defense table and Don would have the volume and the page ready when Pat got there. Pat did not want to sweep dramatically across the courtroom only to end up fumbling through pages of transcript at the table. He wanted every move to flow as if it had been rehearsed a hundred times.

James Morton took care of the medical records.

The defense had compiled hundreds of documents—
medication charts, patient records, nurses' notes,
narcotics orders—and James's job was to have what
Pat needed in these areas when he needed it.

Anne throughout the day jotted notes on her pad
whenever she remembered something about vital
signs, Norma's pain, Hillier, whatever. It made her
feel good to be part of the defense team, not just the
helpless client. She felt needed. And she was thrilled
whenever Pat used something that had come from
one of her notes.

Pat had a tape recording of an interview Hillier
had done with Robert St. Jean, the state trooper who
had investigated the Leanues case for the district
attorney's office. During part of the morning's cross-
examination Pat held in his hand a tape recorder
containing the Hillier tape. Pat did not play it, but he
waved it in front of Hillier's eyes frequently before
placing it back on the defense table.

Returning to the idea that Norma Leanues was a
doomed woman and that Hillier knew it, Pat asked,
"Did you say on the fifteenth that Norma Leanues
looked hopeless?"

"Not that I recall," Hillier said.

"Did you say those words?" Pat demanded.

"I don't recall exactly, no," Hillier said. But then
Pat made a slight move in the direction of the defense
table. Hillier leaned forward. "I . . . I may have," he
added.

"Oh," Pat said, moving back toward Hiller. "You
didn't change your testimony now just because I went
toward my desk for the tape recorder, did you?" The
people in the spectator seats laughed, but Pat knew he
had done more than score points with the audience.
In a small way he had shown Hillier as a man who
might change his mind about what he had said if it
were expedient.

When the laughter subsided, Hillier said, "No, I am answering the question." He sounded offended.

"Doctor," Pat said in a voice as cold as frost, "when may you have said it looked hopeless? Tell the jury when you may have said that."

"Well, Mrs. Leaues's condition—"

"Doctor," Pat interrupted, "when did you say the words 'it looks hopeless'?"

"I don't remember when I would have said those words."

"Did you also say 'She would scream in pain. Every nurse dreaded to see her. If they touched her the wrong way Mrs. Leanues would scream and cry and sob'? Did you say that?"

"I may have."

"And did you also say that every time you saw Mr. Leanues he was at the bedside in a kneeling position holding Norma's hand and crying? Did you say she would scream and you could see the tears running down Edward Leanues's face? Did you say that, too?"

"Yes."

"A pathetic sight for everybody that saw that?"

"It was horrible," Hillier said. "Very difficult, yes."

Now the hawk circled his quarry once more. He was about to expose the most sensational issue of the trial, an issue that he knew would inspire headlines all over the country if he was allowed to pursue it.

Piscitelli and his assistants, along with Anne, had spent night after night poring over medical records and narcotics orders from Morton Hospital, searching always for case histories similar to Norma's. From this mass of material Pat had pulled patient records and narcotics orders—enough, he believed, to show the world that Norma Leanues might have died not from the devious actions of three nurses, but from common practice at Morton. Norma Leanues, he would like to suggest, died from standard operating procedure with terminal patients. However, Pat knew that the relevancy of his material might be seen as tenuous at best and that Judge Prince would not make it easy for him to get it into evidence. He would have to tread carefully.

"Doctor," he said to Hillier, who looked weary from the long stint on the witness stand, "is it your policy in cases where a patient is considered to be terminally ill to give larger doses than normal to attempt to abate or suppress the pain?"

"It is not," Hillier said.

"Is it done by other doctors in the hospital?"

The district attorney certainly knew the sound of a can of worms being opened when he heard it, so he stood up immediately and called out his objection. A bench conference ensued.

MR. PISCITELLI: Your Honor, I am offering this to show the state of mind of my client. The information I am about to bring up about larger doses, goes to her state of mind, goes to her lack of culpability and the fact that others were getting larger doses and getting larger amounts. It was known to her and it was known that terminally ill patients that they gave these. I would show that is why it was increased. It is very crucial to our defense.

MR. PINA: It's all hearsay.

MR. PISCITELLI: I am laying foundation now to bring it in later that this was known to other nurses.

THE COURT: I don't think this is the witness that that question should be required to be asked.

MR. PISCITELLI: Well, I have medications of one patient who was operated on and my client worked on where large doses were given, far in excess of what was given here.

MR. PINA: It's irrelevant, Your Honor.

MR. PISCITELLI: I think it's highly relevant. It is the state of mind of my client in terminally ill cases.

THE COURT: In no way could we pass on good medical practice from another doctor on a hearsay statement of that nature. And I regard it as inadmissable.

For several minutes Pat argued with the judge that he was trying to show common procedure at Morton that would have been known to Anne and would have influenced her actions. Judge Prince agreed with the premise, that state of mind was relevant, but said that the actions of one other doctor or the treatment of one other patient was not. Pat would have to find a more legitimate way to bring this explosive issue into evidence. By the time Pat returned to the witness, the district attorney's temper had been heated almost to the boiling point, and Pina objected to nearly everything that Pat said for the rest of the day.

"Doctor," Pat said, feeling his way around for another door into the issue, "what is a 'no code' order? You have heard of that, haven't you?"

Hillier said, "I don't ever use 'no code' orders."

"I said what is—"

"I don't—"

"Doctor! I want to know what a 'no code' is. What is a 'no code'? Have you ever seen a 'no codes' used at Morton Hospital?"

"NO!" Now Hillier was getting short-tempered.

"A 'no code,' Doctor, is an order given by a doctor to make no heroic efforts to revive or resuscitate a patient who is dying, isn't that so?"

"It can be so, yes."

"Not only can it be so, it is so, isn't it?"

Hillier rolled his eyes. He looked somewhat disdainfully at Pat, as if Pat were a stupid little kid. "It would mean," he explained, "that you don't call what is called a 'code red' when the patient is having an emergency. A code red means you alert through the entire hospital. The resuscitation team goes to the patient's room at a rapid pace. 'No code' would mean you would not call the code red, like not pulling the fire alarm."

"I see," Pat said. "And what about 'comfort orders'? Have you seen them given by doctors in hospitals?"

"Personally, I have never given a comfort order."

"I didn't ask you that, Doctor. I asked if you were aware of them being given."

"I am not aware of that, no."

"What about a 'no time limit' order? Have you ever seen one given at Morton Hospital?"

"Yes."

"Have you seen 'no time limit' orders given where the patient was terminal?"

Hillier told the court that he was unable to answer the question the way it was phrased. Pat rephrased it. Hillier still couldn't answer. Pat changed the wording again. Hillier said he couldn't answer. Pat insisted that he answer. Pina objected. Judge Prince sustained the objection.

"Well, Doctor," Pat said, "did you indicate at some time that part of the plan for Norma was to make whatever time available as pleasant as possible because you knew that Norma was going to die soon?"

"Something to that effect, yes."

Now Pat could feel Hillier weakening on this point. It was time once and for all to bring home the fact that Dr. Robert Hillier, despite any plans for future radiation treatments at Rhode Island Hospital, did regard Norma Leanues as terminal.

"Did you in fact bring in a psychologist, a Dr. Hammer, to talk to Mrs. Leanues as early as December about the possibility that she was going to die?"

Hillier shifted his stance. He paused. "He was not brought in for that reason in December, no."

"Did you bring in Dr. Hammer to talk to Mrs. Leanues about the possibility she was going to die sometime in May?"

"For that and other reasons, yes," Hillier said.

"That was one of the reasons, to get her ready for death, right?"

"No," Hillier said.

Pat moved in. "That wasn't one of the reasons? Didn't you just say that was one of the reasons a moment ago?"

"My reasons—"

"Did you or did you not say a moment ago that was one of your reasons?"

"Not say it the way you said it, no," Hillier snapped.

"Doctor, let me show you again your testimony to the grand jury on August sixth of 1980." Pat walked to the defense table and grabbed the grand jury testimony from Don's hands. He walked back to the witness and began reading loudly, "Question: 'You brought the psychiatrist?' Answer: "Psychologist.' Question: 'Around what period?' Answer: 'In December and I believe again this time to discuss death, dying.' Pat's voice was booming now, and Judge Prince warned him to quiet down. Pat closed the volume of testimony. Instead of staring at Hillier, Pat walked over to the jury. He leaned gently on the rail in front of the jury box, tilted his head slightly to the right toward Hillier, and in much quieter tones he said, "Have I quoted you correctly, Doctor?"

"Out of context," Hillier said.

"Please, have I quoted you correctly?"

"In this context, yes."

"As to what you said? Yes?"

"Yes," Hillier said.

Pat took a deep breath. For a moment things were so quiet he could hear the clock ticking. He moved away from the jury rail and back toward his witness. He knew he had his man reeling against the ropes. It was an ideal time to deliver another mighty blow. All along Pat had implied that Hillier had lied about the conversation with Anne and Nancy Robbins. Now Pat had to answer a question: Why would Hillier lie?

Piscitelli suspected that a deal had been made between Hillier and the district attorney. He couldn't prove it, but he was convinced that Hillier had been promised immunity from prosecution on a manslaughter charge in return for his testimony. Pat thought about bringing the subject up but decided it would do his client more harm than good. Regardless of how it made Hillier look, it would imply to the jury that, in fact, a serious crime had been committed, and that could hurt Anne. So Pat moved instead to a different area of vulnerability.

"Are you aware, Doctor, that you may be civilly responsible in a malpractice action brought against you if in fact the jury believes that you gave an order which might have invested discretion to a nurse who might have given a narcotics order to a patient who might have been accidentally caused to die because of it?"

Pina jumped up and objected. "You've got everything but the kitchen sink in that question," he said to
Pat when they got to the bench. Pina was steaming.

"Do you know what the purpose of cross-examination is?" Pat said. "You must know the purpose of
cross-examination, you're a lawyer. You don't know
the purpose?"

"Assuming this, assuming that," Pina said.
"Really! Put it in evidence."

"I don't know how many cases you've tried," Pat
said. The two men were inches apart.

"What difference does that make?" Pina demanded.

"Well, when you say that, I can't imagine you've
tried many cases."

"Think again," Pina said.

Judge Prince managed to calm the men down.
He told Pat to narrow the scope of the question, and
he sent the attorneys back to their respective places
like a couple of boys who had been caught fighting.

Pat returned to the cross-examination. "Doctor,"
he said, putting the question into a form Judge Prince
would accept, "Have you considered the fact that if
there's evidence that there was in fact a 'no time limit'
order given by you, that you probably could be sued
for negligence, for malpractice?"

"I don't give 'no time limit' orders," Hillier
replied.

"Is your answer yes or no, Doctor?"

"I can't give that an answer."

"Doctor, I said, assuming there is evidence here
to that effect, have you considered the fact that you
might have an awfully large suit for malpractice on
your hands brought by the family of Mrs. Leanues?"

"No, that's not—"

"Has it ever crossed your mind, Doctor?"

"What?"

"That you might be sued for malpractice?"

"It never has."

"Do you mean that?"

"I have given no incorrect orders in this case."

Piscitelli could see that this was going to be another one of those questions that would be as potent unanswered as answered. "Of course, on the other hand," he said, turning away from Hillier and speaking to no one in particular, "if my client were convicted of anything, you'd be off the hook, wouldn't you."

By adjournment on Tuesday Pat was still not done with the witness. Dr. Robert Hillier was, he knew, one of the commonwealth's two most important witnesses, and Pat intended to squeeze from Hillier every drop of testimony that could help Anne.

On Wednesday the crowded courtroom listened intently as Pat spent hours going over Hillier's version of the conversation with Nancy Robbins and Anne Capute, and also a conversation that Hillier had with Dr. David Pottier the following morning. Hillier admitted he had said to Pottier, "I don't expect Norma Leanues to be here when I get back from Europe." But that, Hillier insisted, was a reference to Norma's possibly being transferred to Rhode Island Hospital.

On the taped interview with Robert St. Jean, the investigator from the D.A.'s office, Hillier recalled speaking to Edward Leanues shortly before Norma died and saying, "I think your wife may not live within the week." During a bench conference there was a lot of discussion over whether the phrase "within the week" was substantially different from "within a week." Piscitelli argued that the difference was crucial. "Within the week" implied that Hillier expected Leanues to die before Saturday. That would give credence to Anne and Nancy's statements that Hillier had said that Norma had twenty-four to forty-eight hours to live.

Pat also came down hard on Hillier's failure to sign the medication order.

"On the evening of May sixteenth, when you gave the order that you say you gave to nurses Nancy Robbins and Anne Capute, was there anything preventing you from remaining there and signing the order?" Pat asked.

"No," Hillier replied.

"Was there anything preventing you from writing the order yourself?"

"I wish I had," Hillier said.

"My question was, and would you answer yes or no, was there anything preventing you from taking a pen or pencil and writing that narcotics order yourself?"

"No, there was not."

"I see," Pat said. "So you didn't sign the order even though you knew you were going to Europe for a week."

Pat returned to the issue of a possible malpractice suit but was unable to get much in over Pina's objections.

And finally, when Pat felt he had gotten just about as much as he could from Hillier, Pat said, "Tell the jury again the time, Doctor, when you transferred over total charge of Norma Leanues to Dr. David Pottier."

"That evening on Friday."

"What time on Friday?"

"I don't know the exact time."

"Give us your best recollection."

"Early evening."

166 Gary Provost

"How was that?" Pat asked. "By phone call or verbal order to him?"

"I did not speak to Dr. Pottier," Hillier said.

"Oh," Pat said. "How was the transfer made? What method?" If you didn't talk to him?"

Hillier paused, stared into his hands. Pat stepped closer.

"I called the answering service and stated that I was away, be going away for a week, and to refer my patients to Dr. Pottier."

Now Pat moved to the jury, leaned on the rail, tilted toward Hillier, and said, "And that's all that you did to transfer over the care and the protection and the well-being of Norma Leanues? Your most critically ill patient, dying of cancer?"

Pat stood back a moment, let the silence grip the courtroom. "Your Honor," he said, "I have no further questions."

The defense team was jubilant as they piled into Pat's Mercedes and headed back to Brockton that night. Hillier's direct examination had hurt them badly, Pat knew, and now he felt as if he'd gained back a lot of the lost ground. Don and James sat in back, weary from the grueling day but high-spirited. Anne sat up front with Pat. Though it would have been shorter for Anne to drive from Plympton directly to Fall River each morning, she instead left early and drove to Brockton so she could drive into court with Pat, Don, and James. It just made her feel good to be with them, especially before and after a day in court.

After they had driven about a mile, Pat pulled over and the four of them, as rowdy as a bunch of high-school kids, jumped out and ran into a variety store to buy candy bars. When they were back on the road, munching on their chocolate bars, Don said, "Now, listen, you guys, I have an important announcement to make." Everybody was quiet and Don said, "I think I'm in love with George."

George was a human skeleton. Pat had borrowed the skeleton from Morton Hospital, to be used when he called his own expert medical witnesses to the stand. In the meantime, not knowing quite what to do with a skeleton, he had been driving around with George in the back seat. Now George was stretched across Don's lap, and the rest of the defense team was congratulating him and asking when the wedding would be.

"Haven't set the date yet," Don said. "Pat, is George a boy or a girl?"

"A girl," Pat said. "I call him George because it would be a little tacky to use a female name, since it was a woman who died."

"What a relief!" Don said. "I wouldn't want anybody to think I was strange."

Being with the boys always lifted Anne's spirits, but she often grew morose when she finally got into her own car, alone, and drove from Brockton to Plympton. On this particular night she thought about her growing friendships with Pat and the people in his office. She smiled, thinking about how Don could make her laugh even when she was on trial for murder. She had decided she would kill herself in the courtroom if the jury found her guilty, and it made her sad to think that now there was Pat and Don and James and Donna Piscatelli to be added to the list of people she would leave behind.

Chapter Twenty-two

One afternoon as court was adjourning, Anne decided she wanted spaghetti. She wanted spaghetti and she wanted homemade sauce, and she wanted to cook it herself in her own kitchen, and she wanted all her daughters there to enjoy it with her. What she wanted was a normal family evening.

Getting the whole family to sit down to supper together would have been nearly impossible a few months earlier. But during the trial Anne's girls didn't stay out as late in the afternoon and they didn't go out much at night. They stayed close to Anne. Nobody said it, but everybody thought it: The girls might not have their mother much longer. Even Barbara, who lived in nearby Kingston, often came over after work just to hang around. There had always been tension between Anne and Barbara, largely because Barbara, the firstborn, had been packed up and sent off to live with her grandparents by Anne, who was barely more than a girl herself at the time. Barbara had grown up with Anne's parents, and whenever she came to Plympton to visit her sisters and her mother, she always felt, she says, "like I was from a different branch of the family." Lately that tension had been breaking, and though mother and daughter were still somewhat awkward together, Anne had high hopes that she and Barbara could establish the closeness they had never really had.

When Anne got home that night she called her mother and left a message for Barbara to come for supper. Then she started cooking her spaghetti sauce. As she puttered around in the kitchen, softly singing, she could pretend for a moment that things were normal, that her picture was not on the front page of every newspaper in Massachusetts, that wire services were not telegraphing her plight to the entire country, that films of her would not be shown on the six-o'clock news, that she was just a woman making supper for her family, not a woman on trial for murder.

By the time she put on the water for spaghetti, Anne's family was home. Charlie and the four girls clustered around the TV set in the living room, watching for Anne on the news. Though Anne had gotten in the habit of watching the evening news at the office with Pat and Don and James, she didn't want to watch it at all tonight. She was getting sick of hearing about herself. While she waited for the water to boil, she sat on a stool in the kitchen and read *Messages from Michael*, which her sister-in-law had sent.

For Anne the arrival of the book from Meredith at that particular time had a kind of magical quality. Though Anne and Meredith had never spent much time together—a continent had always separated them—they seemed to be soul sisters. One would always call when the other needed her. Meredith, somehow knowing that something was wrong, had called the night Warren died. And now this book. It was the right thing at the right time. For Anne the book was a key that unlocked parts of her mind that had never been opened before; it was showing her a new set of answers at a time when the old ones didn't seem to be working.

At the supper table Charlie filled Anne in on what the TV news said about the trial, and after everybody caught up with everybody's else's life, Susan asked, "Ma, what's this *Messages from Michael* thing? It says on the cover it's an occult book."

Anne could see that the girls were amused by the word, "occult," but she was ready for them. She had looked it up. "Occult just means 'hidden' or 'unknown'" she said. Anne didn't mind their skepticism. She had always encouraged the girls to follow their own religious paths and not be guided by her beliefs.

"What's it about?"

"It's about these people in California who were fooling around with a Ouija board one night and they started getting messages from this thing called Michael."

"Like a guy who's supposed to be dead?" Meredith asked.

"No," Anne said. "It's what's called an entity. It's made up of a thousand souls, and most of the book is in Michael's words. The book is fascinating. There's a lot of wisdom in there, a lot of ways of looking at things."

"It's supposed to be true?" Meredith asked. "I mean, they're saying it really happened?"

Anne smiled. It was nice to see Meredith getting excited about new possibilities. "You got it!" she said.

"Ma, do you really believe all that stuff?" Lori asked.

Anne thought about it, and when she answered, she spoke not just to Lori but to the whole family. "I don't know," she said. "A year and a half ago I would have said it's all crazy stuff. But a year and a half ago I would have said the idea of me being tried for first-degree murder was crazy, too. And here we are, folks! So I don't know. Maybe it really happened. Maybe the author just made the whole thing up. Maybe a little of both. But I do know that a lot of the things I used to believe haven't worked for me. So let's just say I'm exploring."

Anne had gone exploring before. She had been brought up Catholic, had even attended parochial school. During her teenage years, after a long Saturday of working in the bakery, she used to go to confession. On one Saturday she had started at the bakery at 5:00 A.M., and after twelve grueling hours of work she went to confession and confessed that she had missed Mass the previous Sunday. The priest scolded her harshly, and Anne stormed out of the confessional, muttering "Kiss my ass" almost loud enough for the priest to hear. She never went back to confession and grew more and more disenchanted with the Church. How could wrong become right just because somebody issued an edict? she wondered. During her twenties she read dozens of books about religion, and in 1960 she converted to Judaism. Anne felt comfortable with a religion that, to her mind, had established rules and laws for good reason and would not change them just because the times were changing. But now she had outgrown her Judaism. The religion wasn't changing, but she was.

"Besides," Anne said, after she'd thought it over, "*Messages from Michael* has got a lot of stuff about Taoism, and that's not just a bunch of people in California. That's one of the biggest religions in the world."

Meredith asked, "What's that?"

"Well, I don't know a whole lot about it," Anne said. "You'd have to read a book called *The Power and the Way*. But I looked up Taoism in the encyclopedia. Mostly Taoism says that society's rules are a crock of shit and you should only conform to the laws of the universe."

"Harmony with nature and all that," Charlie said, snatching a piece of the conversation.

"Right, and you have to transcend mundane distinctions," Anne said, remembering the phrase from the encyclopedia.

"Like what?" Lori said.

"Like the distinction between life and death," Anne said.

Her words were as startling as a loud knock on the door in the middle of the night. No one spoke. The whole family knew that Anne had been thinking a lot about death lately. Though she hadn't told anybody her plan, they all knew there was something to worry about.

"Jesus!" Anne said. "Don't look so somber. The jury hasn't convicted me yet."   •

After a moment Charlie looked up from his plate, smiled, and changing the subject, he said, "So how's Pat? Is he still fighting for truth, justice, and the American way?"

After the girls cleared the table, and Susan and Lori figured out whose turn it was to wash the dishes, Anne drifted into the living room with her book. She sat on the couch and tucked her legs up underneath her. She smiled, thinking about how difficult that posture had been when she was overweight. The Anne Capute Diet, she thought. Get accused of murder and lose a hundred pounds.

"Ma," she heard, after she had been reading for a few minutes.

Anne looked up. It was Barbara, standing a few feet away. Barbara looked nervous. "Can we talk?" she said.

"Sure, hon. What's up?"

"Remember what you were saying about how you used to believe some things that you don't believe now?"

"Yes."

"Well," Barbara said, "I know what you mean. I did, too."

"Like what?" Anne said.

"I used to believe that you didn't care much about me."

"Yes," Anne said, "I know." She could feel her heart begin to pound faster.

"Well, I always believed that the fact that we weren't close was okay, you know. I used to think you weren't somebody I wanted to be close to anyhow."

"And now?"

"Well, it's not okay."

"I agree," Anne said.

"Anyhow, when this whole thing happened and you were accused of murder and everything, at first I really felt left out. Everybody seemed to know more about what was going on than I did. But then, after I realized what a horrible thing was happening to you, I decided well, maybe Ma's not my favorite person, but she is my mother, and I'm going to stick by her. That's why I started coming over here more often."

"Well," Anne said, "it's been nice seeing more of you." Her mouth felt dry.

"Watching you go through this, Ma, I see you in a whole new way. I guess I never thought of you as strong. But you are, you've very strong."

Barbara's words floated away, but the silence that remained spoke volumes about what she was trying to say. The relationship between mother and daughter was cluttered with years of tension and fights and misunderstandings, and now it was as if Barbara was trying to push all that away.

Anne's hands were shaking. Part of Anne wanted to run away, think of a few nice things to say and put them in a letter. She had never been as comfortable with sentimental moments as she would have liked, and often the flippancy that rose to cover her discomfort was misunderstood and widened a gap that she was trying to narrow. That had happened often with Barbara. So now Anne chose her words carefully.

"Barbara," she said, "I love you." She looked down into her hands. "I'm not so naïve that I think I can repair years of alienation just by sitting here and saying 'I love you.' We have a lot of work to do. But I'm saying it now because no matter what happens, I want you to remember this moment and my saying 'I love you.'"

Anne stood up. Anne and Barbara hugged each other, and though they were not able to melt fully into each other, Anne noticed that Barbara's arms, and her own, felt a little less rigid than in the past. And as she felt the warmth of her firstborn's body against her, Anne thought, Here is one more reason to live. But it was also one more reason why being imprisoned was unacceptable.

Chapter Twenty-three

The commonwealth of Massachusetts called Dr. David Pottier to the witness stand. Pottier had assisted Hillier during the two operations on Norma Leanues. Pottier had discussed Norma's condition with Hillier on Saturday morning before Hillier left for Paris. And on Sunday morning, Pottier had signed the death certificate. Though Pottier was supposed to be a witness for the commonwealth, Anne liked him. He reminded her of Tim Conway, and she called him "Huggy Bear." Pottier, a former history teacher, seemed to be a reasonable man whose answers were not slanted in favor of his fellow doctor.

"Doctor," Pat asked on Pottier's second day of testimony. "is it fair to say that if a person is terminally ill and in excruciating pain, that it is the policy of the doctors and the hospital to allow that person to die without pain by use of a 'no code' order to the nurses?"

"I use a slightly different terminology," Pottier answered.

"What do you use, Doctor?" Pat said. His approach with Pottier was friendly, one professional to another.

"I write 'death with dignity.'"

"DWD?"

"DWD, yes."

"Please explain to the jury, Dr. Pottier, what death with dignity means when you write that down on the hospital record."

"If I have somebody whose death is imminent, if resuscitation would only prolong a person's life, would mean the continuation of the same procedure, I would write, 'death with dignity.'"

"And," Pat said, "that procedure has been in use at Morton Hospital for some years, has it not?"

"I am aware of it being there for at least three or four years."

"And in effect it is a humane effort to prevent a person who is terminally ill from dying in agonizing, excruciating pain, is it not?"

"That's the way I feel about it," Pottier replied.

"Doctor, would the use of morphine be one way

of carrying out orders to prevent pain in a person known to be terminal?"

"Yes," he said.

During the cross-examination Pat drew from Pottier a number of points damaging to Hillier. Pottier said it was his understanding that a doctor at Morton was required to sign a medication order within twenty-four hours. He also told the court that Hillier had given him the impression that Norma was near death. In fact, Pottier, a witness called by the commonwealth, was so helpful to the defense that a reporter came up to Pat after the testimony and quipped, "So Pat, when does the D.A. start to present *his* case?"

Though Pat was immensely pleased with Pottier's testimony, it was also during Pottier's time on the stand that the trial took one of its most bizarre and potentially damaging twists. Pat and Pina had gone into a bench conference with Judge Prince to discuss a matter of "discovery." Piscitelli wanted to bring in patient records that would show that no-limit orders had been used before with terminal patients at Morton. Pina objected, saying he didn't know anything about the records and hadn't had any time to review them.

As the conversation wound down Pina interjected, "and while we're discussing the matter of discovery, Your Honor, there may be another witness available. I've been notified today. I've issued a subpoena."

Pat was stunned. "Who is this?" he said.

"She's a nurse at Morton Hospital."

"And what's she going to say?"

"I don't know. I just know that her lawyer says it's important that we talk to her."

"A witness?" Pat said. He couldn't imagine how

he could have missed a potential witness. "For whom? For you, or for me?"

"I don't know," Pina said. "I'm just informing the court at this time."

A few minutes later Pat walked over to the defense table, leaned across, looked Anne straight in the eye, and said, "We've got a surprise witness."

"A surprise witness?" Anne said. "Is this real life or a movie?"

Pat shook his head. "Sometimes I wonder," he said.

After Pottier the next witness was Vicki McKenna, the pretty blond L.P.N. who had instigated the entire affair by reporting the high doses of morphine. McKenna was an austere woman; she never smiled during her testimony. There had never been conflict between Anne and Vicki, but Anne always believed that Vicki had been motivated, at least in part, by another nurse, who disliked Anne.

McKenna told the court her story about being at the nurses' station on May 20 and a conversation with Anne.

"Anne said she had taken care of Norma over the weekend," McKenna told the district attorney under direct examination. "And she said she had promised Norma's husband that Norma wouldn't suffer and that she had helped her. And she said, 'If you had a hundred twenty milligrams of morphine, you'd die, too.'"

Pina showed McKenna the doctor's order form, the one that Hillier had never signed. "Now, looking at that record, Mrs. McKenna, as a licensed practical nurse at Morton Hospital, what does that mean to you?"

"It needs to be clarified," McKenna said.

"Why?"

"Because there is no time written on it."

"If you saw that order, what would you do?"

"I would refuse to give it."

After McKenna told the court what she had reported to her superiors and why, Pina led her through the now familiar schedule of morphine shots.

As they went along, Pina referred not to "shots" but to the more provocative "needles," emphasizing the word and glancing at the jury, until Pat objected.

When Pat got Vicki McKenna under cross-examination he asked her about the amounts of morphine she had seen written on Norma's chart, the amounts she had reported to her superiors, and then he startled the courtroom with, "Well that amount would not appear unusual to you, would it, because you have given twice that amount to a patient, have you not?"

Pina objected immediately, and a bench conference followed. Piscitelli offered to prove that Vicki McKenna had once given patients sixteen and twelve milligrams of Dilaudid, a drug four times as strong as morphine. Pat had the patient's records with him. Judge Prince turned Pat down. Pat returned to cross-examination. He tried again and again to prove that McKenna had given narcotics doses similar to, or larger than, the ones she said alarmed her. Pat's goal was not to crucify McKenna. He was simply trying once more to establish in the jury's mind the idea that what Anne had done was not out of step with much of what went on at Morton Hospital. It was the "state of mind" defense, but he was continually stymied by Judge Prince, who saw no relevance. McKenna's testimony had hurt Anne severely, and as Vicki stepped down, Pat glanced at the faces of the jurors. He did not like what he saw.

The afternoon's witness was Alfred Sylvia, Jr., the director of the Morton Hospital pharmacy. Pina used Sylvia mainly to dramatize the amount of drugs that had been pumped into Norma Leanues. Sylvia described the procedure by which narcotics are ordered, delivered, and accounted for. He described the variety of forms used to keep track of drugs and to ensure that they are not stolen or misused.

The one thing of value that Pat was able to mine from his cross-examination of Sylvia was that all of the drugs involved in the Leanues case were accounted for and properly signed out on the proof-of-use sheet at the nurses' station. This could help Anne on the second charge, illegally dispensing a Class B substance," though that charge was of little concern throughout the trial in view of the first-degree murder charge.

Entered into evidence were eighteen tubexes of morphine, a tubex holder, and a ten-milligram Valium syringe. They were not the ones actually used with Norma, but they had a dramatic visual impact, and Pina wanted to have the needles passed around among the jurors. Pat objected. The jurors would have all the evidence in the jury room, so there was no need, he argued. Judge Prince allowed one tubex to be passed around.

Anne sat at the defense table and watched as the jurors passed the tubex along. What's the point? she thought. Nobody's denying that the morphine was given. It seemed to her that the jurors were being given a look at the gleaming needles for dramatic purposes only. It seemed so unfair. It was a bad day for Anne. Her moods lately had been swinging from dark to light, and today's mood was very dark. She was depressed, confused. She thought about how passing around the needles was unfair, and then she thought how absurd it was of her to look for fair and unfair, since the whole idea of her being tried for murder was so monstrously unfair. Her thoughts were muddled.

And now there was a mystery witness to worry about. It was as if they were out to grab her, but she didn't know who "they" were.

Life was not following its own rules, she thought, but she didn't know what she meant by it. She remembered Warren saying, "It's just not fair." And even back then she had said, "Life isn't supposed to be fair. Life just is." She missed Warren terribly. She remembered Beth saying, "Gee, Anne, you're turning into a philosopher." She missed Beth, too. And most of all, she missed being a nurse.

"Anne," she heard. It was James Morton. He touched her shoulder. "You okay?"

"James," she said, "I think I'm losing my mind."

"Just hang in there," he said. "We'll take care of you."

Chapter Twenty-four

Anne's phone rang at two o'clock in the morning. She knew it would be Pat. During the trial neither of them got much sleep, and there were a lot of late-night phone calls. She grabbed the receiver before the phone could ring again and wake the girls.

"Kathy Menard," Pat said.

"Kathy Menard?" Anne couldn't believe it. "That's the mystery witness?"

"Yes. Do you know her?"

"Well, sure I know her," Anne said, "but I can't imagine what she's got to do with this."

"I talked to the D.A," Pat said, "and I've got a copy of Menard's statement to her lawyer. She's going to testify that she overheard the conversation among you and Hillier and Nancy Robbins."

"Is this a joke?" Anne said. "That was a year and a half ago, and she hasn't mentioned a word of this before."

"It's no joke," Pat said. He sounded worried. "She's going to take the witness stand and contradict your version of the conversation."

"But this is absurd. Kathy wasn't even on that side of the ward that night. This is crazy."

"Tell me about her," Pat said. "Has she got anything against you?"

"No," Anne said. "Kathy's okay. She's kind of a *kvetch*. The nurses on the ward used to say that if Kathy spent as much time nursing as she did complaining, she'd be a great nurse. But she's, you know, just a kid. She was only twenty-two when I was there."

"Were you friends?"

"No. Not close or anything, but she used to go out with a bunch of us for a drink now and then."

"Did you spend any time alone with her?" Pat asked.

"No. Oh, just once. Kathy had this friend who made jewelry and one Christmas I wanted to buy gold chains for three of the girls, so Kathy took me to her friend so I could get a good price. That's all."

There was silence while Pat thought it over.

"Well," he said, "can you think of any reason why she'd make up a story like this?"

"I don't know," Anne said. "She always needed the spotlight. Maybe she just wants to get on TV."

Kathy Menard took the witness stand on Monday, September 28, in the fourth week of Anne's trial. She was Kathleen Menard Cyr by then, having been recently married. She was a small, pixielike young lady wearing a heavy sweater and a long plaid skirt. She looked like a schoolgirl. To Anne, she looked like Peter Pan.

Pat had already interviewed Menard at her lawyer's office. Her lawyer, Frank O'Boy, was an old political foe of Ronald Pina. It was O'Boy who had once been quoted in the papers as saying that Pina would someday learn that trials are won in the courtroom, not on the six-o'clock news.

Under direct examination Kathy Menard told Pina that at about six-fifteen on the evening of May 16 she was sitting at the small nurses' station when she saw Dr. Hillier, Nancy Robbins, and Anne Capute come out of Norma Leanues's room, 227. She said the three walked toward her, stopped not far from her, and had a conversation.

"What did you hear?" Pina asked.

"I heard Nancy Robbins asking Dr. Hillier for something stronger for pain for Mrs. Leanues."

"Did you hear a response from Dr. Hillier?"

"Yes," Kathy said.

"What did you hear?" Pina asked.

"He said to change the morphine, which was given orally to IM or s.c. I wasn't sure of the route. He said every three to four hours."

"Excuse me, what did he say?"

"Every three to four hours."

"Did you hear anything else?"

"Nancy Robbins replied to him, 'You mean prn?'"

"And what did he say, if anything?"

"He said, 'Yes.'"

Menard's testimony supported Hillier's claim that he'd said "every three hours," not "no limit." Pina was not going to let it go easily. He handed Menard the doctor's order form and asked her to read it.

"Give MS, fifteen milligrams, s.c, prn, no time limit. Make her comfortable. Give Valium, IM Dr. Hillier. Nancy Robbins, R.N."

"Is that what you heard Dr. Hillier say?" the D.A. asked.

"No."

"How does it differ from what you heard Dr. Hillier say?"

"He said every three to four hours."

"He said every three to four hours?"

"Yes."

"Does that say that, that order to you?" Pina asked.

Pat had had enough. He stood up. "Objection, please. That's the third time."

Judge Prince agreed and struck the question.

Kathy Menard told the court she had seen Anne twice more that night. She said she heard Anne telling Nancy Robbins that she would give Norma something for pain, and later found Anne in the medication closet looking for a six cc syringe.

The six cc syringe had been discussed during Alfred Sylvia's testimony. Pina wanted the jury to infer that use of a six cc syringe instead of a three cc syringe showed an intention to double or triple the fifteen milligrams of morphine.

Pat's turn to question Menard came after lunch. He approached her with a smile, and occasionally he pressed his hand to his mouth as if to suppress a laugh. He wanted to be subtle, but he didn't want to appear to take her too seriously. He knew that any thinking person could see how preposterous it was for a nurse who had heard thousands of patient-related conversations to come forth a year and a half later with a precise recollection of one of them that wasn't even significant at the time. It seemed to him that the whole idea was absurd, and he wanted to keep that sense of absurdity in his tone of voice, his expressions, his entire demeanor, as if he and the jury were adults who were indulging a child who had a silly tale to tell. But Pat also knew that Kathy Menard was a potentially deadly witness and that she would have to be questioned carefully.

Pat brought out a diagram of S-2, which indicated that Kathy's back would have been to room 227 at the time she says she saw the doctor and two nurses come out. He also showed that Kathy would have been fifteen feet away from the conversation during a particularly busy and noisy hour on the ward. Always scavenging for any ammunition he could get from any witness, Pat drew from Menard the statement that Dr. Hillier had once told her that Norma had only two to four weeks to live, and Pat also found ways to talk about Norma's excruciating pain.

Menard told the court that ten minutes after the conversation she saw Nancy Robbins writing on a chart at the nurses' substation. When Nancy was done, Kathy walked over and looked at the chart.

"You saw the order on the chart?" Pat said.

"Yes."

"And that's the one which the D.A. has shown you?"

"Yes."

"Is it fair to say that when you saw that 'no time limit' on the order you did nothing because of it?"

"I can't answer that."

"Well, did you or did you not bring it to anyone's attention?"

"I did not bring it to anyone's attention," Kathy said.

"All right," Pat said. "You have seen in the past, have you not, no-time-limit orders?"

"Objection!" Pina shouted. He could see where Pat was going.

After a long bench conference, Pina's objection was sustained. Pat had been thwarted once more in an attempt to show "no-time-limit" orders as common practice at Morton.

Pat brought out the six cc syringe. The syringe issue had been brought up again and he would have to shoot it down again, as he had with Sylvia.

"This is Exhibit M," he said. "It is a six cc syringe."

"Yes," Kathy said.

"Now, you can put thirty or forty-five milligrams of a drug in a three cc syringe, can't you?"

"Not adequately."

"But you can put it in, can't you?"

"Yes," she replied.

"Because fifteen milligrams of morphine is in fact one cc, is it not?"

"Yes."

"So if you've got a three-cc syringe, you can put three fifteen-milligram tubexes in a three-cc syringe, and you don't need this one for that, right?"

"Yes, that's right."

During the cross-examination Menard told the court that she had been with Vicki McKenna on that Tuesday after Norma's death, and they had looked at the narcotics sheets together. This statement was somewhat startling in view of the fact that Vicki McKenna, in statements to her lawyer, in conversations with Costello and Hickey, and in trial testimony, had never said anything about Kathy being with her.

The statement also suggests that Kathy would have been aware then of the significance of the conversation she overheard but never mentioned it to anybody until after the trial began.

Pat had not given up on his "no limit" question. Hoping to sneak it in, he lulled the courtroom with a lot of questions about Norma's admission to the hospital and such mundane procedures. Suddenly in the middle of a discussion about emergency carts on the ward, he turned to Kathy and asked, "Have you seen no-time-limit orders around the clock before?"

But Pina was alert. He pounced on it with an immediate objection, which Judge Prince sustained.

Pat shrugged. "I tried," he said with a grin, and while the spectators laughed softly, he surprised them again by asking, "Mrs. Cyr, how long have you known Linda Lawrence, the daughter of Norma Leanues?"

The question caused some stir in the courtroom.

Pat had done his homework. He showed that there was a connection between Kathy Menard and Linda Lawrence, but he couldn't get the witness to adopt the word "friend." Menard said that Norma's daughter was "an acquaintance."

Though it never came out during the trial, Kathy Menard had told her lawyer that she was friendly with Linda Lawrence and that after the facts about Norma's death came to light, Linda accused Kathy of being involved in killing her mother. Kathy defended herself, saying that she was one of the nurses who brought the whole thing to the attention of the hospital authorities.

Throughout the day Pat tried every angle he could think of to bring evidence that Kathy Menard Cyr had administered drugs at two-hour intervals and had followed a "no-time-limit" order, just as he had with Vicki McKenna, and just as he would with every nurse who took the stand. During the many bench conferences Pat brought up several points of law. He was impressively well informed, and even Judge Prince, who was getting increasingly annoyed with Pat, offered a grudging admiration. At one point Pat said, "Maybe I'm wrong, but . . ." and Judge Prince responded, "Maybe you are this time. I mean, it's possible. Not probable, but it's possible."

Despite this occasional tension between two men who were trying to do different jobs, Pat and Prince maintained enormous respect for each other. And if there was one thing that Pat and the district attorney agreed on throughout the trial it was that Judge Prince's work on the trial was exemplary and that he personified all that a judge should be.

By the time Kathy Menard finished testifying it was almost four o'clock, and the court was adjourned. After the jury had been dismissed, Judge Prince called Pat and Pina to the bench.

"I just want to get a picture of tomorrow," he said.

"Mrs. Costello," Pina said.

"That will be the rest of the day?"

"That will be the rest of the week," Pat said.

Prince made a face. He was becoming concerned about the length of the trial.

"Your Honor," Pat asked, "is there some way to make Mrs. Costello be responsive?"

"Sure," Pina said. 'I'll ask her questions."

"You know what's she's going to do," Pat said. "She's going to testify."

Pat laughed. "But not for both of us, I'm sure."

"Well," Judge Prince said, "I'll try to keep a tight rein on her, the best I can."

"Could a tight rein be held on Mr. Piscitelli?" Pina asked.

188 *Gary Provost*

"That's a little harder," Prince said.

"I don't need any. It's the D.A. I'm concerned about," Pat said, and the three men parted, smiling at each other for a change.

Chapter Twenty-five

The night before Maureen Costello took the stand, Pat got home at about seven-thirty. He had stayed at the office to watch the evening news with the others. Now, as he drove the Mercedes into the driveway of the gray colonial house he and his wife, Meredith, had bought in the affluent west side of Brockton, something about his image on the TV screen disturbed him. He would have to be more careful with Costello. He didn't want to come across as a bully.

Meredith greeted him at the door.

"Saw you on TV," she said.

"How did I look?"

"Like a lawyer," she said.

He hugged her in the foyer, glancing over her shoulder into the living room where their two sons, Matthew, ten, and Michael, seven, were playing a video game on the television. "Hi, guys," he said. Then to Meredith, "Where's Julie?"

"Upstairs," Meredith said, and she told him what Julie, the twelve-year-old, was doing, but Pat wasn't really listening as he pulled his jacket off and began sorting through the contents of his briefcase.

"Got the Iron Maiden coming up tomorrow," he

said apologetically. It was his way of explaining why he had to look at some papers right away.

"Great," Meredith said coolly. She headed for the kitchen. "Supper's on," she said. "The kids have eaten."

While Pat ate, the kids gathered around him at the table. Each of the boys had a long tale to tell about the day at school. Julie was more subdued. She wanted to subscribe to a new horse magazine and wanted to know if it was okay. "Sure," Pat said, and Julie said little else. After the kids were gone from the kitchen Pat began to glance at the pile of documents, which he had brought in and placed on a chair. Meredith poured him a cup of coffee.

"Just want to check one little thing," he said, and from his pile of papers he pulled out the transcript of Maureen Costello's grand jury testimony.

After he had been reading for a few minutes he heard Meredith say, "I was just thinking how fortunate we are here in Brockton to have the best symphony orchestra around, outside of Boston."

"Huh?" He looked up. "Oh. Yes. We sure are," Pat said, returning to the transcript.

Another minute went by. "My Celtics have started their season," Meredith said. "We really have to get in to a couple of games this year."

"Uh-huh," Pat said, not looking up.

"Jeanine called today," Meredith said. "She and Jim want to get together with us for dinner."

During the time of the Capute case, the Piscitellis' social life had been reduced to dinner out with friends on Friday nights.

"Fine," Pat said without enthusiasm. "Set it up."

"When I got home this afternoon the house was on fire," Meredith said.

Pat looked up. "Huh?"

"Nothing," she said.

"Oh." He turned the pages. "Costello's going to be an interesting witness," he said. "You ought to try to get to the trial a couple of days."

When his coffee was gone, Pat tucked his pile of papers under his arm and stood up. He leaned down and kissed his wife on the cheek. Then he walked into the living room, where the boys were.

"Got to work," he said. It was his way of signaling Matthew and Michael not to disturb him and not to make a lot of noise. Then he went into his study, as he did on most evenings, and closed the door behind him. He spread his papers out on the desk. He had read them all before, some several times, but in other trials he had often come upon useful points on a third or fourth reading. He didn't want to overlook anything.

As he stared down at the documents and tried to read, his normally strong powers of concentration failed him. He got to the bottom of one page of transcript and realized he had no idea of what he'd just read. Something was nagging at him. Merry, he thought, using his pet name for Meredith. What was it she had said about the Brockton symphony? The Celtics? The more he thought about it, the more he realized she'd been underscoring an issue between them. Neglect. He had been neglecting her and the kids ever since the day Anne Capute walked into his office. Merry had told him often, and in gentle ways. Now, by hinting at places they could go together, she was trying a different strategy. He smiled. Just like a lawyer, he thought.

But Merry understands, he thought, trying to push his thoughts back into his work; I was like this when she married me. Still he could not concentrate. He thought about Julie.

"She's at an age when she needs a lot of attention from her father and she's not getting it," Merry had said less than a week ago. "She's going through a hard time." So Pat had taken an hour alone with Julie, and they'd had fun together. But then, plowing back into his work, he had forgotten to give her another hour, or even fifteen minutes, the next day.

For an instant he didn't much like himself. He sat back in his captain's chair and stared at his life. Success had brought him wealth. He had a house on Cape Cod, and another in New Hampshire, where he and the family went skiing on winter weekends. He had three great kids and a wife who could take care of just about everything with his help or without it.

But he was a man with an issue, and he always had been, though he didn't often deal with it. The issue was how to balance family life and obligations with career life and the obligations he had to do the best possible job for his clients, some of whom were depending on him for their lives. Like Anne, he thought. The issue had always been there, long before he'd met Merry. Back in law school he had thought often about it, and that, in part, was why he never got married until he was thirty-five.

Pat was proud of his success. But he knew there were other successful men around, plenty of them, who were sick with regret for the things they hadn't taken care of. He remembered a judge whose son had died in a car crash at age twenty-five. The judge had been a lawyer just like Pat. And the judge, in a moment of sadness, had told Pat that he hurt most of all because even when the son was alive he had seen little of him because of work. He hadn't really seen his son grow up. A lot of men had said the same thing to Pat, and now as Pat thought about them, and the looks on their faces, a mild panic began to sweep through him. He bolted from his chair and pulled open the door.

"Julie!" he called, stepping into the hallway. "Julie!"

Meredith came in from the living room. "What's wrong?" she said.

"Where's Julie?"

"She's out. Why? Is something wrong?"

"No," Pat said. "I just . . . I was just going to spend some time with her."

"She'll be home in an hour," Merry said.

"Good," Pat said. "Good. Let me know when she gets in."

He went back into his study.

After he sat down he thought he should go and spend some time with the boys. But no, he thought. I'll take them somewhere on the weekend. Again he opened the Costello transcript. He read four pages before he slammed the volume shut. "Weekend, hell!" he said out loud. He knew he was addicted to his work and would be no less likely to forsake it on the weekend than he was now. He pushed himself away from the desk, as if the trial papers could reach up and grab him if he got too close. Finally, resolving to leave his work and spend some time with Meredith and the boys, he loaded everything into a desk drawer and slammed it. Before he could get up, there was a knock on the door to his study. It was Meredith, and she was not smiling.

"Honey," she said, "the time for subtlety is over. I'll get right to the point."

"What's up?" Pat said, though he had a pretty good idea.

"I feel like a widow," she said. "That's what's up. And your three children feel like abandoned kids."

"Honey—"

"In fact, they *are* abandoned kids," she said.

"Honey, I—"

"Pat, you have neglected us ever since this damn Capute thing started. I am fed up."

"I know," he said, "it's just that this case is so damned important."

"Don't," Meredith said. She put her hand up in front of him, signaling him to stop.

Pat shrugged. He knew it was hopeless to try to defend himself. This was a case even he wouldn't take on.

"Don't tell me," Meredith said. "I know all that. It's important for the office, it's important for you, it's important for our future. A woman's life is at stake. I understand all that, I do, but you've got a family. You are not just P. J. Piscitelli, attorney-at-law. You are my husband. You are a father."

Pat could not speak. The moment was making him terribly sad. Can you be the best possible lawyer and still be a good family man? he wondered. He had always tried, but there had been many days and weeks when he had failed. And Anne's case, which could become his greatest victory as a lawyer, could also represent his worst failure as a family man. He had been obsessed with it, even more than the others, and because of it had been that much more neglectful of his family.

"I take it you are pleading guilty," Merry said. Her voice had softened somewhat.

"Yes," Pat replied meekly. "Are you one of them hanging judges?"

"No," she said. "Not yet, anyhow. I've devised a work-release program for you. Tomorrow morning, during the first recess, you are going to call your friend at the ticket agency and you are going to order four tickets for a Celtics game. And I don't mean one in March. I mean one this month."

"Can't you call them, and—"

"No!" Meredith said. "You will make the call!"

"Okay."

"And then," she said, "I'm going to give you a pardon. But only until the Capute trial is over. Do you understand?"

"Yes," he said.

"And after that, you and I and your children are going skiing after the first snowfall."

"Okay."

"For a week. Right after Christmas."

"A week?" Honey, I can't get away for a week—"

"Pat!"

"Okay," he said. "For a week."

Meredith rose on her toes to kiss his cheek. "You do plan to have this trial done before Christmas, don't you?"

Pat shook his head. He laughed as he led Meredith out of the study and into the living room, where the boys were playing. "Sometimes I wonder," he said.

Chapter Twenty-six

During Maureen Costello's first morning on the witness stand she told the court that she supervised 430 nursing personnel at Morton. She then rattled off her long list of nursing and administrative positions, explained the nursing hierarchy, and described the various regulatory commissions that govern nursing procedure. Costello told the jury what was in a nursing policy manual and what should be in nurses' notes, medication records, and doctors' orders. And she said, "If a nurse determines that the doctor's order could potentially jeopardize a patient's safety based on her nursing knowledge, she has a responsibility to do everything she can to clarify it." Costello also said that at the time of Leanues's death the hospital did not have a written procedure for clarifying a physician's order.

Costello was prim, well tailored, and as precise as a scalpel. She spoke slowly, leaving space between each word, and she responded to questions in such painstakingly formal language that anybody who didn't know better would think that she was a lawyer.

Anne was still in awe of her.

The district attorney handed Costello the nurses' notes, medication records, and the other documents that Costello had reviewed before interviewing Anne on the night of May 22. Then he asked her about that night.

"I met with Anne at ten-thirty," she said. She described how Anne got there, who was present, and where they were positioned in the room. "I noted that Anne's color was pale, that she had a marked pallor. She appeared rigid. She appeared to be shaking. When I told her that she was there on a patient-care matter the observation I made was that Anne rolled her eyes in recognition—"

"NO!" Pat shouted. "Objection!"

Judge Prince warned Costello. "Don't characterize. Just tell us what she did." It was a warning he would have to give her several times.

Costello said she questioned Anne carefully about the condition of Norma Leanues and the information contained in the nurses' notes.

"During this discussion I asked Anne about morphine sulfate," Maureen Costello said. "I asked her what she knew to be the normal adult dose, and I asked her what she understood to be its side effects. She said that the usual adult dose was ten to fifteen milligrams, and she knew that the side effect of the drug was respiratory depression."

"Did she indicate anything else?" Pina asked.

"She indicated that thirty milligrams was in excess of what the usual dose is."

By bringing Costello through her conversation with Anne about the nurses' notes, District Attorney Pina was once again able to create the drum roll of drug injections. What time? How much? What comments were written? The jury had heard the list many times by now, but it made good theater, and as the amounts of morphine increased and the injections became more frequent, the courtroom once more grew tense.

MR. PINA: What did you discuss about that notation, ten-fifteen on Saturday night?

MRS. COSTELLO: We discussed Anne's understanding. Again we discussed Anne's understanding of the presence of apnea.

MR. PINA: What did she say?

MRS. COSTELLO: She indicated to me as I previously testified, her understanding of apnea.

MR. PINA: Was what?

MRS. COSTELLO: Absence of respiration.

MR. PINA: Did you discuss anything else about the ten-fifteen notation?

MRS. COSTELLO: I don't remember specifically that we did.

MR. PINA: What did you discuss next?

MRS. COSTELLO: We discussed the "eleven-fifteen morphine sulfate, forty-five milligrams, s.c., in right arm, nail beds are bluish, extremities warm, apnea ten to fifteen seconds in duration. Not responding. Condition very poor. Valium ten milligrams, IM times two at six P.M. and nine forty-five."

MR. PINA: Would you tell us what that discussion was?

MRS. COSTELLO: I asked Anne to describe to me the effects of that dose, forty-five milligrams, on the patient, on Mrs. Leanues. And Anne stated to me that it would kill her. "My God, it would be enough to kill an elephant." After this discussion Anne recognized to me, "I must have killed her."

Later that day in the direct examination Pina asked Costello if she recalled any questions that Tom Bosanquet, the personnel director, had asked Anne.

"Yes," she said, "after Anne had said to me, 'I must have killed her,' Mr. Bosanquet asked her, 'Did you realize that you had killed her?' or 'Do you feel that you killed her?' And Anne's response was, 'Yes, I do.'"

Pina moved on. He covered the interviews that Costello had done with eight other nurses, and the phone calls between Costello and Anne.

For Anne the worst moment of the day came at three o'clock.

"Mrs. Costello," Pina said, "based on your training and your experience as assistant administrator for nursing services at Morton Hospital, do you have an opinion as to whether or not safe nursing practices were used by defendant Anne Capute in her nursing care of Norma C. Leanues on May sixteenth and May seventeenth, 1980?"

"I have an opinion," Costello said.

"What is that opinion?"

Anne held her breath.

"My opinion is that safe nursing practices were not followed."

Anne was crushed. Here was the woman she practically worshiped, the ultimate nurse, saying to the world that Anne was not a good nurse. A terrible sadness fell upon Anne. It was worse then being accused of murder. For a long time Anne could not even listen to the testimony. It hurt so badly to have that woman say she was not a good nurse. But in time the sadness turned to anger. Goddamn it, Anne thought, I *am* a good nurse. I have always been a good nurse. Even at Morton, she had always been con- sidered a good nurse. She grabbed her notebook and ripped off a piece of paper. She wrote, "If I'm such a lousy nurse, why did they give me a step and a half pay raise?" and she handed the note to Pat. She knew he would use it.

For the rest of the day Costello, responding to Pina's questions, listed the points on which she had based her conclusion about Anne. From time to time Pat reached around Don to squeeze Anne's shoulder. He had known all along that Costello's testimony would be the most difficult part of the trial for Anne. Pat took notes, too. At one point Pina and Costello both referred to the word "unresponsive" in the nurses' notes. It didn't sound right. "Unresponsive?" he wrote on a piece of paper, and he slipped it to Anne. She crossed it out. "Not responding," she wrote, and she slipped it back to him. Costello was misquoting the nurses' notes. It was the first sign that she was fallible.

On the drive home that night Pat was steamed. "Now hear this," he announced to the defense team, "a state of war exists between us and Morton Hospital."

Though Pat had been, as his wife says, obsessed with the case right from the beginning, he had tried not to let himself get too involved with Anne and her plight. But underdogs had always tugged at his heartstrings, and Anne, more than the others, brought out the protective instinct in him. They were picking on his little girl, and he was enraged. For Pat "they" meant the district attorney and the Morton administration, a vague, collective enemy he often referred to as "the forces of darkness."

And now he had reached his limit, because all afternoon they had dared to criticize Anne over minor procedural points, such as whether she had initialed every line on a medication record or had merely signed for a whole series of medications. Pat was enraged at this because he knew that the hospital's hands were far from clean. In his briefcase he had a long list of hospital violations, and he intended to use them.

The next morning, after Pina finished with Costello, Pat went to Judge Prince with his list of violations. They were contained in a letter that had been sent to Larry Ross by the Department of Health, Education, and Welfare. Pat wanted to bring this information into evidence. Though not as startling as his other material concerning terminal patients, this also was part of his "state of mind" defense. He wanted to show that Anne, like other nurses at Morton, had performed her duties in an atmosphere of slipshod procedure. After a long bench conference, and over the objections of Ronald Pina, Judge Prince allowed Pat to use the material if he made

specific reference and limited himself to nursing
matters. He was not, for example, to talk about the
plumbing.

Pat began by pointing out that Costello had used
the Department of Public Health and the Department
of Health and Human Services standards the day
before in defining good nursing practices. He then
asked her if she was familiar with a review of policies
and procedures at Morton conducted by the Department of Public Health and the Department of Health,
Education, and Welfare.

Costello said yes, she was familiar with the
review.

And then Pat opened fire on the enemy.

The hospital's procedure for documenting medication had been criticized. Its procedure for the
narration of nurses' notes had been criticized. Nursing care policies were often in conflict with other
policies. One physician did not write progress notes
until after the patient had been discharged. Another
was using a rubber signature stamp on case histories
and physicals.

"Was there a deficiency noted that telephone and
verbal orders were not used sparingly and were not
initialed by the physician as soon as possible?" Pat
asked.

"That's correct," the Iron Maiden said.

"Was there also a deficiency to the effect that
there was no listing of nurses qualified to administer
intravenous medication?"

"That's correct."

"Was there a deficiency concerning the policy of
reporting adverse effects of drugs?"

"That's correct."

"Was it also noted that six hundred ninety-six
records were not completed and filed within fifteen
days?"

"Yes."

The assault continued. Pat pulled out volumes of nurses' notes showing that all the minor mistakes Anne had made were being made almost daily by dozens of nurses.

"And again," he said, "the same mistake I have been indicating before, none of these charts contain the names of the doctors that they are supposed to, right?"

"That's correct," Costello said.

"And again, on the ninth, no doctor's name mentioned again, right?"

"That's right."

"And that's for about ten different lines, right?"
"Yes."

"Same thing on another chart for the tenth? Another mistake? No one signed the doctor's name?"
"Yes."

"And again, here, you've got someone who only signed once instead of every time, the way she is supposed to, right?"

"That's correct."

"And by the way," Pat said after he'd been hammering away for three quarters of an hour, "did you know that Mrs. Leanues had a thoracic laminectomy?"

"Yes," Costello said.

"I notice on the medication record of Mrs. Leanues, it says at the top 'lumbar laminectomy.' They didn't give her the wrong operation, did they?"

The spectators laughed.

"I cannot testify to that, Attorney Piscitelli."

"Well, would you call that an honest mistake?" he said.

"I would prefer not to characterize it."

Pat went on. "Now I show you the other proof-of-use sheets for Norma Leanues. I ask you whether or not there is a doctor's name next to the column where there should be."

"No, there's not."

"So all the nurses there, they all made a mistake, too, is that right?"

"Yes."

"And I ask you to look through each of these other sheets. You see the same mistake made there?"

"Yes."

"Do you see three or four other nurses' names?"

"Yes."

"But my client's does not appear there?"

"No."

Pat showed no mercy. He pointed out four and five mistakes at a time. Before long it grew into hundreds, hundreds of stupid little mistakes of the type that Anne had been criticized for. And Costello, as emotionless as a computer, was helpless. All she could do was sit there and say that Pat was correct.

Anne was stunned. She had thought of the Iron Maiden as perfect, a woman who ran not just a tight ship, but a flawless one as well. And now Pat was rattling off this incredible number of mistakes that Costello had not caught.

"And on this one," Pat was saying, "no doctor mentioned for twenty-five different spaces beside the times medication was given."

Pat flailed away at the violations all morning and into the afternoon. There seemed to be no end. Finally, unable to stand it any longer, District Attorney Pina stood up and said, "Objection, Your Honor. I am going to object at this time. I think the point has been made."

Pat smiled. It was a victory. He apologized to the court for being repetitious but slyly glanced at the notes in his hand, as if to tell the jury that there were plenty more.

The decimation of Maureen Costello went on all week.

On Wednesday afternoon Pat grilled her about the word "unresponsive."

"Now, the district attorney asked you yesterday about the word "unresponsive' in the nurses' notes. Do you remember that?" he said.

"Yes, I do," Costello replied.

"And you told us that it meant Mrs. Leanues could not articulate her needs at that time and that she was probably comatose, not complaining, right?"

"Yes."

"That is how you defined 'unresponsive'?"

"Yes," Costello said.

"Now, Mrs. Costello," Pat said, "I show you the nurses's notes for that day, and I ask if you will please put your finger on the word 'unresponsive.'"

Costello stared at the notes. After a moment a look of bewilderment filled her face. Anne, sitting at the defense table, smiled. She had never seen Costello flustered. Finally the Iron Maiden looked up. "I can't put my finger on it," she said.

Pat turned to face the jury. "That's because it's not there, isn't that right?"

"That's correct," Costello said. "'not responding' is there."

"And for all you know, when Anne Capute wrote 'not responding' she could have meant that Norma Leanues was not responding to the medication, right?" Pat swung around and looked Costello straight in the eye. "Isn't that a fair statement?"

Costello glanced down. "That's a fair statement," she said.

For a long time they recounted the night of Anne's traumatic interview in Costello's office.

"Mrs. Costello," Pat said, "when you questioned Anne Capute on May twenty-second, did you ever tell her that after she left Norma Leanues on the previous Saturday night that another nurse went in and gave an additional forty-five milligrams of morphine to Mrs. Leanues? Did you tell Anne that before she made the statement 'I must have killed her'?"

"I don't remember that I told Anne that."

"So if my client said, 'I must have killed her,' she said it without knowing that another nurse went in and gave forty-five milligrams about an hour later, right?"

Costello stood up straighter. Choosing her words carefully, she said, "It is possible that Anne may have made that statement without knowing that another nurse had entered Mrs. Leanues's room and had administered forty-five milligrams."

Now Pat shouted. "Didn't you think it was important to tell her that?" The judge disallowed the question, but Pat didn't care. He could feel the adrenaline careening through him. He was excited.

At the defense table Anne was caught up in Pat's excitement. She was mesmerized by the fall of Maureen Costello. Anne listened intently, leaning forward all the time, as Pat went over the long list of interviews that Costello had conducted with other nurses and supervisors who had been on S-2 during the crucial days.

"And so that comes to eight people," Pat said when they were done. "Did anybody who was present take any notes at all of those conversations?"

After a pause, Maureen Costello said, "There weren't any notes taken during the interviews."

Anne was stunned. How, she wondered, could the efficient, the thorough, the meticulous Iron Maiden possibly allow such a thing to go unrecorded?

Pat turned to the jury and made a face as if he, too, were stunned, though in fact he knew the answer to every question he asked before he asked it. Shaking his head in mock disbelief, he leaned on the jury rail and looked at the jurors but directed his voice toward the witness stand.

"You have related to us about eight people, each of whom was interviewed for an average of two to three hours over the course of several days, and not one single, solitary note was taken of any one of those conversations?"

"That's correct," Costello said, as if she were telling a student who had gotten the right answer.

The Costello image continued to crumble. Pat showed that the first notes had not been taken until ten days after the first interview and that Costello had never gotten around to interviewing the surprise witness, Kathy Menard.

By the end of the day Anne's illusions about the Iron Maiden had been nearly shattered. Costello had taken no notes, she had not talked to Menard, she had failed to correct work habits that accounted for hundreds of technical violations, and she had spent time on the witness stand defining a word that didn't even appear in the nurses' notes.

On Thursday and Friday, Costello fared no better.

Piscitelli spent much of Thursday developing the fact that dozens of people were aware, or could have been aware, of the amount of narcotics that Norma Leanues was receiving. The list included nursing supervisors who were advised daily about patient medication but had seen no reason to issue incident reports. The Bailey of Brockton pounded home his point again and again: Nobody had been alarmed until Vicki McKenna read the chart on Tuesday the twentieth. Pat also spent a good deal of time on Norma's pain. He asked Costello what the other nurses had said about Norma's screams, her agony. He belabored the point for as long as he could until an exasperated Ron Pina finally told the judge, "I will agree that the woman was in pain," and Judge Prince order Pat to move forward.

Pat had made sixteen photocopies of the nurses' notes. He handed them to the jury and asked Costello to discuss them line by line, explaining terms and abbreviations to the jurors. Pat wanted the jury to hear how often references to pain were written.

By Friday morning Pat was still not out of ammunition.

"Mrs. Costello," he said, "you have told us that you tried to be as comprehensive as you could in putting down what you recall in the notes which you finally made, correct?"

"That's correct," Costello said. For three full days she had been on the witness stand, her voice, for the most part, as steady as a pulsar. During the three days on the stand Costello never sat down and never drank water. Only now was she beginning to look weary from the ordeal.

"Did you leave some stuff out that you thought was important?" Pat asked.

"Yes, I did," Costello said. The sounds of surprise swept through the crowded courtroom.

"You knew that this was a serious patient-care situation that you were inquiring into?"

"Yes, I did," said the Iron Maiden.

"And you knew that the report might later be used in case you wanted to penalize Anne Capute if you thought she did something wrong?"

"That's correct."

"And yet," Pat said, "you want the jury to

understand that you intentionally left out stuff that you thought important in those notes."

Pat shook his head, took a few steps, stretched his arms in front of him. He, too, was getting weary. But he knew he was into the last round with Costello, and he could feel the excitement rising in him. This, he thought, is what I became a lawyer for. He strode back to the witness stand.

"Mrs. Costello," he said, lining his words with a carefully modulated tone of importance, "did Anne Capute tell you there had been poor results with Mrs. Leanues because of her inability to swallow the forty milligrams of oral morphine?"

"Yes."

"Did she tell you that Mrs. Leanues could get no relief from her pain?"

"Yes."

"Did she tell you exactly what happened when Dr. Hillier came on the floor of S-2?"

"Yes," Costello said, "she did."

"But you didn't tell this jury the other day that Anne said on May twenty-second that Dr. Hillier had said fifteen milligrams, subcu., prn, no time limit, did you."

"My answer today is that she might have said that."

Pat walked away and came back. He turned once more and glanced at Anne. Then he looked at Costello again.

"Did she tell you that she had reassured Mr. Leanues that the doctor had ordered a change in medication? Did she say that to you, Mrs. Costello?"

"Yes, she did."

"And did she say that she told him it would make Mrs. Leanues feel more comfortable, she put her hand on his shoulder and said that to him?"

"Yes."

"And did she tell you that she felt tremendous compassion and sympathy for Edward Leanues, this poor man having to watch his wife die in a hospital room? Did she tell you that?"

"Yes, she did."

"And the family and the daughter, did she not feel sorry for the daughters there having to watch their mother slowly dying? Did she say that as well?"

"Yes."

"That's in your notes, isn't it?"

"Yes, it is," Costello said.

"But, you didn't tell that to the jury when you were asked about the conversation two days ago, did you?"

"No," Costello said, "I didn't."

Pat stood silent and looked at the jury. The answer, he felt, required no further comment. He could feel the tension spreading through the courtroom. Timing, he thought, timing is important here; Anne's life is at stake. And when he thought he could feel the wave of tension crash against the back of the courtroom and begin to roll back toward him, he began to speak slowly to the witness.

"Now," he said, and he paused. "Mrs. Costello," and he paused. "At some time do you recall the question being asked by Tom Bosanquet, 'Anne, did you intend to kill her?' Do you remember that question being asked?"

"Yes," the witness said.

"And did Anne answer in reply to that question, 'No, of course I didn't intend to kill her. I mean, I wasn't trying out for euthanasia nurse'? Did she say that?"

"Yes," Costello said. "That was an important point that I have not testified to."

"You forgot about that one," Pat said. "But you had just reviewed your notes before you took the stand so that you could be as accurate as possible when you told the jury about this conversation, right?"

"Yes. That's correct."

"Mrs. Costello, does it appear anywhere in your notes that Anne said, 'No, I didn't intend to kill her. I mean, I wasn't trying out for euthanasia nurse.'? Does that appear in your notes?"

"I don't believe that—'

"Mrs. Costello, does it appear in your notes?"

"It's—"

"Is it in your notes?"

"No."

Again the combined sound of a hundred whispered comments filled the courtroom. Pat strode to the defense table and stood drinking from a glass of water while he waited for the noise to seep away.

When he walked back to the witness stand he said to Costello, "Did you not think it was important that she had denied intending to kill that woman, is it not important that the jury be made aware of that fact?"

Costello evaded the question, but it didn't really matter. Pat had swung his sword at the forces of darkness. He had done what he had hoped to do. He had shown the jury that on May 22, 1980, long before she had a lawyer, long before she even knew what was going on, Anne Capute was saying the same things that she was saying now. And if she had made some incriminating remarks that night, there was a context to be considered, a context that, intentionally or not, had been manipulated by those same dark forces. Anne Capute, he would like to say, was not guilty; the hospital was.

As he was getting near the end of his cross-examination, Pat stood close to the jury and far from the witness.

"Mrs. Costello," he called, "you have been provided with immunity for any prosecution for anything that's happened as a result of the Leanues matter, have you not?"

"I have," Costello said.

"You refused to disclose any information until such time as you were given immunity. Is that so?"

"That's correct."

Pat turned away as if he were through with the witness. He could feel his hands shaking, and his entire body felt weak. His emotions were gaining fast on his intellect. For months he had been inches away from Norma Leanues's pain, and now more and more he was feeling what Anne had been going through. He took two steps toward the defense table. He looked at Anne, and he smiled. Then he turned back. There was one more thing he had to do.

"Mrs. Costello," he said, "at the time you spoke to Anne, she told you that she felt that she had cared about her work and had been a good nurse and had tried to do the best job she could in the time that she was with Morton Hospital. Did she say that to you?" Pat could feel the tears crowding into his eyes.

"Yes, she did."

"And as a matter of fact, she did get a one and a half step increase just a few months before?"

"Yes, she did."

"Which is a half step more than what is normally given, right?"

"That's correct," Costello said.

"Because," Pat said. He stopped. His voice was cracking. "Because the quality of her nursing performance did support that?"

"Yes."

"Thank you very much," Pat said. "No further questions."

It was noon on Friday. The witness was dismissed, and Judge Prince declared a recess for lunch. Pat, exhausted but triumphant, moved slowly back to the defense table. Anne rushed around to meet him. She wrapped her arms around him and pulled him down close to her. "Thank you," she said.

Chapter Twenty-seven

The trial continued.

"I'm learning what's bullshit and what isn't," Anne said to James Morton one day at Gale's. Gale's, a mom-and-pop restaurant five blocks from the courthouse, had become the regular lunch spot for the defense team. They went there almost every day at recess, and the owners fussed over them as if they were celebrities.

"I think if I come out of this thing okay, then maybe it was even worth it," Anne said. "I mean, if things were normal it would have taken me years to grow this much."

James said nothing. One of his jobs was to keep Anne as emotionally steady as possible by just listening to her when she needed to talk.

"Taoism teaches us to live simply," Anne said. "You know, be more spontaneous and get rid of all that junk we carry around in our heads. I don't know why it takes us so long to learn what's junk."

"You know," she said a few minutes later, "I'm beginning to see death as freedom. It's kind of like being out in the wilderness permanently. And you know how much I love the wilderness."

After she read *Messages from Michael*, Anne had turned to other occult books—by Ruth Montgomery, Edgar Cayce—books about reincarnation and psychic phenomena. The books described events that, like her own murder trial, did not fit neatly into the pattern of "the way things are supposed to be."

Each time Anne closed a book, she wondered: Is such a thing possible? Are there people who can somehow plug into a vastness of cosmic wisdom? Or is it all the fraudulent or naïve imaginings of writers? Sometimes she felt like a gullible nitwit who could be convinced of anything as long as it was in print. At other times she felt as if she had finally cast off the shell of restrictive thinking and was closing in on some sort of truth. And the more she wondered about the validity of the books she read, the more it didn't matter. Like the Taoism that attracted her, all this reading was a path, not a place. As she continued to search the spiritual realm, the Roman Catholicism of her childhood and the Judaism of her adulthood receded into her past, and when she looked back at them she thought of them as games she used to play.

The more Anne read, the more she believed that she would live again. She knew that a psychiatrist would say that this newly formed belief in reincarnation was a device, a trick of the mind to make suicide easier. While everybody around Anne believed that Warren's death had convinced her not to kill herself, Anne still had a suicide plan.

"One of the great things about believing in life after death," she said to James, "is that if you're wrong, you never know it."

Though Anne spent much of her time during the trial immersed in this sort of contemplation, there were a good many mundane matters to be dealt with. Her family was her greatest concern, and she worried about the effect of all the publicity on the girls.

"Anne did not want the girls to attend the trial," Charles Capute says. "She was worried about all the reporters hounding them. She was especially worried about Meredith, the youngest, because Meredith has the Capute name and because she endured all those sick phone calls. Anne told the girls not to come to the trial. But Susan and Lori went anyhow. They took turns going. Barbara, who was working, did not attend. Pat was happy. He wanted Anne to have family in the courtroom. He figured it would make the jury more sympathetic."

Charlie did not go to the trial. The weather was good, and he was a carpenter who had to take work when it was available. Each morning he wished Anne luck, then headed out in his van, cheerfully beeping his horn as he left the driveway. Charlie thought he could best serve the family by going to work and earning money to pay off the enormous debts that were piling up. Anne, however, did not see it that way. Though she said little about it, she was deeply hurt by what she saw as Charlie's lack of support. Although she was trying to eliminate anger from her vocabulary of feelings, she became very bitter about his response and often made cutting remarks that she regretted later.

As the trial progressed, press coverage increased. Anne's picture flashed on TV screens every night, and excerpts of testimony appeared in every morning's paper. Anne felt as if she were under a microscope.

Anne usually went back to the office to watch the

six-o'clock news with the rest of the defense team. Everybody on Pat's staff was caught up in the drama, and by the fourth week they were taking turns attending the trial. Pat's mother started showing up at the trial. Even Pat's wife, Meredith, despite the stress that the Capute case was putting on her household, could not resist the lure.

"It was an extraordinary time," Meredith Piscitelli says, "I have to admit that. Pat was obsessed with the trial. After a while that's all there was. The trial. Pat got up early every morning, even though he'd had only three or four hours' sleep. Right away he'd have his nose buried in some medical records or grand jury transcript. I'd help him pick out his suit for the day. The clothes were always picked carefully, for the best effect on the jury. And then he was gone, never really having been home. His family then was not me and the kids. It was Anne and Don and James. The four of them had formed a kind of marriage. They lived in their own world."

Just as he took care in choosing what to wear in court, Pat took care in everything where the jurors were concerned.

"We used to park in the same place every day, on a side street near the courthouse," he says. "One morning as we neared the courthouse we saw one of the jurors, an elderly white-haired gentleman, standing on a corner about a hundred fifty yards ahead of us and directly in our line of travel. We would have had to go straight up the street and take a turn right in front of him. In my Mercedes. I had carefully created an image of Anne as this low person on the totem pole fighting the hospital, and I didn't want to spoil it by having a juror see her riding in the front of a Mercedes with this supposedly big-time lawyer. Sometimes a little happening like that can alter the jury's thinking about you. So I put the car in reverse and I backed down the street about a hundred yards and I took a route that was about a mile and a half out of our way to avoid being seen. Long after the trial was over I ran into this juror at a party and he told me that he had seen us that day and wondered why we didn't drive by him."

Attending the trial every day were also the daughters of Norma Leanues.

"When the trial began there was no contact at all between Anne and the daughters," Piscitelli says. "But as the trial went on and the evidence began to come out to show that maybe Anne was not guilty of killing their mother, it was interesting to watch how they softened, at least one of them did. After a while it got so that Anne and one of the daughters would nod hello to each other. Anne also wanted to speak to Edward Leanues. She was so filled with compassion for that man and so sorry that he had to go through what he went through. But I wouldn't let her talk to him."

Pat wouldn't let Anne speak to the press, either. The reporters came around each day and tossed a few perfunctory questions at her, but she stuck to her silence, and they did not harass her. Anne grew to like the newspaper reporters. But she wasn't so sure about the television people. She was still irked by the memory of the Channel 6 news team pounding on her door. Her opinion of television people plunged even farther when a well-known Boston newswoman befriended Susan and Lori, gave them a tour of the TV studio, and then put in her pitch for an interview with Anne.

Anne didn't sleep much at night. She listened to tapes, Neil Diamond mostly, and sometimes she talked to Pat on the phone for hours. At home the girls offered the emotional support she needed, but in many ways Anne could feel herself distancing from them, getting ready to leave them. It occurred to her often that one way or another she would soon be separating from her daughters. If the jury found her guilty, she would kill herself in the courtroom. If the jury said she was innocent, she would pack up and drive to California. If any of the girls wanted to go with her, that was okay. But if they didn't, that was okay, too.

Though Anne was cheerful most of the time and often made wisecracks about the witnesses, she was often depressed. A strand of pessimism ran through her humor. When people tried to reassure her that everything would be okay, that she would not be sent to jail, she often quipped, "That's what they told Jean Harris."

Harris, the headmistress of a prestigious private school near Washington, D.C., had been convicted the previous February for murdering the "Scarsdale Diet" doctor.

"She had money, connections, everything," Anne would say, "and they put *her* in jail. So what chance do I have?"

Pat Piscitelli was also often moody. Though he rarely let on to Anne, there were times when he could feel the trial slipping away, and he was haunted by visions of the jury bringing in a guilty verdict.

Pat had been hit hard by Judge Prince's refusal to let him wield one of his mightiest weapons in the "state of mind" defense: his proof that much of what Anne did was common practice.

"Part of our strategy was to show that large amounts of morphine and Dilaudid, which is four times as strong, had been administered to terminal patients before Leanues," Piscitelli says. "We had secured from a nurse at the hospital the names of at least three patients who had died. One patient had been given twelve milligrams of Dilaudid, IM, around the clock every three hours, and also every three hours in between was given a Brompton's cocktail. That's a solution of cocaine and vodka. The Dilaudid was later increased to sixteen milligrams every three hours and later to twenty milligrams, equal to about eighty milligrams of morphine. The patient built up great tolerance to the drugs, and the nurse told us that the last she knew he was getting thirty-two milligrams of Dilaudid before he died at home. We always suspected that he died of the narcotic. The evidence was not allowed by the judge.

"We also had evidence of another patient who had a 'no code' order and died in 1975. It was unusual to have it written down because most doctors don't want to put it in writing that they are saying it. On that one there was an order for ten to fifteen milligrams prn and the words 'no time limit' written in. When these were not allowed in, it was a great setback to our case. I was rather devastated, though I made an offer of proof to protect the record. It never got across to the jury that this was common practice."

For most of the trial Pat felt helpless on another significant matter: Anne's testimony.

Anne was terrified of going on the witness stand and testifying in front of the jury, the spectators, and the millions of people who would see her on television. After Hillier's testimony there had been a brief period of feistiness when Anne wanted to testify, she was so enraged. "Put me on the stand, Pat," she had said in the car, "I'll show that lying son-of-a-bitch. I'll give them all hell."

"That's what I'm afraid of," Pat had said, and after a few minutes Anne retreated and once again was urging Pat to keep her off the witness stand.

Pat's dilemma, however, had nothing to do with whether Anne wanted to testify. The problem was her name.

"I was concerned about putting Anne on the stand right from the outset," Piscitelli says. "Anne had told me about using someone else's records to get into nursing school and that she had adopted the phony name. The problem is that if she had to take the stand she would be sworn in and would have to give her real name. If she didn't, the first words out of her mouth would be perjured statements. The D.A. would have a field day with that. I could just imagine him telling the jury, 'You heard from her, and the first things you heard were lies.' I could not put her on the stand and have her perjure herself. That would have been improper. And if she admitted that she lied to the nursing school that would have tainted everything; our credibility would be jeopardized. The great crisis was determining how to get over that hurdle if the evidence came in so compellingly and so convincingly that we had to put her on the stand."

Anne once told Pat that she was afraid the D.A. might find out about her name change. Pat laughed.

"Find out? I'm sure he's known about it for a long time," he said.

"How could he?" she asked.

"Anne, your picture's in the paper every day. It's being seen by dozens of people, maybe hundreds, who know your name is Mary Patricia. There's got to be at least one busybody out there who would let Pina know."

"I guess you're right," Anne said. "Why hasn't he said anything?"

"He's waiting for you to take the stand so he can shock the jury with it."

"And what if I don't take the stand?"

"Then," Pat said, "he'll probably leak it to the press when the trial's over. Anything that makes you look bad will make his actions look more justifiable."

After a moment Anne said, "Then you're telling me that even if I'm acquitted I'll probably lose my nursing license?"

"Anne," Pat said, "let's deal with that when we get to it."

But the weeks of the trial were not all somber. If Pat, Don, James, and Anne were like a combat team behind enemy lines, they were also often like drunken soldiers on a three-day pass. Affection and good humor flowed freely among them. There was, for example, "The Great Wink Defense."

"See," says James Morton, "during the first week of the trial the district attorney would not look at Anne. He did everything he could to avoid her eyes. He'd gaze away whenever she looked at him. Anne always thought this proved that he felt guilty about what he was putting her through. 'I think he's afraid of me,' she told me once. She was determined to catch Pina's eye. She said if you're going to accuse somebody of murder, you ought to be able to look that person in the eye. So on the day that we went to the hospital with the jury, there were two elevators, and Anne and I got in one with the judge and a couple of court officers and Pina. She had him trapped in the elevator, and when she finally got him in her sights she looked him straight in the eye. She winked and said, 'Hi, Ron!' Pina's face turned red and he started twitching. He was totally unnerved. Anne was ecstatic. And from then on it became a game. It was a challenge to her to get Pina's eye and wink at him. One time she got in four winks in one day. She was like a little girl, she was so pleased with herself."

And Don Harwood recalls "The Magic Hershey Bars."

"One night we were driving home after court, talking about the case, and Anne shouted, 'Hey, Pat, you forgot your goddamn candy bars.' And Pat had to turn the car around and drive all the way back to the grocery store where we bought our candy bars every night. Getting the candy bars had become a ritual, and we didn't want to break the spell, because it could mean bad luck. Pat and James and Anne always got Hershey Bars because of their obvious mystical powers. I always got a Milky Way because I wasn't superstitious. And George, the skeleton, never got anything. She was on a diet."

During the third week of the trial, Anne started finding letters from strangers in her mailbox. At first there would be just one letter every couple of days, and then they started coming three and four at a time. The letters were from Iowa, Tennessee, Michigan—everywhere. And they were different. She had gotten a lot of hate mail when the story first broke, scrawled notes that said she was a murderer. But these were messages of support. Some people offered their prayers; others, advice. Most of the letter writers said that they had a friend or a relative who died in terrible pain and that they wished that someone had had the compassion to put that loved one out of pain. Anne answered every letter.

And one afternoon when she was coming out of court two middle-aged women walked up to her. One handed her a flower. The other said, "We're with you, Anne." Anne cried most of the way home. She was beginning to sense that the people were with her.

Chapter Twenty-eight

Piscitelli looked Judge Prince in the eye.

"An old English jurist said that once you let loose a skunk in the courtroom, how can you tell the jury to forget the skunk is there?" he said. "The smell still permeates the courtroom."

Pat was worried. He and Don sat in the Judge's chambers with the prosecutors, trying to shoot down testimony that could send Anne to jail.

The skunk in this case was a conversation on May 16 between Anne Capute and Martha Rice, an R.N. who worked on S-2. During the conversation, according to Rice, Anne described acting as charge nurse for cancer patients at Lemuel Shattuck Hospital and giving terminal patients a combination of Thorazine and Dilaudid intravenously by a method known as an "IV push"—that is, by pinching off an intravenous tubing and injecting both medications into the IV tube that goes into the patient's bloodstream. Martha had told the district attorney that Anne described this and then said, "That will do it," and "Martha, it gives me goose bumps to think about it." Martha had responded, "It gives me goose bumps also."

Pina wanted this testimony admitted to show Anne's knowledge, her intent, her state of mind.

Piscitelli thought the conversation carried hints of dark motives and the suggestion of a prior crime.

He told Judge Prince the testimony would make the jury think Anne had been involved in euthanasia before and that once that idea was planted in the jurors' minds, a cautionary instruction from the judge could not erase it any more than it could erase the smell of a skunk.

Judge Prince told the men he would make the decision by the next morning. Pat went home that night certain that Prince would not let Rice's story in, but he stayed up late planning his cross-examination just in case.

In the morning Judge Prince met Pat and Pina in chambers and told them he had decided to allow the Rice testimony. Pat was shocked and distraught. The defense team fell into despair.

"It was," says Don Harwood, "one of the worst moments of the trial."

The despair, however, did not last long. When Pina got Martha Rice on the stand he "missed the opportunity," according to one of his own staff people. The potential dynamite was little more than a firecracker.

MR. PINA: Would you tell us what that conversation was?

MS. RICE: We were standing at the nurses' station and we were talking about cancer patients in general.

MR. PISCITELLI: Well, Your Honor, may that go out? I am going to ask that the conversation be related.

THE COURT: Yes, the statement as to the nature of the conversation must go out. So far as possible, you must recount to the best of your recollection just who said what and what the response was and so forth. Try to.

MR. PINA: Would you tell us what the conversation was?

MS. RICE: Anne said, "Dilaudid and Thorazine," and she made a gesture like she was giving it intravenously with a syringe, like it's called an IV push.

MR. PINA: It's called what?

MS. RICE: IV push. It's that method of administering medication. And she said, "That will do it." And she said, "The thought of it gives me goose bumps." And I said I had goose bumps, too. And that was the end of the conversation.

Pat was thrilled. He had stayed up half the night worrying about this testimony, and now it had come out in such a way that it had virtually no impact on the jury.

Pina tried to lead Rice back into the conversation, to get another shot at it, but Pat objected, and that was the end of it. The defense team was gleeful, and they smiled at each other as if they had done something wonderful. "Martha," Anne said to no one in particular, "how did you get so screwed up in your head?" During the next recess, Assistant D.A. Dave Turcotte walked over to the defense table and said, "You have got to be the luckiest guys in the world." He shook his head and walked away. (Throughout the trial, as relations with Pina deteriorated, the defense team viewed Turcotte with high respect and no animosity. As far as they were concerned, Turcotte was a good guy doing a good job; he just happened to be on the wrong team.)

The absurdity of the entire "IV push" incident is compounded by the fact that Anne's conversation with Martha had nothing to do with experience at

Lemuel Shattuck. Anne had been talking about a scene from a book. The book, *Nurse*, by Peggy Anderson, was a popular and controversial account of a nurse's daily life, and it had been making the rounds at Morton.

"Martha Rice was just confused, though not intentionally so," Piscitelli says. "Anne showed me the parts from the book. But I didn't want to bring the book into the testimony if I could avoid it because there were a lot of other damaging things in there about the dispatching of patients. I was afraid that once I brought it up, the D.A. might utilize it; he might say that events in the book are similar to what Anne was being accused of and that maybe the idea originated when she read the book."

Martha Rice was followed to the witness stand by four more nurses: June Machnik, Annetta Marie LaBrun, Susan Santos, and Rosemary Miles.

Machnik was an R.N. whose testimony added nothing new to the trial.

LaBrun was a clinical manager at Morton; her testimony was so innocuous that even Pat wasn't sure why Pina had called her as a witness. LaBrun had worked the day shift on May 17. The district attorney established her background, asked her a few questions about Norma Leanues, and dismissed her. Don Harwood, trying to hold back a grin, leaned over to Pat and said, "Pat, we're sunk. The D.A.'s got us. He has proved beyond any reasonable doubt that Norma Leanues was in fact a patient at Morton Hospital and did, in fact, have a room." Pat smiled. It was nice to have a harmless witness for a change.

As he did with the other nurses, Pat used LaBrun's presence on the stand as an opportunity to take potshots at Hillier, whom he regarded as the real villain.

"Mrs. LaBrun," he said, "is it fair to say that Dr. Hillier is one who is accustomed to giving very large orders of narcotics to patients?"

The witness did not have an answer, but the thought had been expressed.

Susan Santos, an R.N. who had taken care of Leanues on the seven-to-three-thirty shift during Norma's last weekend, was a slightly more dangerous witness.

Pina asked, "When you saw Mrs. Capute come from the area of room two twenty-seven, Mrs. Leanues's room, did she say anything to you?"

"Yes, she did," Santos replied.

"What did she say?"

"As she walked by, she stated to me that she had just given Mrs. Leanues one hundred ninety-five milligrams of morphine in an eight-hour period."

Anne began to study the jurors' faces. She tried to guess who was with her and who was against her. She had given them names such as "White Hair" and "Chubby Cheeks," and when these incriminating statements were made in the courtroom, she tried to guess how each of the jurors was affected. This particular one scared her. The implication, and she could see it in the jurors' faces, was that she wouldn't have mentioned the 195 milligrams unless she knew it was an extremely large and unusual amount.

When Pat cross-examined Susan Santos, the first thing he said was, "You were aware that Norma Leanues was a terminal patient, were you not?"

"Yes, I was," she said.

"And in fact," said Pat, "the whole staff who was treating her was made aware of the fact after her operation that she was going to die imminently, were they not?"

"Yes," Santos said.

Then, getting back to the crucial conversation, "And after Anne Capute said to you, 'I have just given Mrs. Leanues one hundred ninety-five milligrams of morphine during an eight-hour period,' you did nothing with that information, right?"

"That's correct," Santos said.

"And I assume if you had thought it unusual you would have done something about it, right?"

"Correct."

"As a matter of fact," Pat said, "Anne told you, did she not, that she had just given Mrs. Leanues forty-five milligrams of morphine in one shot?"

"That's correct."

"And again, if that had been unusual, you would have done something or said something?"

"That's correct."

"In fact, isn't it fair to say, Miss Santos, that there were a lot of people, twelve, eighteen people during Friday and Saturday who would have been aware of the dosages, the frequency, and the particular drugs which were being given to Norma Leanues on Friday and Saturday because of all the ways which this was communicated?"

Pina objected, and the objection was sustained.

"Miss Santos," Pat said, "do you recall Anne stating to you at some time on Saturday when you came in that she was concerned that Mrs. Leanues had not been medicated enough by the girl on the day shift?"

"I can't remember."

Pat stopped then and glanced around at the spectators, as he had with the other nurses.

"Miss Santos, isn't that your lawyer sitting there, Mr. Frank O'Boy?"

"Yes, it is."

"He has been paid for by the Morton Hospital, has he not?"

"Yes," she said.

"Along with several others?"

Santos was not required to answer the question, but Pat had again reminded the jury that the hospital was hiring lawyers for nurses who took the stand.

Rosemary Miles, a clinical nursing supervisor, also had a damaging statement to make. Speaking in a voice so low it could not be heard at the back of the courtroom, she told the jury that on May 16 she was on S-2 to start an IV on a patient.

"And Anne said something about how she wished I could start an IV on her, and she nodded her head toward Mrs. Leanues's room, so that she would get her medication more effectively and it would be able to help her along the way."

The words "to help her along the way" echoed in Anne's mind as she studied the faces of the jurors. She was beginning to realize how powerful offhand words could be when someone was looking for meaning in them.

Though Miles acknowledged under cross-examination that Norma's pain was so bad that her screaming could be heard throughout the ward and that she knew Norma was terminal, the testimony still hurt Anne's case.

As she listened to the testimony of the nurses, Anne tried to discern what it all said about the sisterhood of nurses' view of her. Half believing that Rice, LaBrun, and Miles could speak for nurses everywhere, Anne examined each word, each tone, searching for signs of support or signs of condemnation. Certainly the nurses who took the stand didn't appear to be "out to get her." Yet there they were testifying for the commonwealth. Pat assured Anne that all the nurses had been interviewed by Costello or Lorraine Hickey back in May 1980, and they were called to the stand only because the district attorney thought they had something damaging to say. "The nurses are with you, Anne," Pat said, as he had before. But Anne wasn't so sure. She was beginning to feel the support of the general public, the people who watched TV news and read the newspapers. But what about the nurses? Had she somehow let them down? Had she tarnished their image? Being a nurse was what she had always dreamed of, and now she hoped most of all that when the dust settled, even if nobody else understood what she had gone through, at least the nurses would.

Norma Leanues's daughters, Linda Lawrence and Cheryl Frost, took turns on the witness stand.

Though the two young women had little of substance to add to the immense body of evidence, their testimony packed an emotional wallop. Both appeared shaken, and Cheryl Frost when she spoke had to bite her lower lip to hold back tears.

Linda Lawrence testified that a nurse gave Norma a shot while Norma was sleeping. Pat saw this as a point for the defense, since the shot was given by a nurse not involved with the case and would indicate common practice. But when Cheryl Frost later testified that Anne Capute had given Norma Leanues a shot while Norma was asleep, it caused a stir in the courtroom and inspired a headline the next day: DAUGHTER TESTIFIES MOTHER INJECTED WHILE ASLEEP.

Mrs. Frost's testimony pulled at the heartstrings of the jurors.

"Mother was sleeping," she said at one point. "My father was sitting next to the bed, crying. I tried to wake her." Frost's voice quavered, and she spoke barely above a whisper. "She never woke up. I squeezed her hand. She didn't respond. She just laid there motionless. I left sometime after four P.M."

Pina, recognizing the emotional grip he had on the jury, used it to the fullest. He pulled out a photo of Norma Leanues with her husband, both of them smiling. In the photo Norma looked happy, healthy, and full of life. He asked the daughters if the photo showed what their mother looked like in May 1980. They both said "Yes." The picture was shown to the jury. Pina also showed the witness a photo which Pat had brought into evidence. Taken when Leanues was a patient in Rhode Island, the photo showed her as a thin, hunched-over woman wearing a hospital johnny.

"Is that your mother?" Pina asked.

"No, it isn't really her," Linda Lawrence said. "It's not what she looked like in May 1980."

Though the daughters of Norma Leanues remembered her as the smiling woman of Pina's picture, the nurses who treated her remembered something very different. Rosemary Miles, for example, said that Pina's picture looked nothing like the Norma Leanues she had seen. The Norma she saw was the Norma of Pat's picture, with her face sadly sunken in, her cheeks hollow, and her skin pale and waxy-looking.

By the time the nurses and daughters had testified, news reporters were beginning to speculate that Anne's trial would be the longest in the history of the commonwealth. They compared it to Lizzie Borden's, which it had already surpassed; the Brinks trial, which ran for forty-five days; and the trial of Sacco and Vanzetti. Court reporter Mark LaPlante told one newsman that he already had 2,500 pages of transcription. "And I expect to double that before this trial is over," he said. It was the biggest trial he had been on, and he was transcribing the equivalent of 150 pages a day. Clerk magistrate William Grant told the

Brockton Enterprise he thought the trial would be the longest in his 22 years of court work. District attorney Ronald Pina told the press he had a list of 47 potential witnesses, and Piscitelli said he would bring 36 witnesses to the stand. Judge Prince told a reporter, "I'll never see that October foliage I had planned to see in western Massachusetts." And Pina, predicting the trial would be the longest his office had ever had, said, "I've stopped taking notes. I've put my pen down."

By this time Pat had made his most important decision of the trial. He revealed it to Anne one afternoon on the way to lunch.

Anne had fallen slightly behind the others that day as the four members of the defense team walked to Gale's Restaurant. She had become well known up and down North Main Street, and she was buoyed by the occasional "Hi, Anne,' from a shopkeeper or a stranger who recognized her. But she had fallen behind just to put a little extra space around her. She missed the wilderness. As she strolled along the sidewalk, Pat and the others ahead of her, she remembered how even they had seemed threatening on the first day of the trial. She had felt then that they had power and that she didn't and that that made them dangerous. But now that feeling was gone. Partly it was because she no longer felt powerless. She had inner power, she knew. She was willing to die, and if you're willing to die, she thought, there's nothing they can do to you. But—and this was more important to her—these men were in no way frightening because she loved them. She had come to love Pat and Don and James. All of them, Anne felt, had been kind to her far beyond the call of duty. And, ironically, she had begun to dread the end of the trial because it would be the end of this beautiful kind of marriage the four of them had created.

Pat glanced back, and thinking she was depressed, he came and put his arm around her.

"Got some good news for you, kid," he said as they walked along.

"Norma is still alive and hiding out in Argentina?" Anne said.

Pat laughed. "Not that good. But I've gone over Costello's testimony and I think I've done what I wanted. I've told your story through her recollections."

"And?"

"And that means I'm not going to put you on the stand," he said.

"Oh, Pat!" Anne cried. She let out a whoop and threw her arms in the air. A guy across the street shouted, "You tell 'em, Anne!" She put her arms around Pat. "That is super," she said. "That is just super."

Pat was delighted to see Anne so jubilant, but as he hugged her, he felt a little bit guilty. Because even though he wasn't going to make her take the witness stand, he was trying to arrange for her to do something even more difficult. He wanted her to speak directly to the jury.

Chapter Twenty-nine

Joseph Goldrick of the Taunton Police Department took the witness stand. Goldrick had witnessed the Norma Leanues autopsy. Because Ambrose Keeley, the man who had performed the autopsy, was now dead, Goldrick was in court mainly as a witness to the fact that an autopsy had taken place. Goldrick's testimony was a grisly reminder that Norma Leanues, who had suffered so much before death, was exhumed and carved up after death.

"I saw Dr. Keeley remove kidney tissue and dissect it and place it in two glass vials," Goldrick said. "I also saw him remove intestine, which was dissected and placed in two glass vials. He also did the skull. The brain was removed, dissected, and placed in two glass vials."

Pat regarded Goldrick's testimony as a few small points for the prosecution. There was nothing controversial about it, but throughout the trial he could feel much of the testimony coming in waves of sympathy toward Leanues or toward Anne. He felt that Anne's case was hurt by anything that portrayed Leanues as a victim, even after death.

The next witness was Robert St. Jean. St. Jean, a state police officer assigned to the Bristol County district attorney's office, had done much of the early investigating on the case.

Throughout the trial Pat had tried to shift the

spotlight from Anne to others. He had tried to
portray Hillier, Costello, and Morton Hospital as
villains. But the commonwealth, personified by D.A.
Pina, could also be presented as a villain, Pat knew,
and he wanted to make the most of it. He wanted to
show Pina as a man who lusted so desperately for a
conviction in this high-visibility case that he would go
to extraordinary lengths at taxpayer expense to make
the evidence come out the way he wanted. Robert St.
Jean was as close as Pat would come to having Pina on
the stand. Pat came out fighting.

"Did Dr. John McHugh, a chemist with the
Massachusetts Department of Public Safety, do a
chemical analysis on various parts of the body of
Norma Leaneues?" he asked St. Jean.

"He tells me he did, yes, sir."

"You know he did, don't you?" Pat said. "And
you got a report back from McHugh June the twenty-
fourth of 1980, did you not?"

"Yes, sir."

"You weren't satisfied with that report, were
you?" Pat said. "It didn't say what you wanted it to
say?"

Judge Prince struck the question.

"So ten months later," Pat said, "you sent another
jar of body parts down to New York for analysis,
right?"

"Yes," St. Jean said.

"You could have brought the jar to John
McHugh, couldn't you?"

Pina stood up and objected. The objection was
sustained.

"Did you bring the jar to McHugh?" Pat said.

"No, sir, I did not."

"Got any other chemists that work for the state
here in Massachusetts?" Pat said. He paused, then

added, "Here in the commonwealth of Massachusetts."

"Yes, sir."

"You didn't take the jar to any of those guys, did you? Sent it down to New York instead, right?"

"Yes, sir."

"I see," Pat said. He glanced at Pina, so that the jury would know who he was really trying to talk to. He walked to the defense table for a drink of water. When he came back he asked, "Mr. St. Jean, was immunity of some sort given to four administrators of Morton Hospital?" In his hand he had the letters of immunity he had gotten from Pina.

"I understood that to be true, yes, sir."

"In fact," said Pat, "they were promised that no matter what the grand jury did by way of indictments, the D.A. would drop the charges if they revealed all they knew about the incident involving the death of Norma Leanues, is that right?"

Pina's objection was sustained, and Pat had no further questions for St. Jean.

After St. Jean there came to the witness stand a series of medical experts, eight in all. They were physicians, toxicologists, pathologists, men and women who each had more higher education than the entire jury. They were highly qualified and well-paid experts. They were impressive, they were fascinating, they were often boring. Most of all they were thorough, and it took them two weeks of court time to tell the jury what they knew and how they knew it, about the condition of Norma's body, the findings of the autopsy, the severity of her illness, and the amount of morphine that had been given to her.

The prosecution called George Katsas to the stand. He was a pathologist at Waltham Hospital. He had known Ambrose Keeley, and he told the jury about problems connected with an autopsy; he described the background a pathologist must have and the procedure he must follow. He explained the abbreviations and codes to be found on an autopsy report.

Next came Dr. William Q. Sturner, chief medical examiner for the state of Rhode Island. Sturner had studied the autopsy report, and under questioning from Pina he told the court, "My opinion is that Norma Leanues died of morphine poisoning. I base that on the autopsy report, which indicates the cancer did not involve the vital organs." He said the records showed that Norma had been given seventeen hundred milligrams of morphine during the last eight days of her life, two hundred in the last six to eight hours, and that it had killed her.

This was a direct assault on Piscitelli's outermost wall of defense, the defense that said cancer, not drugs, killed Leanues.

"Dr. Sturner," Pat said, "did the autopsy report anything about finding morphine in the body?"

"There is nothing mentioned about finding morphine, no."

"And the chemist's report indicates no morphine was found in the body?" Pat said.

"That's correct."

"Is it not a fact that the chemist's report does not support your conclusion that Mrs. Leanues died of acute morphine poisoning?"

"I'd say that's correct," Sturner said. "It does not support my opinion."

"Doctor, are you telling us that solely upon the autopsy and the chemist's report, you could conclude that Norma Leanues died of morphine poisoning?" Pat said, raising his voice to rattle the witness.

Sturner, whose conclusions were based largely on

the medication records, seemed to back off on several points under Piscitelli's attack.

Though Anne was frightened of Sturner's testimony, Pat was not.

"Sturner didn't seem as knowledgeable as he should have been," Pat says. "He was a nervous type, and every time there was an objection he would step back off the stand. After a while I would glance at his feet, and it became kind of humorous to see him bounce back and forth like that, like a jack-in-the-box. Anytime you can get the jury laughing a little bit like that, it will help your case."

Piscitelli kept the heat on Sturner. He knew this was an important witness for the commonwealth, for if they couldn't convince the jury that Leanues had died of the morphine, they couldn't get a conviction.

Sturner, who had been critical of the autopsy, admitted under cross-examination that spinal X rays of Mrs. Leanues's body had not been taken to determine the extent of the cancer.

"So Doctor," Pat said, "then we don't know if it was a tumor on the back part of the spine which caused depressed respiration and death, do we?"

"Well," Sturner said, "we do know there's a tumor there."

Pat raised his voice. "My question," he said, "is a very simple question for a very intelligent man. We don't know, based on the autopsy, Doctor, how high up on the spine that tumor might have gone, do we?"

"Yes, counselor, we do not know," Sturner replied.

At one point Pina jumped up and shouted an objection to Piscitelli's courtroom technique. Judge Prince overruled Pina. "The fact that you don't try a case as Mr. Piscitelli does is not a basis for an objection," Prince said.

Before Sturner left the stand, Pat took another shot at Pina's handling of taxpayers' money.

"Doctor," he asked, "how much are the people of Massachusetts paying for your testimony?"

"I charge any attorney two hundred fifty dollars an hour."

"I see. Four dollars and seventeen cents a minute," said Pat, having figured it out the night before for the benefit of blue-collar jurors, many of whom didn't make $250 in a week.

The commonwealth's next witness was also not from Massachusetts. He was Dr. Leo Dalcortivo, a toxicologist from New York.

In the tense and crowded courtroom, Dalcortivo told the jury that the morphine given to Norma Leanues was "an enormous drug insult to the human individual." The morphine, he said, had killed her. He was sure.

Though the previous witness, Sturner, had not found morphine, Dalcortivo had. He explained that the morphine had been dissolved by the embalming fluid pumped into Norma, so the morphine was to be found in the fluid, not in the tissue. He stood in front of a blackboard drawing graphs to show the effects of the increased morphine dose. The short time intervals between injections, he said, did not allow the drug's peak effect to decline, and Norma had no time to recover from the side effects. In other words, she couldn't breathe.

Pat had telephoned Anne at two o'clock that morning to tell her to bring a whiskey shot glass to court, since he didn't have one at home. Now, with Dalcortivo under cross-examination, Pat held up the shot glass for the jury to see. Dalcortivo had described the amount of morphine he found as two hundred nanograms in five cubic centimeters of solution. Pat

showed the jury that five cc's would equal only one
sixth of the glass and that finding one nanogram of
morphine in there would be the equivalent of finding
one person in three quarters of the population of the
United States.

"And that," he said dramatically, "is what you
based your opinion on!"

Pat also took a swipe at Dalcortivo's qualifications.

"You are not a pathologist, right?"

"Yes."

"You were interpreting a pathology report which
documents the autopsy of Norma Leanues, and
reached an opinion of matters not in your purview, is
that correct?"

The judge struck the question.

The next witness was Dr. Marianne Prout. She
took the stand on Tuesday, October 13, a month and
four days after the trial had begun. Dr. Prout was a
cancer specialist on the staff of Boston City Hospital,
and a professor of oncology at Boston University
Medical School.

"Anne thought she was like a female Hillier,"
Piscitelli says. "She came across as if Mrs. Leanues was
in much less pain than the nurses said."

Dr. Prout, a sallow-faced woman with straight
dark hair, told the jury that she didn't think Norma
Leanues was terminally ill. She based this, she said, on
"the low volume of cancer that was seen in the
autopsy" and on her own knowledge of cancer
treatment.

"The cancer was not life-threatening," she said.
"If Mrs. Leanues had responded to therapy we could
expect her survival to have been prolonged for
anywhere between six months and up to perhaps
years. I think there is good evidence to say you could
shrink her tumor, and the odds are very good that it

would have relieved her pain." Dr. Prout also told the
courtroom, "side effects are well tolerated by the vast
majority of people."

Pat perceived a certain coldness in the woman,
and he tried to bring it across to the jury.

"Does the nurse's notation 'she is writhing in
severe pain' mean to you that the patient has been in
great pain?" he asked.

"I must have direct quotations from the patient,
or see the patient myself to tell," Dr. Prout replied.

"If Dr. Hillier described what he observed in his
patient as 'excruciating pain in the midback area
every time she took a breath,' would you still say
Norma Leanues was in no kind of severe pain?"

"Again," Dr. Prout replied, "I cannot quantitate
without knowing the patient, Dr. Hillier, and the
nurses."

As he moved toward the end of the cross-
examination, Pat brought up the subject of Dr.
Prout's book *Dilemma on Dying*, which deals with how
doctors treat seriously ill patients and make nontreat-
ment decisions that allow patients to die. Pat asked
about "no code" orders and "death with dignity"
orders, but Pina objected and Prince sustained it.

But in the silence of a courtroom grown tense
from the momentum of all the weeks of testimony,
Pat asked one of those questions that fell upon the
jurors' ears with more impact than any answer could.
He first glanced at Anne.

"Doctor," he asked, "how many doctors have
been indicted for murder?" Judge Prince struck the
question, and it was never answered.

In the morning Ronald Pina told Judge Prince
that the commonwealth of Massachusetts was resting
its case.

Chapter Thirty

Pat Piscitelli called only two witnesses to the stand.

Though he had talked about "thirty-six witnesses" to keep Pina on his toes, and in fact did have several waiting in the wings, Pat saw no need for more. During the last week of the commonwealth's prosecution, almost everybody agreed that momentum was building in Anne's favor. But Pat had known this feeling before, and he knew that moods can change rapidly in a trial. He wanted to get to the end before the wave receded.

But even more to the point, Piscitelli had said almost all he had to say. All of the points in Anne's favor he had made through Pina's witnesses. Pat felt that he had turned many of the enemy's weapons against him.

Pat's two witnesses were also medical experts: Dr. Alan L. Schiller and Dr. David Watkins.

Dr. Schiller was a pathologist at Massachusetts General Hospital and Harvard Medical School. A rather lively and good-humored man, he stood next to George the skeleton and explained to the jury that it was not morphine that killed Norma Leanues but a combination of ailments. He listed them. One, the widespread cancer of the breast, which he said was growing rapidly. Two, the tumor that had serious effects on her breathing and her heart. Three, coronary artery disease. Four, curvature of the spine.

"Five," he said, "she already had the telltale effects of pulmonary damage, secondary to emphysema, and possibly to kyphoscoliosis."

"All of these things taken together can lead to death," he said. "I think there is evidence of enough disease in this unfortunate patient to lead to her demise without incriminating another cause."

When Pina got his first chance to cross-examine a witness he recited a list of Norma's ailments and then asked Schiller if any one of them alone had killed her. He derided Schiller's use of "could," "might," and "may." When Schiller told the court that heartbeat irregularities as a cause of death was "conceivable," Pina smiled. "Is that like 'possible' and 'could be'?" he asked.

Schiller retained his sense of humor, however. When he left the stand he picked up the judge's gavel and slammed it down. "Case dismissed," he announced, and everybody, including the district attorney, laughed.

Dr. Watkins, a physician, anesthesiologist, and toxicologist at Massachusetts General Hospital, testified that it was impossible to nail down the cause of Norma's death. "Morphine was certainly a possibility," he said, "but of all the possibilities, I don't see it as being number one."

Watkins said there was a strong possibility that Norma had died of a blood clot, and he noted the variety of other medical problems that could have brought on her death. Watkins also said that, by his reckoning, Norma was a terminal patient as of May 1980.

Pat asked him if he thought giving Norma 195 milligrams of morphine in one evening was acceptable medical practice.

"I think it was not unreasonable," he said. "I

think that it was compatible with reasonable medical practice if one adopts the concept that one employs the dose of drugs that is necessary to alleviate pain."

For Don Harwood, sitting at the defense table, this was the most emotional moment of the trial, and he could feel himself getting choked up. He was glad he didn't have to speak to anyone just then.

"That was a real emotional point for me," he says. "All along we had these witnesses and these experts and they had all just kind of dismissed Anne's training and her skills, especially the nursing supervisor, and they had given the impression that Anne was not a good nurse. And she was a good nurse. And now, here was this highly respected and honest-sounding expert, a physician from Mass. General Hospital, saying that what Anne did wasn't wrong, saying that what she had done was proper. It was such a vindication for Anne to finally have someone from the medical profession stand up for her. It almost made you want to cry."

After Watkins, Pat stood before Judge Prince and said, to the surprise of almost everyone, "Your Honor, the defense rests."

There were two more witnesses.

Pina's rebuttal witness was Dr. Joseph Cochin, who told the court that he thought the morphine was the cause of Norma's death.

Piscitelli's surrebuttal witness was Dr. David Greenblatt. Greenblatt, who refused to accept a fee from Pat for his work on the trial, said there were several other possible causes of death. Greenblatt, thirty-six years old, was, arguably, the most qualified of all the experts. He is quoted several times in a book that Pina's witness Cochin had described as "the Bible of pharmacology."

During that final week of testimony Pat took

Anne into the side room during a recess. He brought along Don, James, and the court stenographer. Anne sat at the end of the long conference table. Pat paced.

"Anne," he said, "I have to ask you to make a very important decision."

Pat explained to Anne that the law allowed the jury to come back with one of three guilty verdicts. They could find her guilty of first-degree murder, which carried a mandatory life sentence. They could say she was guilty of second-degree murder, which also would sentence her to life in prison, with a chance for parole after fifteen years.

"Or," he said, "they could find you guilty of involuntary manslaughter. That could mean anything from twenty years down to a suspended sentence.

"Anne," he said, "I don't want to give the jury any room for compromise."

"What are you getting at?" she asked.

"I want to ask the judge to instruct the jury to bring you in on first-degree or nothing. The D.A. is saying you are guilty of first-degree, premeditated murder. I say either you're guilty of that, or you're guilty of nothing."

Anne said nothing. She had already decided that one day without her freedom was one day too many.

"It's a big risk," Pat said. "I brought the stenographer in here so there would be no misunderstanding later about whether or not you were properly advised. Most lawyers would be more conservative on this and give you that safety net of a possible involuntary manslaughter conviction."

"Go for it," Anne said.

"First-degree murder?"

"You got it," she said.

"You don't have to decide now," he said. "Think it over. Let me know tomorrow."

"I don't have to think it over," she said. "I'm innocent. If they want to convict me of something I didn't do, they might as well make it first-degree murder. No sense being wishy-washy about it."

"You're sure?"

"I'm sure," Anne said. She wanted to tell him that as far as she was concerned, any sentence was a death sentence, but she was afraid he might try to stop her.

A few minutes later, when Pat and Anne were alone, she stood by her window and stared at the street below. She liked to watch the cars and the people during breaks. It had become symbolic of freedom, the ordinary people going about their business. Anne longed to be an ordinary person again. Pat was packing up his briefcase. She could tell he was nervous.

"Oh, Anne," he said, "there's just one other little thing."

She turned to face him. "What?"

"You're not going to like it."

Anne smiled. "To tell you the truth, Pat, I don't much care for any of this."

"Well," Pat said, "there's an old law in Massachusetts that allows a defendant in a capital case to make an unsworn statement to the jury if the judge allows."

"NO," Anne said. She cut him off.

"It hasn't been used for years, but it's still on the books."

"No," she said. She felt the panic rising.

"You wouldn't be under oath," Pat said, "and there wouldn't be any cross-examination."

"No." She was frightened, just the way she was when he asked her to go to Morton Hospital with the jury.

"It will help immensely," Pat said. He had that look of being annoyed with her.

"I can't do it," Anne pleaded. "You don't need it. You said things looked good."

"They do, Anne, they do. But we could still lose. That jury hasn't heard your voice. They don't know you as a person. They know you as a defendant. I want them to be able to really look you in the eye and see what kind of person you are."

"Pat," she said, trying to be funny even though she was scared, "I don't make good first impressions. They'll hang me for sure."

"Anne!"

"Don't ask me." She held out her hand. "Look," she said, "my hand's trembling just thinking about it."

"Do it, Anne. Talk to them."

"I'll screw it up," Anne said. "I know I will." She fumbled in her pocketbook for a cigarette. "All those people watching me. And that damn television camera."

Pat started shouting. "Are you telling me you're afraid of a television camera? Are you telling me you've got a little bit of stage fright after all you've been through?"

"Yes," she said. "You find that strange, do you, that a fat girl from Jamaica Plain doesn't want millions of people watching her?"

"Christ, Anne! Don't pull that poor little fat girl stuff on me!" Pat hollered back. "You know as well as I do that she died a long time ago."

"Oh, what the hell do you know about it?" Anne cried. "Huh? You, with your Mercedes and your goddamn suits. You're gorgeous, for God's sake, you look great on television."

"I get scared, too, you know," Pat said, lowering his voice.

"Oh, sure."

"I do," he said. "I get up there every day and I'm

supposed to be accurate and I'm supposed to have all these facts at my fingertips and I'm supposed to make sense and speak well. Anne, do you know how many chances I get every day to make a fool of myself in front of the world?"

"But I'll be a nervous wreck," Anne said. "Can't you see that?"

"You'll only be nervous for a few seconds. Once you get going, you'll be fine."

"I'm not doing it."

"Yes, you are," Pat said. "This business of being nervous, of not wanting to be on television, of being afraid of all the people watching you—do you know what that is, Anne?"

"No," she said, "but I bet you're going to tell me."

"It's bullshit," Pat said. "That's what it is. And you made me a promise a long time ago, and you made yourself a promise, there would be no more bullshit."

"You know," Anne said after a moment, "sometimes you can be a real pain in the ass."

They glared at each other. Finally Anne threw her hands in the air. "Oh, go ask the judge," she said. "I hope he turns you down."

"I already did," Pat said. "And he didn't."

"Oh, great," Anne said.

Pat grabbed his briefcase and headed for the door before she could change her mind.

"Are you going to write something for me?" she called.

Pat turned around and smiled. "If I write it, it will sound like a lawyer wrote it. Write it yourself."

"Me? What am I going to write?"

"Write what you feel," he said.

Chapter Thirty-one

Pat Piscitelli rose from his chair behind the defense table. He strode slowly, almost arrogantly, to the front of the courtroom. There he stood before the jurors. He held the rail for several seconds as if waiting for the room to quiet down.

"May it please the court," he said, "Mr. Foreman, members of the jury. Anne Capute is charged with murder. Since biblical times murder has been the most horrible offense known to man. It calls for the most severe punishment that the law allows. And that, in short, sums up why I stand before you this very pleasant October morning."

Thus began the most important and dramatic summation of Pat's career. He had been tense. Now he was glad to be into it.

Pat had stayed up late, as usual, searching for ammunition to fire in this crucial summation. He had made a list of contradictions in testimony, weaknesses in the prosecution's witnesess, and points that could make Pina look bad. These formed the stage from which he launched a virulent attack on the commonwealth's case.

"What does this case boil down to?" Pat asked the jurors. "A nurse, the mother of seven children, an L.P.N. for three years, who medicates a terminally ill patient and then proceeds to document everything she does."

Pat looked the jurors straight in the eye. He could see that they were as weary from the seven-week trial as he was.

"The district attorney is shotgunning you," he said. "He's spray-canning you. He's throwing out to you anything that can hurt Anne Capute, never mind that it contradicts some other part of his case."

Holding the jury rail with one hand, Pat swung the other through the air like a symphony conductor as he enumerated the contradictions.

"Who do we believe?" he asked, glancing toward the prosecution table. "Do we believe Dr. Hillier, who said that Leanues was terminal? Or do we believe Dr. Prout, who said she was not? They were both witnesses for the commonwealth.

"Do we believe Dr. Hillier when he tells us that most of the cancer was removed from Norma Leanues? Or do we believe Dr. Pottier when he tells us that most of the cancer was left in? The commonwealth called both witnesses."

"Do you know what this is?" he asked, taking a step back, smiling devilishly, "this case of the commonwealth's? It's a multiple-choice quiz, that's what it is."

Pat went on hammering at the "multiple-choice quiz" angle. He didn't expect any laughs; the moment was too serious for that, but he hoped that he could amuse the jurors two or three times during his summation. It would help.

By the time he'd been standing in front of the jury for close to an hour, holding the rail and leaning in close most of the time, the pile of emotions inside him was steep indeed. A weak, almost hollow feeling had invaded his arms and legs, and he felt as if he were in a race with an emotional wave that had passed the horizon long ago and would overtake him before the day ended.

During the trial he had taken a definite dislike to some of the commonwealth's witnesses, and now he portrayed them for the jury as a rogues' gallery. His attack was rancorous.

"What about Dr. Hillier?" he said. "There's the one who should be on trial. Hillier!" Pat grinned. "Do you remember how quickly his memory returned when I held up the tape recorder and the transcript? Hillier! If Anne Capute is convicted, he'll be off the hook. He will avoid one enormous malpractice suit."

Pat was pleased. The words were coming to him in the easy, fluid style he had cultivated, flowing for him in the way they had never flowed for his father. Pat glanced out at the spectators and caught sight of his mother sitting there, smiling proudly. He thought for a moment that maybe his father was sitting somewhere, smiling proudly, too. After all, he thought, anything's possible.

Putting two hands on the rail, Pat leaned in toward the jury. "Hillier had given up on Norma," he said. "Pain wasn't paramount in his mind. Paris was. Pleasure in Paris, not pain in Taunton."

When Pat got to Martha Rice, he did not elaborate. He believed the jury had given little weight to her testimony, and he did not want to raise its credibility by arguing with it at length.

"Martha Rice's testimony," he said simply, "is a disjointed statement which I want you to ignore."

Then there was Marianne Prout. Pat had not liked her at all, and he hoped the jury felt the same way. "If you believe the D.A.'s witness, Dr. Prout, Norma Leanues wasn't in pain at all," he told the jurors. "Why? Because she hasn't verbalized it for you. Had to write it out, you know. Dr. Prout doesn't believe in pain unless she hears the patient herself. Nonsense! Nonsense!"

"And what about this guy Sturner," Pat said. "Here's a guy purporting to give you a pharmacological basis for his opinion and he tells you there are thirty milligrams in a gram. There are *sixty* milligrams in a gram. The guy doesn't even know pharmacology.

"And how come the D.A. has to get this hired gun out of Rhode Island, anyhow?" Pat asked, raising his voice, gesturing toward Pina. "All he lacked was the two guns and the holsters. How come he had to—" Pat stopped, scanned the faces of the jurors—"*we* had to—pay him two hundred fifty bucks an hour? For what? As jurors, you make sixteen dollars a day, and we're paying him two hundred fifty dollars an hour. Don't we have any good medical examiners in Massachusetts?"

While Pat had Pina against the wall, he figured he might as well take another slap at him.

"Did you know that Vicki McKenna's statement had been sent to Dr. Cochin?" he said. "What kind of medical testimony is that? You might almost think that somebody was suggesting what Cochin might say."

By the time he got to Maureen Costello, Pat had mellowed. He knew that making fun of witnesses could go just so far. The jurors would enjoy it and stay with him for a while, but there was a point, and he didn't want to get to it, where he would become the villain. He would sound vindictive. He would sound like a bully. So he changed his tone while the jurors were still with him. Costello was the perfect place because, in fact, he liked her. Throughout Costello's days on the stand, though it was his job to assault her constantly, a peculiar respect and admiration had quite obviously flowed between them.

"Maureen Costello!" he said now to the jurors.

"A charming woman. And a strong woman. You saw her up there three days on the stand, never sat, never drank water. A woman of intelligence and charm. But how would you feel facing that woman in her office that night the way Anne Capute had to? How would you feel? Frankly, I'm surprised that Anne didn't confess to shooting Ronald Reagan."

A few jurors laughed, but they seemed embarrassed by that fact.

As Pat retold the story of Anne's visit to Costello's office, he heard the emotion in his own voice. It both pleased and frightened him. He had done a lot of acting during this trial, but he was not acting now. True emotion, he knew, could be a great asset in a summation, but only if the attorney controlled the emotion, and not the other way around. He needed to stay in control, at least until it was over.

"So Anne left Costello's office that night," he said. "They told her she was being suspended for three days, that's all. But instead of being called back to work, she got a phone call. They told her, 'Your interests and the hospital's have diverged, Anne." Do you know what that means? It means the hospital is afraid. The hospital does not know what happened. The hospital has got to be careful. The hospital wants to wash its hands of Anne Capute. Like Pontius Pilate."

Pat stepped back from the jury rail. He had been talking for an hour and a half. Now the end was in sight. He allowed a moment of silence to do its work. Through years of trial work he had learned that silence can often speak as eloquently as words. He glanced at Anne. She looked neither happy nor sad. but she did look peaceful. She knows I'm doing my best, he thought, and the thought made him happy. He knew Anne well, and he knew that no matter what happened she would never look back and second-guess his work on the trial. Pat was exhausted. He was getting to the point where he wanted to cry. Slowly, subtly, he began to narrow the scope of his summation, began to move the focus from the villains to the defendant, began to shift the tone from the logical to the emotional.

"How absurd," he said, "how very absurd it would be for Anne and Nancy Robbins to write down a false doctor's order that would be seen by dozens of people. If you wanted to give someone a large dose of morphine, all you'd have to do is take three tubexes, administer it, go back and drop two on the floor, and record two broken tubexes on the proof-of-use sheet. You could have covered up that happening ten hundred ways. And that's the strength of the case of the defendant, that it was done so openly."

Pat reminded the jury about the hundreds of violations at Morton, and then he reminded them about the step and a half pay increase that Anne had gotten.

"That tells you what kind of a nurse Anne Capute was," Pat said. "Underpaid and overworked. All nurses are. They are fine people who care. You have to be a special kind of person to be a nurse."

Finally, with the weight of two hours of summation, seven weeks of trial, and nine months of deep, obsessive involvement pushing on him, when he knew he had to finish up or lose his race with that wave of emotion, Pat reached into himself for the last words he would have to speak in defense of Anne Capute.

"Anne Capute is not guilty of anything!" he thundered. And then, his hands trembling on the jury rail, he said, speaking softly, "I take that back. She is guilty. She is guilty of loving and caring for her patients; she is guilty of having compassion, pity, sympathy, and love for Norma Leanues and Mr. Leanues and the Leanues family. That is what Anne Capute is guilty of, and nothing more. Thank you."

As the last words fell from his mouth, Pat pulled his hands from the jury rail. Tears spilled into his eyes, and even the "Thank you" had been forced out in a nervous rush. Pat spun around quickly and put his hand in front of his face. He didn't want the jurors to see him crying. The tears were real, the emotion genuine, but he was afraid that the jury might see his crying as an attempt to manipulate them. He rushed back to the defense table, his legs shaking beneath him, and he sat down with his face in his hands. Anne put an arm around him. The courtroom was silent.

Finally Judge Prince, speaking almost apologetically for disturbing the hushed moment, said, "Ladies and gentlemen, we will take a brief recess, and then the district attorney will address you."

By the time the recess was over, Pat had pulled himself together and was, even at this late moment, working on the trial. He held his notes in front of him, and ready to jump up with an objection any time the district attorney strayed to matters not in evidence. "It's not over until it's over," he said to Anne.

Though the jurors had clearly been moved by the passion of Pat's summation, they gave no sign that they would be swept up in a wave of sympathy for Anne. From the first day of the trial the men and women of the jury had projected to everyone the impression that they were proud and intensely serious about the job they had been given and that they would carry out their duties precisely as the law commanded. During Pat's summation they had listened carefully to every word. And now they leaned forward and listened just as intently as Ronald Pina approached them with the commonwealth's final argument.

Pina had not been rattled by Pat's presentation. Pina was calm, accurate, precise, impressive, and convincing. Pina's success in politics could be traced largely to his public-speaking skills. He knew how to hold an audience. Pina brought back into sharp focus a good many reasons why the jury should convict Anne of murder. And as he spoke, and as jurors now and then offered a subtle nod of agreement, he seemed to pull in the sails that had been carrying Anne to safety.

"Norma Leanues was not dying of cancer," Pina said. He quoted Dr. Prout, the only cancer expert who had testified. "Norma Leanues had a future. Anne Caputo took that future away."

Pina defended his experts, and he rattled off a list of their credits that, indeed, was impressive. He told the jury that Pat's witnesses never said that cancer killed Norma Leanues. "They just didn't know."

He explained that he had gone to Rhode Island for Sturner because Keeley's death had left the whole commonwealth of Massachusetts with only one state pathologist. He told the jury that Keeley's report showed "that there is no cause of death anatomically in the body, other than chemically."

"Use your common sense!" he said. It was a refrain he used often.

He told the jurors to consider the record, the nurses' notes, the dosages, he reminded them that Dr. Dalcortivo did find morphine.

"And I asked him his opinion," Pina said, "I asked his opinion on the cause of death. And he said, 'She died of morphine poisoning.' And what did he tell you? He told you it was a 'chemical insult to the body.' You can't breathe is what he told you, your lungs are not operating, you reach a point on an hourly basis where your body just cannot respond.

And Dr. Cochin told you the same thing. Dr. Cochin! Chairman of the National Council of Drug Abuse, a committee that advises the entire Food and Drug Administration of the United States of America on drugs. That's Dr. Cochin."

"Norma Leanues couldn't breathe," Pina said. He paused. "She could not breathe. And Dr. Dalcortivo told you that the notations 'bluish nail beds, ten to fifteen seconds of apnea, not responding' indicates to him that Norma probably would have died, based on the eleven-fifteen shot." Pina glanced at Anne.

"Anne rolled her eyes, she was pale, she seemed to have respiratory problems when she talked to Mrs. Costello," Pina said. "It was ten minutes before she started to calm down. And keep in mind, it's not the doctors who brought this case. Look at the evidence. It was Vicki McKenna, another licensed practical nurse, who looked at something and made a report."

Then Pina tore into Anne with all the statements she had made.

"Anne said, 'My God, it would kill you. My God, it would be enough to kill an elephant.' She was asked, 'Do you think you killed her?' and she said, 'Yes, I do,' and she said, 'I must have killed her."

Pina recounted Kathy Menard Cyr's testimony supporting Hillier's statement. And then Martha Rice.

"Anne said to Martha Rice, 'Thorazine and Dilaudid together, an IV push, that will do it. It gives me goose bumps.'

"Anne said to Rosemary Miles, 'I wish I could give her an IV medication, to send her along the way.'" Pina stopped and stared at the jurors. "To send her along the way," he said with a sneer. "Not trying out for euthanasia nurse?

"And when Anne was asked about ten to fifteen

seconds of apnea, she said to Mrs. Costello, 'The morphine is doing her in.'

"And in a phone call with Mrs. Costello, Anne asked, 'Who else is involved?' and when Costello didn't tell her, Anne said, 'Well, it's only Nancy Robbins and me. I am primarily the one, and she encouraged me.' She encouraged me! Anne also said, 'I made an error in judgment, I didn't cover myself legally.' Mrs. Costello testified to that right here."

"Use your common sense," Pina said again. "Take into consideration the doctor's form. It says fifteen milligrams, no time limit. Even if you assume she followed that, 'no time limit' is the frequency. It doesn't mean change the dose to thirty milligrams or forty-five. Look at the nurses' notes, thirty milligrams, an hour goes by, thirty milligrams . . . I don't have to go on. Look at the chart, watch the peak effect. See what happens. Could Norma tolerate that every hour? Use your common sense.

"The needles are over there, they're in evidence," Pina said. "Take them. Inject them into a body. Put it all in. It will stop respiration. Nail beds are turning bluish. Respiratory distress. The patient not breathing, not getting oxygen, not responding, lying there. Mrs. Costello used the word 'comatose.'" Pina thrust out his arm and announced, "Anne Capute knew what she meant when she said, 'the morphine is catching up to her.' She's a nurse, she knew exactly what she was doing."

Like Pat, the district attorney shifted from an appeal to logic to an appeal to the emotions as he moved toward the end of his speech.

"What did Norma Leanues have on that Saturday night that she didn't have when she came to the hospital?" he asked. "She already had cancer, the emphysema, the operation.

"But," Pina said, dramatically raising his voice, "there were a few things she didn't have. She didn't have the defendant Anne Capute as her nurse, and she didn't have one hundred ninety-five milligrams of morphine. Do you think that would kill somebody?

"Norma Leanues," said Ronald Pina, "was not given the chance to decide about further treatment because that woman over there, Anne Capute, took away whatever future Norma had on the evening of May eighteenth . . . whatever flicker of hope, whatever belief that there was a possible treatment for her cancer, whatever chance there was that something could have been done, whatever time to see her children again . . . all of it, taken away by the defendant. Use your common sense."

By the time Pina was finishing up his summation, Anne was a nervous wreck. She had not been affected by his words simply because the petrifying knowledge that she would have to stand up next and talk to the jury in front of everybody blotted out everything else.

"Norma never had a chance," Pina was saying. "So who decides who lives and who dies? A woman has died, fifty-one years old, two boys at home, two daughters married. Who decides? The doctor? No 'no code' here, no 'death with dignity' order here. Who decides? A licensed practical nurse made a decision for somebody else. Does the defendant have the right to make that decision? Does she have the right to take away that woman's life and take whatever hope, whatever future she had? Norma Leanues isn't here today. The charge is murder. I request, on behalf of the commonwealth, a guilty finding on both counts. Thank you."

At the defense table Pat, Don, and James glanced at Anne. They had all stayed up late at Pat's house

listening to Anne practice her statement. Now Lori
and Susan were in the audience. The daughters of
Norma Leanues were there, too. "Now it's up to you,"
Pat said. Anne was scared. But she knew she could do
it.

Chapter Thirty-two

THE COURT: At this time I address now the
defendant, Anne Capute. And I say to you that,
Mrs. Capute, in accordance with a longtime
practice in capital cases, you are hereby granted
the right to address the jury. What you say will
not be taken by the jury as any evidence but will
be in the nature of a second argument, so to
speak. You have the right to suggest to the jury
by way of argument and address anything that
you would like to say to them. The privilege is
yours. And you may exercise it as you see fit. You
may consult with your counsel if you choose to do
so at this time.

Do you wish to address the jury?

DEFENDANT CAPUTE: Yes, I do, Your Honor.

THE COURT: All right. She may do so. She will not
be permitted to take the witness stand and she
will not be sworn. She may address the jury.

DEFENDANT CAPUTE: Ladies and gentlemen of the
jury, excuse the notes. But I am afraid I will go
blank.

Since I was six years old, the ultimate dream of my life was to be a nurse. My husband, Charlie, who is a carpenter, and myself, raised seven children between us over the years in between being a wife and mother. I worked seventeen years in various fields. For six years I drove a school bus and finally in 1977, I graduated nursing school.

It became a reality. I loved my patients and I loved nursing. And I loved Norma Leanues as I have any of those that I've cared for. Since May sixth, when Norma was operated on, it was common knowledge amongst the staff that she was a terminal cancer patient.

And her screams of agony only proved to those hearing it in charge and myself that she wanted an increased dosage and she was medicated with it not only on May sixteenth but on May seventeenth in an effort to ease her agony.

Norma Leanues was not comatose when I medicated her at eleven-fifteen on the seventeenth. When I went back and checked her at eleven-thirty, I made the notation in her chart later that her nail beds were bluish, that she was having periods of apnea, and it wasn't uncommon for her.

I also made the notation "not responding." That was my reference to the fact that I felt she wasn't responding to the medication.

No one here, not the nurses, not my lawyer, not the district attorney can possibly imagine the pain and agony that she was going through because they weren't there. But I was.

The district attorney has accused me of willfully and intentionally killing Norma Leanues. Not only here and in the media and for weeks you have been hearing it, but my children have been hearing it. We have been hearing it for a year and a half now.

And I stand before you today and I beg of you only one thing. If you believe the district attorney when he says that I killed Norma Leanues, I ask you to bring back a guilty verdict. But if not, if you believe as I swear to you is true, that I did nothing other than try to help Norma Leanues with her agony and her suffering, then set me free and return me to my family.

Thank you for listening.

Anne stepped back from the jury rail and looked out at the silent faces in the courtroom. She shrugged, as if to ask, What more can I say? Her hands were still shaking when she got back to the defense table.

Pat studied the faces of the jurors. Several of them were in tears. He thought for sure they would find Anne not guilty.

Chapter Thirty-three

The next morning Anne listened stoically as Judge Prince gave his charge to the jurors. The jury had been trimmed to twelve by the dismissal of the four alternates. Anne felt sorry for the alternates. It must have been hard on them, she thought, to sit there for seven weeks listening to testimony and then have no vote in the verdict. Anne had grown fond of the jurors. It was a lousy job they had, and she admired them for their stamina. She glanced often at their faces as Judge Prince explained the law to them.

Prince told the jury what to consider and what to disregard. He also told them what verdicts they could return.

Judge Prince had turned down Pat's request for a "first-degree murder only" charge to the jury. Pat had griped for hours about it, but Anne had been largely unaffected. More and more she was learning simply to accept whatever came along. Prince advised the jury that they could find Anne not guilty, or they could find her guilty of first or second degree murder, or of involuntary manslaughter. At ten o'clock the jury left the courtroom.

"Well," Anne said, turning to the cluster of people who had come on this momentous day. Charlie and the girls were there, along with two of Pat's secretaries. "So what do we do now? Go home and watch *General Hospital*?" She was feeling flippant, but she was also very scared.

"We wait," Pat said. "They'll be back in four hours."

"You don't say," Ann replied. "Four hours, huh? You got your crystal ball working today?"

"I feel lucky," Pat said. "Besides," he added, "if they're not back in four hours, I'd . . ." He stopped.

"You'd what?" Anne said.

"Nothing."

"Nothing, huh?" She looked him in the eye. "Pat, I love you dearly, but don't you think it's a little late to start with the bullshit? You were going to say you'd worry."

"Yes."

"Why would you worry?"

"Because they should go into that jury room looking for a way to find you not guilty. They can find it in four hours and still maintain their integrity. If they're out much longer than that it means there's strong support on both sides."

"In other words, someone doesn't like me," Anne said.

"You got it," Pat replied, mimicking one of Anne's favorite phrases.

"And?"

"And that could mean a compromise of some sort."

"Second-degree murder?" she said.

"Or manslaughter," Pat said. "The compromise situation is what I wanted to avoid."

There was awkward silence while everybody stared down into their hands, as if they'd just been notified of a death.

"Hey, let's not be so glum," Anne said. "It won't happen. Pat says four hours."

After the jury had been out for ninety minutes, a note came down for Judge Prince. There was a moment of excitement. Ron Pina, sitting in the jury box playing with a Rubik's Cube, looked at Dave Turcotte and said, "If it's a verdict, we're sunk."

But it was not a verdict. The jury was merely asking for more instructions from Prince.

Anne and Charlie and the girls sat at the defense table. They took turns reminiscing, and they all held hands. But Anne's mood darkened with each minute. She felt closer than ever to Charlie and her daughters, and yet in another sense she felt a million miles away. They had all gone through the trial together, but it was Anne and only Anne whose life was being decided in the jury room. Pat and Don and James paced. Pina played with the Rubik's Cube. Lori glanced over at the district attorney once. "I hate him," she whispered, and Anne looked sternly back at Lori and said, "Don't. Never hate anybody." Were they actually hoping to hear a guilty verdict? Anne wondered. The thought made her sad, not for herself, but for them.

At three o'clock the jury told Judge Prince they had reached a verdict on one charge but were still considering the other.

"It's the drug charge, isn't it?" Anne said to Pat.

"Yes," he said, "most likely."

"They took five hours with that one. "That's not good, is it?"

"No," Pat said, "it's not. But we don't know that it took five hours. They might have reached the verdict a long time ago. They're just telling Prince about it now."

Though Pat tried to find positive things to say, Anne could see that he was getting worried.

At five o'clock the jury still had not reached a verdict. Judge Prince ordered them to deliberate longer. Anne played cards with the girls, but her heart was not in it. Now and then she stepped out into the corridor for a cigarette. She watched fearfully as the lawyers started tugging at their ties, putting their feet up, dozing off. Everybody was bored. Reporters milled around the courthouse corridors hoping to get some kind of story. And they got one.

The story they got was that Anne Capute had falsified records to get into nursing school, and it broke long before the verdict. Though the TV stations and the newspapers that ran the story never named the source, there was no doubt in Pat's mind that the source was the D.A.'s office.

A reporter who was there confirms Pat's suspicions.

"Pina gave out the information in a hallway conference while the jury was locked up," says the reporter. "I think he was clawing at something dramatic. His ego was so damaged because he had been so outclassed all through the trial. It couldn't help Pina's case; the jury was already out, but I think he wanted to get even. The public loved Anne, and I guess he wanted to say, 'See, she's not the woman you thought she was.'"

Suppertime came, and still no verdict. The sky grew dark beyond the tall court windows. And still Anne waited with her family.

At eight o'clock Pat and Don went for a walk. Things looked grim, and they needed to talk about it away from Anne. As the two men walked along North Main Street, bundled up now against the first cold evening of the season, their spirits were close. They had both put enormous amounts of work into the case, and now, with the long deliberation, they knew that they had lost. Anne would be found guilty. Not of first-degree murder, they were sure of that. But there would be a compromise, and the jury would return with a verdict of guilty of second-degree murder or involuntary manslaughter. They tried to tell themselves that beating first degree was a victory, but they knew better. They talked about appeals they would make, but the sense of failure hung heavy on them both.

"I was very angry that night," Pat says. "I was angry that the judge hadn't let us go in with the first-degree charge only. We could only keep our fingers crossed and hope that the people who were for Anne would hang tough and not compromise. We walked for quite a while around the courthouse area, and when we were a couple of blocks away we looked back and there on the second floor was a lighted room, and we could actually see the jurors deliberating. We could see figures standing, but we couldn't determine anything. Nobody seemed to be making wild gesticulations or anything like that. Don and I just stood for two or three minutes, watching, and thinking how odd it was that we were walking around discussing a case that had occupied our lives for months, and there up in that window were these twelve strangers deciding the whole thing. Finally, after we'd been there a few minutes, almost hypnotized by it, Don said, 'Let's throw a rock through the window with a note on it that says, 'The Doctor Did It,' and we both started laughing. It was a funny moment at a desperate time."

At nine-thirty the jury told Judge Prince it could not reach a verdict that night. Judge Prince sequestered the jury. The jurors were put up in a motel. Everyone else went home. No one had much to say.

Late that night, when the girls and Charlie were sleeping, Anne went into the kitchen. She sat alone in her nightgown and wrote a note to her daughters.

"My dear daughters," she wrote, "all I really want to write is, 'Gee folks, it's been swell, so long!' You know me, always ready with a joke. And besides, by the time you read this I will have pulled the biggest joke of all. But I guess I can't just be flip. You wouldn't let me get away with it. By now you have seen something horrible and your mind is full of questions. I can't answer them all. All I can tell you is that I love my freedom more than anything and I could not bear to be in prison. I would just shrivel up and die. If I have to die I want it to be my way. Remember that when Warren died it seemed like the world was closing in on us all and there was so much despair. But we survived. We were strong. All of you girls are strong, and you will survive this. The other thing I want to say is that I love you, I love you so much, all of you. I know that you know that, and that's one of the things that would make prison so unbearable. I love you, and that is what you should remember always. Love, Ma."

She tucked the note into an envelope. Then she went downstairs to Charlie's workroom in the basement, where the gun cabinet had been moved after Warren's death. She took out the .38-caliber revolver and loaded it. She left one chamber empty so that nobody would get hurt if the gun accidentally went off.

In the morning Anne drove to Pat's house early. Charlie would be driving the girls to the courthouse, but it was important for her to drive in with Pat, James, and Don. They had come this far together. Pat's family was just finishing breakfast. James and Don were already there. Pat, incredibly, was working. He was reading documents from the trial just in case an appeal was needed. He's scared, Anne thought, that's why he's working.

She stood in the living room for a moment, looking at everything but focusing on nothing. The Piscitellis stared at her. Everyone was tense, not knowing what to say. Today the verdict would surely be in.

"Anne, is there anything I can get you?" Meredith Piscitelli asked.

Anne looked at Matthew Piscitelli, Pat's nine-year-old son.

"Do you have any Neil Diamond records?" she asked.

"I think so," Matthew said, and he ran off to look for one.

"Anne was very strange that morning," Pat says. "Very quiet, very distant. You could almost say she was calm. I don't know where she was, but she wasn't with us."

Anne was really out of it that morning," Don Harwood says. "I thought maybe she had taken some drugs or something."

While she was waiting for Matthew to return, Anne slipped the envelope containing the note into James Morton's hands.

"If I'm found guilty I want you to give that note to my girls," she said.

James wanted to explain to her that if she was found guilty she'd have plenty of time to give them the note, herself. Nobody was going to drag her out of the courtroom in chains. But Anne looked so distraught that James thought he might as well take the note, anything to make her feel better.

None of them knew that Anne had the loaded gun in her pocketbook.

Matthew came back, proudly presenting Anne with the only Neil Diamond album in the house. It was still early, and everybody except Anne gathered in the kitchen. Anne stayed in the living room. She put the record on and she stretched out on an easy chair and put her feet up. She thought of lighting a cigarette, but then decided, no, it wasn't right to smoke in someone's house without asking first, and she didn't want to go in and ask. Instead, she put her head back and listened to Neil Diamond and felt the warmth of morning sunshine that flowed through the window and landed on her arm.

How sad, she thought, to have a dream and have it lead to this. Her mind swept back across all that had happened, and she barely heard the first two songs on the album. And then she returned to the moment. She loved Neil Diamond, she thought. Listening to him sing was one of the great pleasures of her life, and here it was, one more thing she was doing, possibly, for the last time. Pushing other thoughts from her mind, and with a knuckle jammed into her mouth to hold back the tears, she listened more intently to the music. Anne wept.

The drive to Fall River that morning was the first one that was not enlivened by Anne's joking and laughing. Though she had often been sad, she had never been completely lost to the others the way she was this morning.

Through the morning they did much the same things they had done the previous day. They talked. They paced. Gradually the courtroom filled up. Meredith Piscitelli and several people from Pat's staff came for the verdict. Charlie and the girls filed in sadly, took their seats. Reporters came. Members of the Leanues family arrived, somber-faced, looking less concerned with what the verdict was than the fact that one came in and put an end to it all. People from Morton Hospital came, perhaps seeking some sort of vindication for their institution. And curious mobs of people who had come to know Anne through the newspapers and the TV news, streamed in from the back of the courtroom. They waved to her and smiled. Even though Anne didn't know them, hers was a familiar face to them. Everybody wanted to see how the story came out. They waited and waited. Noon arrived, but nobody went out for lunch.

At twelve fifty-five the jury filed in. Anne could feel the room go tense.

"I hope the state bought them a nice dinner last night," Anne whispered to Pat. It was her first light comment of the day.

"They deserve it." Her heart was thundering in her chest, as it had that night in Costello's office. She clutched her pocketbook close to her. The gun was getting heavy. One chamber was empty. She would have to cock it. Just stick the barrel in her mouth, cock the gun, pull the trigger. It would take only a few seconds. And then she'd be free. Anne was feeling kind of crazy, but she understood that. The thought came to her: I'd have to be crazy not to be feeling kind of crazy right now.

The jurors filed into their places in the jury box, remained standing. The clerk waited for silence in the room, then he faced them.

"Ladies and gentlemen of the jury, have you reached a verdict?"

"We have," said Robert E. Richman, the jury foreman.

"On the charge of murder, how say ye?" Is the defendant guilty or not guilty?"

Pat reached over and squeezed Anne's hand as tightly as he could.

Chapter Thirty-four

"Not guilty," the foreman said.

Anne felt numb. A magnificent roar rose up from the crowd around her. And, as if from the end of a tunnel, she heard people clapping and shouting, almost singing, "ANNE, ANNE, ANNE." She felt herself swimming out of the tunnel. The tumult grew louder. Pat was coming into focus. Only a second had passed, but everything was in slow motion. Anne fell into Pat's arms. She hugged him desperately and cried. She felt her daughters, each of them sobbing uncontrollably, rush to her and slip their arms around her in a single loving knot. When she flowed from their embrace, Charlie came to her, his arms large and hard, pulling her in; he felt now like a boy as he cried into her shoulder. Anne, still limp, moved from one person to another. Everybody needed to hug her, and she needed to hug everybody. She hugged Don, wanting to hug him forever; she hugged James, wanting to hug him forever. The clapping continued around her, getting louder as she drew closer to a true awareness of what had happened. Already the reporters were shouting out their questions. The bedlam was snapped only long enough for the foreman to announce "not guilty" on the second charge, the illegal-drug charge, and the crowd let out another joyous roar.

The jurors were in tears. Through the crushing crowd around her Anne moved toward them. When she got to the jury box she reached out to caress their eager hands. They pulled her to them; she hugged them, she kissed them. "Thank you, thank you," she cried over and over, and she threw them kisses as she was swept back into the crowd.

Everywhere people were jumping up and down as if they, themselves, had been acquitted of murder. Someone had dashed out the doorway and begun spreading the word up and down the street. Already horns were hooting out on North Main.

Minutes later Anne, at the center of a single jubilant crowd, moved to the doorway, through the hall, down the stairs. By the time she got to the door, more than a hundred people had gathered in front of the courthouse. Anne couldn't believe it. They cheered. "Anne!" they shouted, "Anne!" and they applauded as she came through the courthouse doorway for the last time. She stood out in the afternoon sunlight and threw them kisses. Reporters were all around.

"Were you scared?" one asked.

"You bet!" she replied.

"Are you angry with the Leanues family?" some-one asked.

"I'm not angry with anyone," Anne said. "I don't have time to be angry. My heart goes out to them." She was breathless. "I hope they can put all this behind them now. I am sure they have suffered as much as I have."

And then a woman with a notebook moved in close to her and asked her about the effect of it all on the family. Anne told her that everybody had gone through very hard times.

"Especially your husband?" the reporter asked.

"Why do you say that?" Anne asked, still feeling bitter about the fact that Charlie hadn't come to the trial until the last two days.

"Well," the woman said, "it must have been like standing by helplessly and watching his wife get raped."

"I guess," Anne said, somewhat stunned by the remark. "I hadn't thought of it that way."

Anne and Pat and the others pushed their way through the crowd and began walking toward Gale's. People everywhere called her name. Cars slowed down. Drivers beeped their horns or leaned out the window to shout, "Congratulations, Anne!" One man pulled his truck to the curb, left it sticking out into the road, and jumped out and ran up to Anne. "I've been watching it all on TV," he said, jamming a wrapped present into her hands. "This is for you." By the time Anne tore the present open, he was gone. It was a name and address book from the five and ten, and she never knew who the man was.

Word of Anne's acquittal traveled at remarkable speed. By the time the family and the defense team reached Gale's, there were photographers standing on the tables to snap them as they came through the doorway. The owners, who had served them lunch almost every day, rushed to greet Anne and hug her. By the time the party had jammed into three booths to order lunch, which was on the house, the news had reached ABC's *Good Morning, America* show. A producer from the show had called Pat's office and been given the number of Gale's. Five minutes after Pat sat down at Gale's he was called to the phone. When he came back he announced to Anne, "David Hartman wants to interview us on *Good Morning, America.* Are you up for that?"

"You got it," Anne said.

After lunch they drove back to the office, laughing and shouting all the way. They stopped at Morton Hospital first and bade farewell to George the skeleton, which Pat was returning to Larry Ross.

Pat's staff had ordered champagne, and when Anne arrived for the party, there were flowers everywhere, and telegrams of congratulations.

"The place looks like a damn funeral parlor," Anne said. She stepped into the main waiting room, where once she had sat with Beth Whitehead waiting to see Pat Piscitelli. Huge bouquets covered the area. There were twenty people gathered in the office, Pat's staff, Anne's family—and they all went silent as Anne approached the flowers. Everybody knew where most of them had come from.

Anne approached one huge bouquet and plucked the card from it. She read it, moved on to the next. Then more quickly she stepped to the next bunch of flowers, and then another and another.

"Oh, my God," she said, "they're from nurses." Groups of nurses from all over the country had sent the flowers. She stood, teary-eyed, facing everybody, and her heart felt light again.

"That night we went out to dinner at a restaurant

in Brockton," Pat Piscitelli says. "The whole bunch of us. A reporter from Channel Five came down and interviewed us while we were having dinner. Later that evening we went for drinks to Christo's in Brockton. The place is frequented by nurses from the Brockton Hospital, and it's always packed on a weekend night. We walked into the large room and after about sixty seconds someone started to clap, and then someone else, and before long everybody in that place was standing up, applauding for Anne. It was amazing. I couldn't get over the outpouring of love and feelings that had followed Anne all day. All those people. Applauding."

And as she listened to the applause that night, Anne knew that she couldn't just pack a bag and head off to Montana, as she had fantasized all through the trial. She would go, she was sure of that, but not just yet. And through eyes wet with tears she stared out at the applauding strangers. And she thought, how sad that Warren could not be here to see this. And then she thought, well, maybe he is. Anything's possible. And she reached for Pat's hand and held it, and she waved to the crowd and threw them kisses.

Epilogue

A few days after the trial ended Anne appeared on the *Good Morning, America* program. She told David Hartman that her trial had been "a living nightmare," and that since the acquittal she felt like a new woman. "I feel like Cinderella," she said, "and I'm hoping the clock never strikes twelve."

In December the jury that had freed her held a reunion. They invited Anne to be their guest of honor. The jurors and their spouses, along with two court officers, gathered at the Gang Plank restaurant in Fall River.

"I expect a very compassionate person," one juror told a reporter while they were waiting for Anne. "Hopefully, we'll see a happy person. We certainly didn't see a very happy person during the trial." Another juror said, "I'm happy for her that it's Christmas and she's free. It was a long time for her and I think it will be a merry Christmas."

At eight o'clock Anne showed up, with Pat and Meredith Piscitelli, Don Harwood, James Morton, and Donna Piscatelli. The jurors stood and applauded.

A month after the trial Bristol County District Attorney Ronald Pina announced that he was dropping murder charges against Judy Foley and Nancy Robbins.

"Jurors' views of nurses, doctors, hospitals, and

the subject of cancer make it virtually impossible to obtain an impartial jury," Pina said.

Despite the jubilation that followed the acquittal, Anne's ordeal was not over. The trial had left permanent scars. Morton Hospital refused to rehire her. News stories about her fake name and transcript continued to surface until the Massachusetts Board of Registration in Nursing decided to look into it. In July of 1982 Anne voluntarily surrendered her practical nurse's license after admitting that she had used another woman's name and records to enter nursing school.

"After two years of almost constantly being in the public eye of controversy, I want desperately to find some peace of mind and some semblance of order in my life," she told the press.

Though she has had occasional non-nursing jobs since the trial, Anne has found it impossible to get a good job.

"They see the name 'Capute,'" she says, "and they don't want me."

Anne acquired her high school equivalency certificate, but was still not allowed to reapply for a nursing license. In September of 1984 Pat and Anne appeared before the state's Board of Registration in Nursing to seek reinstatement for Anne. On February 3, 1985, Anne received a letter from the board telling her she would not be allowed to reapply.

"I was devastated," she says. "I mean, I expected it, but when it actually happened I got terribly depressed. Things had not been going well at home. I had no job, and now they were taking away my last hope."

The next day a story about Anne's troubles appeared in the *Boston Herald*. Then the Boston television stations took an interest. Anne went on TV with Pat and talked about her life since the trial. The public sided with Anne. Letters of support came in. Pat decided to give it one more shot and make one last appeal to the board even though he had little real hope.

On April 24, Piscitelli and Anne met with the Board of Registration, and Pat made his pitch. Working the board as he would a jury, reaching back for some of the same phrases and emotions he had used four years ago in the historic trial, Piscitelli tried to convince the board that Anne was a woman who had been brutalized by a system and then discarded after she proved them wrong. Anne, for her part, expressed remorse for her mistake and apologized to the board. The individual board members asked questions, and after an hour went into executive session.

"We knew they were going to turn us down," Anne says, "but we had to give it a try."

When the session was over the board called Anne and Piscitelli into the room and told her they had decided to reinstate her.

"I couldn't believe it," Anne says. "Something had gone right. I was so excited. It was like being found not guilty all over again."

"I'm sure the publicity helped," Piscitelli says.

The board set down some requirements, which were standard. Anne would have to propose a course of study in nursing which would bring her up to date for practice. But she would not have to go through another hearing. After she has completed the courses in three or four months, she will be reinstated.

"So, I'm back at the books," she says, "and I love it. Of course, it hasn't been all bad. A few good things have happened since the trial. I'm a grandma now. My daughter Lori had a baby girl, Danielle, and she's precious. And most important, I've got that sense of inner peace. Hell, they damn near killed me, didn't they? And I'm okay. Inner peace. They can't take that away from me."

So now Anne Capute spends her days studying and taking care of the house and helping Lori with the baby. And she dreams of that day when she will again be a nurse.

Rusty's Story

By Carol Gino
Author of NURSE'S STORY

When Carol Gino first met Barbara "Rusty" Russell, the young woman was working as a nurse's aide in a nursing home. Immediately, Carol was impressed by Rusty's compassion and understanding of her often difficult elderly patients, and the two women quickly became friends.

As their friendship deepened, Carol began to uncover the layers of Rusty's life. At the age of fifteen, Rusty suffered a seizure at a football game and the incident propelled her into a medical nightmare. Rusty was institutionalized, overmedicated, and misdiagnosed as everything from a paranoid schizophrenic to a dangerous psychotic. Struggling to maintain a normal life, Rusty fought back against the medical system and appeared to have won by the time Carol met her. But, her nightmare was just beginning . . .

Rusty's Story

The harrowing true tale of the friendship between two women who join forces for the fight of their lifetime.

Available December 18 wherever Bantam Books are sold.